Knights of Columbus
122nd Supreme Convention
Dallas, Texas
August 3 – 5, 2004

Catholic Texans is being provided as the registration gift in commemoration of
Knights of Columbus 122nd Supreme Convention
and
Texas State Council Centennial Anniversary.

We are sure you will enjoy the history of Catholicism in Texas that is uniquely captured in the commemorative issue of this very special book.

Steve Landregan, the author, is a Brother Knight and the archivist for the Catholic Diocese of Dallas.

We hope you will have many wonderful memories of the Knights with whom you share this convention.

Thank you for your participation.

Your presence has helped to make this event a great success.

Catholic Texans
Our Family Album

Author
Steve Landregan, M.A.
Archivist
Catholic Diocese of Dallas

Educational Consultants

Toni Underwood, M.S., M.Ed.
Assistant Director of Catholic Schools, Diocese of Dallas
Saundra Sillaway, B.S., M.S.

History Consultants

Donald Chipman, Ph.D.
Susan Eason, M.S.I.S.
Rev. James Talmadge Moore, Ph.D.
Rev. Robert Wright, O.M.I.

Bibliography

Patrick Foley, Ph.D.

Catholic Diocese of Dallas, Texas

Author
Steve Landregan

Illustations
Gianpietro Costa

Design and Layout
Bayle Communication

Photoengraving
Éditions du Signe - 104868

Publishing Director
Christian Riehl

Director of Publication
Joëlle Bernhard

Published by
Éditions du Signe
1, rue Alfred Kastler
B.P. 94 – 67038 Strasbourg cedex 2
France
Tel. (33) 3 88 78 91 91
Fax (33) 3 88 78 91 99

2003 Éditions du Signe
ISBN: 2-7468-1285-1
Printed in China by Sun Fung Offset Binding Co., Ltd

Table of contents

Introduction .... *page 5*

 1 The Age of Exploration
and Discovery .... *page 10*

 2 Missions and Settlements .... *page 26*

 3 Independence, statehood
and civil war .... *page 42*

 4 Expansion and growth .... *page 76*

 5 Changing Church .... *page 88*

 6 The Church in Texas today .... *page 102*

Index .... *page 136*

This book is dedicated to my wife, Barbara, for her support, affirmation and patience; to my bishop, Charles, whose only charge was to "make it good;" to all my collaborators, particularly Father Bob Wright for his work as chief historical consultant and his numerous suggestions that improved the book, and Toni Underwood, coordinator of the teacher review committee, for her demand for excellence and great endurance. Finally, I wish to acknowledge the assistance, encouragement and patience of the Éditions du Signe staff, Christian Riehl, Joëlle Bernhard and Marc de Jong.

Preface

Texan Catholics

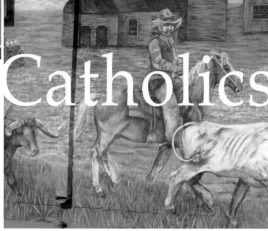

When the first Europeans came to Texas in the early sixteenth century, the world was very different from the one we live in today. It has been described as a world lit only by fire because there was no electricity. Fire, in one form or another, was the only source of heat and light. There was no indoor plumbing; water had to be carried into your home from a well, a lake or a river. Bathing was in a stream or in a wooden or metal tub with hot water that had been heated on the fire.

Getting around was difficult, too. People walked, rode on horseback or in horse-drawn vehicles. Of course, there were no airplanes or trains. There were few roads; mostly trails that were either dirt or mud, depending upon the season, that were used for travel. There were no public schools; there were only a few private ones. Wealthy people had tutors who lived in the home and taught the children. Books were very rare, but there were very few people who could read. It had been less than 100 years since a primitive form of printed books and papers replaced hand-lettered ones. Since there was no television or radio, there were a lot of storytellers.

What were the Spanish and French sailors and explorers who first came to Texas like? They were mostly very young, since average life expectancy at birth was 32 years. They were either very wealthy or very poor. Expeditions were normally financed by the leader or a wealthy patron. The captains and lieutenants were usually aristocrats. Sailors and soldiers normally came from poor families. All of them saw exploration and discovery as a possible source of riches and a better life. Religion was very different at this time also. People who lived in Europe, and in countries that bordered the Mediterranean Sea, were either Christian or Muslim, and the choice was not theirs. Jewish people were tolerated, but were treated badly.

The king or ruler generally determined the religion of the country's subjects. Catholic Christians were passionate about spreading the Christian faith to those who did not know Christ. Both Christians and Muslims did not hesitate to force people to change their faith, in the belief that they were doing God's will and the person would experience a real conversion.

Just as exploration and discovery offered the opportunity for wealth and fame to many, for others it offered the opportunity to preach the Gospel of Christ. The two causes are not always compatible as we shall see in our story of Texan Catholics.

The world of the sixteenth century was Eurocentric. That means that European culture was perceived as superior to all others and conquerors were therefore not only justified but obligated to impose it on others who often possessed a rich culture of their own. At this time in history many actions were based on the mistaken idea that the end justifies the means. As a result, many injustices and even crimes were committed in the name of nationalism and religion and considered justified.

History must be true to the facts as known, but the actions of nations and individuals should be considered in the light of the times in which they occurred.

• Our Family Album

A family album is a book that tells the story of a family. It is filled with pictures and stories of grandparents, aunts and uncles, brothers and sisters and moms and dads. It tells the story of how our family became what it is today. We Texas Catholics are a family, and this book is our family album, filled with pictures and stories of Catholics who brought their faith and love of God with them to their new home. It reminds us of important events on the path of Texas history that made Catholicism the largest religious denomination in Texas today. This is the story of the grandparents, aunts and uncles, brothers and sisters and parents of our faith and this is their story... but it is also our story... because we are part of the family of Texas Catholics.

In one sense, our first Catholic family album is the New Testament, the story of Jesus Christ, the Son of God, and his mission on earth as recorded by his followers. It tells of the first heroes of our faith. We have been called Catholics since the second century after Christ. The word means universal or world-wide, and it was used to describe our church because it had spread throughout the world by that time. But the New Testament is more than a family album, it is the Good News or Gospel, that is the foundation of our Catholic faith.

Our Texas Catholic family album is the story of men and women of our faith, who through their ordinary and extraordinary lives fashioned our Catholic heritage in Texas.

B.C.= Before Christ and refers to dates prior to the year 1 A.D.
A.D.= Anno Domini (the year of the Lord) and refers to dates following the year 1 B.C.

1 Exploration and Discovery   2 Missions and Settlements

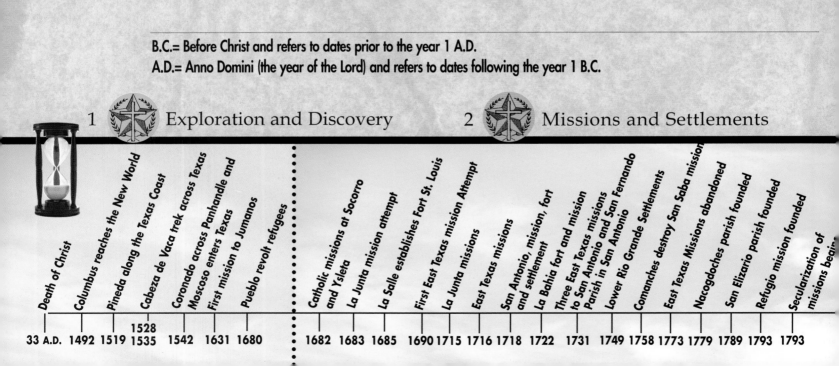

Death of Christ	Columbus reaches the New World	Pineda along the Texas Coast	Cabeza de Vaca trek across Texas	Coronado across Panhandle and Moscoso across Texas	First mission to Jumanos	Pueblo revolt refugees	Catholic missions at Socorro and Ysleta	La Junta mission attempt	La Salle establishes Fort St. Louis	First East Texas mission Attempt	La Junta missions	East Texas missions	San Antonio, mission, fort and settlement	La Bahia fort and mission	Three East Texas missions to San Antonio and San Fernando Parish in San Antonio	Lower Rio Grande Settlements	Comanches destroy San Saba mission	East Texas Missions abandoned	Nacogdoches parish founded	San Elizario parish founded	Refugio mission founded	Secularization of missions begin
33 A.D.	1492	1519	1528 1535	1542	1631	1680	1682	1683	1685	1690	1715	1716	1718	1722	1731	1749	1758	1773	1779	1789	1793	1793

How our Texas Catholic family got here

CONQUISTADOR con media armadura y silla de guerra, en la expedición a tierra firme de México, 1519. Tiene jerarquía de capitán de grupo, por ser propietario de un caballo. Cargadores indígenas al fondo. CONQUISTADOR in half armor and war saddle, during expedition to the Mexican mainland in 1519. As owner of a horse, he held group captain's rank. Native bearers in background.

J. HEFTER

Catholicism is woven into the history of Texas so completely that it is virtually impossible to separate the two. Spanish explorers, who "happened" on Texas in 1519, while looking for a short cut to the Orient, were agents of the Catholic King and Queen of Spain and were charged with the dual mission of exploring and Christianizing by spreading the Gospel.

Spanish conquistadors, whose task was to plant the flag of Spain in the new land, marched side-by-side with missionaries whose charge was to plant the Catholic cross. Their Catholic culture is reflected in the names they gave to the land: Corpus Christi, the Body of Christ; rivers named for the Most Holy Trinity, the "Trinity"; and the Arms of God, the "Brazos".

Often times the missionaries were the advance guard, their missions the first outposts in the wilderness. In many instances Hispanic settlements grew up around the missions and forts, or were even developed independently as at Laredo.

Like the Spanish, the French explorers brought with them the Catholic Faith. Their only settlement in Texas was named Fort St. Louis. It was at Fort St. Louis that the first child of European parents was baptized. Many Indians were baptized, some readily accepted Baptism and even sought it; others were hostile to the European invaders and many priests and lay people became martyrs to the Faith.

3 Independence, Statehood, Civil War and Reconstruction

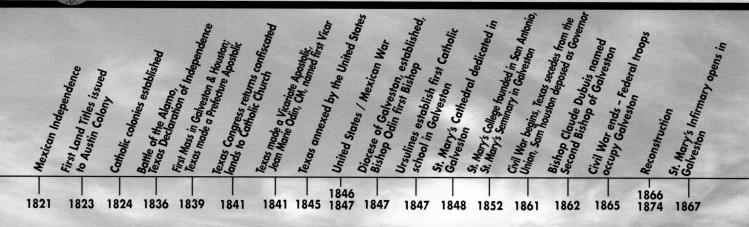

Mexican Independence	1821
First Land Titles issued to Austin Colony	1823
Catholic colonies established	1824
Battle of the Alamo, Texas Declaration of Independence	1836
First Mass in Galveston & Houston; Texas made a Prefecture Apostolic	1839
Texas Congress returns confiscated lands to Catholic Church	1841
Texas made a Vicariate Apostolic; Jean Marie Odin, CM, named first Vicar	1841
Texas annexed by the United States	1845
United States / Mexican War	1846 1847
Diocese of Galveston, established, Bishop Odin first Bishop	1847
Ursulines establish first Catholic school in Galveston	1847
St. Mary's Cathedral dedicated in Galveston	1848
St. Mary's College founded in San Antonio, St. Mary's Seminary in Galveston	1852
Civil War begins, Texas secedes from the Union; Sam Houston deposed as Governor	1861
Bishop Claude Dubuis named Second Bishop of Galveston	1862
Civil War ends – Federal troops occupy Galveston	1865
Reconstruction	1866 1874
St. Mary's Infirmary opens in Galveston	1867

Remember the Alamo

Texas' most important historical landmark, the Alamo, was a Catholic mission, San Antonio de Valero, which had been converted into a military garrison. Many Catholics were among the heroic defenders. Catholics helped draft and were among those who signed the Texas Declaration of Independence. Catholic legislators worked to restore church lands taken over by the Texas Republic after the war of independence from Mexico.

Under the Spanish and Mexican governments, all new settlers had been required to become Catholic. Many became Catholic in name only to qualify as immigrants. After independence, some Texans identified the Catholic church with the Mexican government, and the Church suffered. Soon church authority was transferred from Mexico to clergy from the United States, and many missionary priests, sisters and brothers primarily from France replaced the remaining Mexican clergy.

Catholic business leaders and politicians worked closely with the French clergy to reestablish Catholicism in the Republic of Texas. The Pope appointed a vicar for the new republic.

Upon entering the Union, Texas was given its own diocese, the Diocese of Galveston, and many religious orders came into the state to establish churches, schools and hospitals. Even during the Civil War, new priests and nuns came into the state by running the Union blockade or slipping through the front lines.

There were still hostile Indians. Missionary priests, called circuit riders, frequently traveled by night to avoid discovery. They suffered terrible hardships from the rugged country, disease, the weather and hostile Indians.

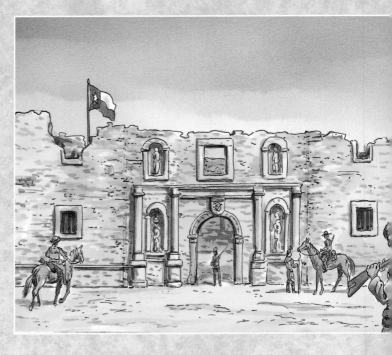

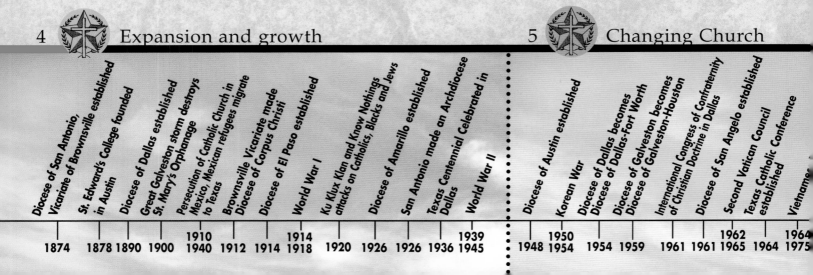

Diocese of San Antonio, Vicariate of Brownsville established

St. Edward's College founded in Austin

Diocese of Dallas established

Great Galveston storm destroys St. Mary's Orphanage

Persecution of Catholic Church in Mexico, Mexican refugees migrate to Texas

Brownsville Vicariate made Diocese of Corpus Christi

Diocese of El Paso established

World War I

Ku Klux Klan and Know Nothings attacks on Catholics, Blacks and Jews

Diocese of Amarillo established

San Antonio made an Archdiocese

Texas Centennial Celebrated in Dallas

World War II

Diocese of Austin established

Korean War

Diocese of Dallas becomes Diocese of Dallas-Fort Worth

Diocese of Galveston becomes Diocese of Galveston-Houston

International Congress of Confraternity of Christian Doctrine in Dallas

Diocese of San Angelo established

Second Vatican Council

Texas Catholic Conference established

Vietnam…

1874   1878 1890 1900   1910 1940   1912   1914 1918   1920   1926   1926 1936   1939 1945   1948   1950 1954   1954   1959   1961 1961   1962 1965   1964   1964 1975

• Immigrants from many lands renew the Church

After the Civil War, large numbers of new settlers came into Texas from other states and many European countries. Catholics came from Germany, Ireland, Poland, Czechoslovakia, Italy, Belgium and France to establish communities in the state, often bringing their priests with them.

Texas' population first tended to be along the Gulf coast and the Mexican border, but this new influx of settlers quickly populated the rest of the state. The coming of the railroads brought more Catholic settlers to Texas as laborers and merchants.

When it became evident that the growing Catholic population could no longer be served from Galveston, which was at the southeastern corner of the state, a new diocese was established at San Antonio. A vicar was appointed for the Brownsville and Corpus Christi area.

It was not long before the number of dioceses multiplied as the population of Catholics increased. Dioceses were established at Dallas, El Paso, Amarillo and other cities. By the year 2000 there were 15 dioceses in Texas, more

than any other state, and the number of Catholics had increased to over 5 million. In the ebb and flow of history, populations change. Today the Hispanic Catholic population is increasing as new immigrants come from Mexico and Central America. Catholics from Asian countries are increasing. New churches have been established for Catholics from Vietnam, China, Korea, India and the Middle East.

That is a quick look at our Texas Catholic family history; we know where we came from, and where we are now. But, there are many interesting stories along the way, stories of men and women whose lives and faith have provided the threads from which our family history has been woven.

TEXAS!!

Emigrants who are desirious of assisting Texas at this important crisis of her affairs may have a free passage and equipments, by applying at the
NEW-YORK and PHILADELPHIA HOTEL,
On the Old Levee, near the Blue Stores.

Now is the time to ensure a fortune in Land: To all who remain in Texas during the War will be allowed 1280 Acres.
To all who remain Six Months, 640 Acres.
To all who remain Three Months, 320 Acres.
And as Colonists, 4600 Acres for a family and 1470 Acres for a Single Man.
New Orleans, April 23d, 1836.

TEXAS BROADSIDE   *The University of Texas*

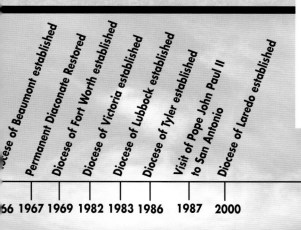

Diocese of Beaumont established
Permanent Diaconate Restored
Diocese of Fort Worth established
Diocese of Victoria established
Diocese of Lubbock established
Diocese of Tyler established
Visit of Pope John Paul II to San Antonio
Diocese of Laredo established

66 1967 1969 1982 1983 1986 1987 2000

1

The Age of Exploration and Discovery

> Americans before Columbus

North America was discovered tens of thousands of years ago, probably by people who walked across a land-bridge between Siberia in Russia and Alaska. These people gradually spread over North and South America, and many settled in what is now Texas.

They hunted great woolly mammoths, giant buffalo and other large beasts using only spears. Archeologists have discovered the bones of people who lived in Texas eight to ten thousand years ago. There is some evidence that the first Texans arrived long before that, possibly as long as 37,000 years ago.

Gradually they learned to control fire and developed better hunting weapons like the bow and arrow. Some built villages, while others learned to cultivate the land and became farmers. Many continued the nomadic ways of their ancestors. These were the kinds of people who lived in Texas before the arrival of the first Europeans.

Far across the ocean, Europeans traveling to China and India had returned home with spices, silk, jade and precious jewels. Trips from Europe to the Orient by land took months, sometimes years. Sailors and explorers from Portugal and Spain thought that a faster route to the Orient could be found by sea.

Portuguese sailors sailed south, down the west coast of Africa in search of a route. Christopher Columbus, from Genoa (in present day Italy), was convinced that the world was round, not flat. He believed that the best route to the Orient would be to sail west, around the world. King Ferdinand and Queen Isabella of Spain thought that Columbus was correct and agreed to finance his expedition of three small ships called caravels.

"land-bridge"
A neck of land joining two large land masses, in this case Siberia and Alaska.

"archeologist"
One who studies human history and pre-history through the excavation of sites and the analysis of physical remains.

Christopher Columbus makes his proposal for reaching the Orient to King Ferdinand and Queen Isabella.

"nomadic"
The custom of pastoral peoples who roam from place to place seeking fresh pasture.

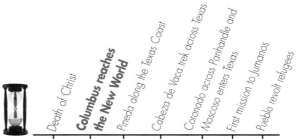

Death of Christ	Columbus reaches the New World	Pineda along the Texas Coast	Cabeza de Vaca trek across Texas	Coronado across Panhandle and Moscoso enters Texas	First mission to Jumanos	Pueblo revolt refugees
33 A.D.	**1492**	1519	1528-35	1542	1631	1680

> The call to spread the Gospel

Many in Spain were interested only in finding a shorter, faster route to the Orient to gain wealth and fame. However Ferdinand and Isabella were especially interested in spreading the Catholic faith to lands where Jesus was not known, and the Gospel had never been preached. Indeed, Ferdinand and Isabella were so committed to the Church, that they were called "their Catholic majesties."

Columbus, certain that he had found a new route to the Orient, arrived on the island of Guanahani in the Bahamas, which he renamed San Salvador or "Holy Savior." Believing he had found India, he called the land the Indies, and the people there, Indians. Today we use the term Amerindians, to distinguish them from the people of the Asian nation of India. Once the conquistadors found that the natives possessed gold, the New World became a source of riches in itself.

Spanish explorers, following Columbus, soon realized that he had not reached India and began searching for a way around or through this land that had become such an obstacle to reaching their goal. Spain's first contact with Texas was made by one of these explorers, Alonso Alvarez de Pineda, naval adjutant to Francisco de Garay, the governor of Jamaica. In 1519 Garay outfitted an expedition led by Pineda, who, with four armed vessels, sailed north from the Island of Jamaica to Florida and westward along the Gulf coast to Mexico. The primary purpose of Pineda's expedition was to establish Garay's claim to a share in the riches that Cortés had reportedly found among the Indians in Mexico. A secondary purpose was to find the elusive (and legendary) Strait of Anian that would provide passage to the Pacific and to the Orient.

> **Alonso Alvarez de Pineda**

1494 > † 1520

Alonso Alvarez de Pineda is shown drawing the first map of the Gulf of Mexico.

Little is known about this Spanish explorer who was commissioned in 1519 by Francisco de Garay, governor of Jamaica, to lead an expedition to explore the coast of the Gulf of Mexico from Florida to Mexico. During his voyage of exploration, he mapped the Gulf of Mexico from Florida to the Yucatan peninsula, established that Florida was a peninsula and not an island and became the first European to sail along the Texas coast. He also attempted unsuccessfully to establish Garay's claim to lands surrounding the Río Pánuco. He is sometimes referred to as the "Discoverer of Texas." A year after his historic voyage he was killed near the Río Pánuco by Huastec Indians.

CLICK-LEARNING

> **caravel**
> **Columbus' journal**
> **Ferdinand and Isabella**
> **conquistador**

"Catholic Majesties"

A term referring to the kings or queens of Catholic countries.

"Gospel"

The first four books of the New Testament (Matthew, Mark, Luke and John.)

"conquistador"

One of the Spanish soldiers or adventurers who conquered portions of North, Central and South America in the 16th century.

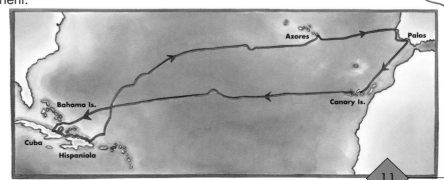

Columbus' first voyage to the New World.

> First Europeans reach Texas coast

Pineda did not find the strait, because it did not exist, but he did become the first European to sail along the Gulf coast of Texas and Northern Mexico. It was speculated by some historians that Pineda landed and later established a colony at the mouth of the Rio Grande, sometimes identified as the Río de las Palmas. Recent research by Dr. Donald Chipman of the University of North Texas, has established beyond a reasonable doubt, that Pineda did not land at the Rio Grande, or anywhere in Texas. The site of his colony, according to Dr. Chipman, was the Río Pánuco, near the present Tampíco, Mexico.

For six or seven weeks Pineda and his ships remained at the Río Pánuco, while they cleaned and caulked the hulls of their ships. When the expedition returned to Jamaica, Governor Garay immediately sent Pineda back to Río Pánuco to establish a colony. The Huastec Indians apparently destroyed the colony and killed Pineda during a revolt in 1520.

In 1523 Garay established another ill-fated colony at the Rio del las Palmas, the present day Rio Soto la Marina, between Pánuco and the Rio Grande. There is no indication that Pineda ever set foot on Texas soil, or that the Rio del las Palmas was the Rio Grande. The coming of the first Europeans to Texas would await the arrival of Nuñez Cabeza de Vaca and the remnants of the ill-fated Narváez expedition.

Alonso Alvarez de Pineda and his crew land at the mouth of the Rio Pánuco.

CLICK-LEARNING

> **Friar Juan Suárez, OFM**
> **Hernán Cortés**
> **Hispaniola**
> **New Spain**

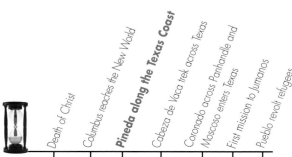

Death of Christ | Columbus reaches the New World | **Pineda along the Texas Coast** | Cabeza de Vaca trek across Texas | Coronado across Panhandle and Moscoso enters Texas | First mission to Jumanos | Pueblo revolt refuges

33 A.D.   1492   **1519**   1528-35   1542   1631   1680

In this print of Friar Juan Suárez, the bishop-elect is shown with the bishop's mitre, a book of Catholic doctrine and the crucifix.

> Plans for the first Catholic dioceses in the New World

King Carlos I, who became King of Spain in 1516, was anxious to establish the Catholic Church in the new lands, which by that time had been named New Spain. Bishops had been appointed on the islands of Hispaniola (Santo Domingo) in 1511 and in Cuba in 1522. There was no bishop on the North American mainland. The king petitioned Pope Clement VII to establish a diocese on the mainland at Las Palmas and nominated Friar Juan Suárez (a Franciscan priest) to be the first bishop. Friar Suárez had spent time in Mexico and was well loved by the natives among whom he worked.

King Carlos sent Friar Suárez and four companions with the Pánfilo de Narváez expedition, to explore and settle the Gulf coast from Florida to the Rio de las Palmas. Narváez' charge was to establish three forts and two towns in the territory, one of which would be Las Palmas.

In addition to Friar Suárez and his band of Franciscan friars, the king also appointed a treasurer, to look after the royal interests. The treasurer, Alvar Núñez Cabeza de Vaca, was destined to become the hero and the historian of the expedition.

"bishop"
The highest clerical rank in the Church - normally the head of a diocese.

In June, 1527, Narváez set sail from Jamaica for Hispaniola with five ships and six hundred soldiers and colonists to establish the forts and settlements required by his royal charter.

"diocese"
A geographical area where a bishop has the responsibility to teach, govern and sanctify the Catholic people.

"Franciscan"
A religious order of priests and brothers founded by St. Francis of Assisi.

"friar"
The title by which members of certain religious orders of men are called. It means "brother."

"historian"
One who studies the history or chronicle of an event.

> A troubled voyage and doomed expedition

Pánfilo de Narváez' expedition experienced many difficulties from the beginning. Storms drove them off course and destroyed two ships and supplies. Sixty men were drowned, and others deserted. They finally landed on a peninsula near Tampa Bay on the West Coast of Florida, thousands of miles east of their intended destination.

Upon landing they encountered indigenous people wearing trinkets of gold. Narváez decided to move the expedition inland in search of the source of the precious metal. Against the advice of Cabeza de Vaca, Narváez sent the ships to search along the coast for the mouth of the Rio de las Palmas while the men proceeded overland. The ships were dispatched with instructions to rendezvous with the overland expedition later.

It was a tragic decision. The ships were never seen again, and the members of the expedition were forced to begin a journey that would involve eight years of great suffering, sickness, death and unbelievable hardships as they wandered the Southwest.

"rendezvous"
An agreed upon place for meeting or assembling.

The Spanish Christians were regarded as healers because many of the sick recovered after Cabeza de Vaca and his companions prayed with them.

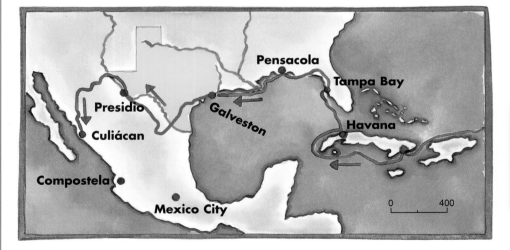

Route of the Narváez-Cabeza de Vaca
Journey in 1527

CLICK-LEARNING

> **Cabeza de Vaca**
> **Esteban the Moor**
> **Pánfilo Narváez**

Death of Christ — 33 A.D.
Columbus reaches the New World — 1492
Pineda along the Texas Coast — 1519
Cabeza de Vaca trek across Texas — **1528-35**
Coronado across Panhandle and Moscoso enters Texas — 1542
First mission to Jumanos — 1631
Pueblo revolt refugees — 1680

> An incredible journey

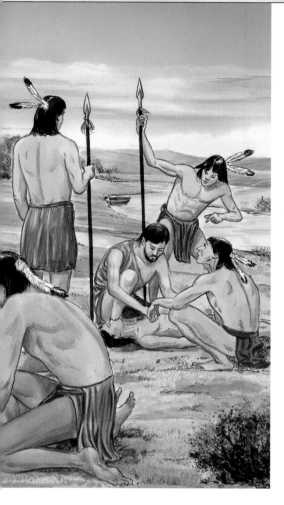

Believing that they were only a short distance from the Rio de las Palmas, Narváez and his men headed west toward New Spain. They traveled along the Gulf coast, by foot, and then in crude barges which they had built themselves. The barges became separated and landed at different places along the Texas coast. These men were the first Catholics to set foot upon Texas. Cabeza de Vaca and two of the barges came ashore on Galveston Island, which, as history would have it, would become the launching place of the Catholic Church in modern Texas.

Texas was no place of refuge for the survivors. Their journey turned out to be a death march for most of the several hundred men. Many lives were lost as the barges were wrecked or sunk, others were killed or captured by Indians and disease and starvation took a large toll. Eight years later, Cabeza de Vaca and three other survivors, including Esteban the Moor, reached a Spanish outpost in New Spain.

> **"New Spain"**
> The name given to Mexico by the Spanish government.

> **"Moor"**
> A member of a Muslim people of northwest Africa who conquered and occupied Spain and Portugal.

Bishop-elect Suárez and his Franciscan companions were among those who perished. The Diocese of Rio de las Palmas was never established. Instead Mexico City became the first diocese in New Spain in 1530.

Cabeza de Vaca returned to Spain and gave a detailed journal of his incredible journey to the king. In his journal he refers to his companions, not as Spaniards, but as Christians. He wrote of how some of the native people were suspicious and hostile, but of how others were open and helpful. He taught them about the Christian faith and baptism.

On their journey the Spaniards encountered many sick whom they prayed over and blessed. Because they often recovered, Cabeza de Vaca and his companions came to be regarded as healers. Cabeza de Vaca developed a great respect for the Amerindians and became a defender of their cause before the king. He wanted to lead a new expedition to the area he had explored.

The king, however, had already granted a charter to Hernando De Soto for exploration of the lands from Florida to New Spain. It is said that Cabeza de Vaca refused an invitation from De Soto to join the expedition.

> **"journal"**
> A daily record of happenings.

> **"healer"**
> A person who heals, especially through prayer or faith.

> Alvar Nuñez Cabeza de Vaca
1490 > † 1557

This Spaniard, whose name means "head of a cow", survived and recorded one of the most astonishing explorations in the New World. It took him eight years to make the journey during which he was enslaved by the natives. He taught them about Christianity, and learned about their culture. Cabeza de Vaca's strange name was given to an ancestor who helped the King win a battle by marking the entrance to a hidden mountain pass with the head of a cow, a "cabeza de vaca".

Alvar Nuñez Cabeza de Vaca.

> Early explorations of Texas and New Mexico

Hernando De Soto succeeded where Narváez failed. His expedition explored the interior of the new lands (present day Florida, Georgia, Mississippi, Alabama, Louisiana, Tennessee and Arkansas), but at a terrible price. The Spaniards' cruelty to Amerindians, in the form of inhumane treatment combined with exposure to devastating diseases, left

behind a trail of blood and misery. De Soto never reached Texas. He died of a fever after a five-year journey overland from Florida. His lieutenant, Luis de Moscoso, led the expedition into Texas with several missionary priests. They explored much of Northeast and East Texas including the lower reaches of the Trinity River before eventually returning to the Mississippi. Carlos Castañeda wrote that they built seven small boats and descended the Mississippi to the Gulf and sailed along the coast to the Río Pánuco.

Three hundred of the six hundred who started in Florida reached New Spain. Castañeda reported that five priests accompanied Moscoso into Texas and that none survived, but that some 500 Indians were baptized during the journey.

From a distance, the desert sun makes the adobe pueblo appear golden to Friar Marcos de Niza.

Death of Christ | Columbus reaches the New World | Pineda along the Texas Coast | Cabeza de Vaca trek across Texas | **Coronado across Panhandle and Moscoso enters Texas** | First mission to Jumanos | Pueblo revolt refugees

33 A.D.　1492　1519　1528-35　**1542**　1631　1680

> Quest for gold

Portugal had won the race to discover a sea route to the riches of the Orient, but Spain had changed its goals to a search for the mineral riches of the New World. Cortés' conquest in Mexico brought him not only wealth, but power and acclaim. Hopes of similar conquests and wealth inspired others to do the same.

Hopes are fueled by legends, and the legend of the Seven Cities of Gold was no exception. The legend resurfaced in a story told to Cabeza de Vaca.

> **"missionary"**
> A person who teaches the Christian faith to people in another land.

Esteban the Moor (or Estebanico), one of Cabeza de Vaca's companions, and Friar Marcos de Niza, a French Franciscan missionary, were sent by the Viceroy of New Spain, to investigate the story of seven cities of great wealth to the North. Because of his knowledge of the land, Estebanico traveled far ahead of Friar Marcos. Some of the natives traveling with him returned to tell the priest that Estebanico had been killed when he attempted to enter Cíbola, one of the seven cities.

> **"Viceroy"**
> represents the king in New Spain.

Friar Marcos retreated to Mexico and told the Viceroy that he had gotten close enough to see the golden city from a distance and had planted three crosses claiming the territory for Spain. But, fearing for his life, he returned to Mexico to report the events. The desert plays strange tricks on your eyes, and it is not impossible that Friar Marcos could have seen a mirage of the great pueblo in the golden sunset and that it truly appeared to be a "city of gold."

> **"mirage"**
> An illusion caused by atmospheric conditions.

Route followed by De Soto/Moscoso expedition from Florida to New Spain

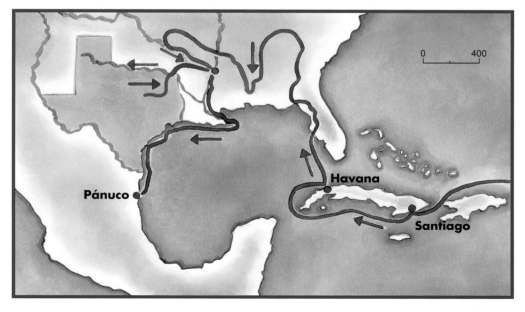

Pánuco · Havana · Santiago

0   400

> Estebanico the Moor

Unknown > † 1539

One of the four survivors of the Narváez expedition, Estebanico was a native of Morocco and a Moor who had been baptized. A slave, he accompanied his master on the expedition. Both survived the eight-year journey from Florida to New Spain. Zuni Indians killed him when he tried to enter one of their pueblos while looking for the Seven Cities of Gold.

Estebanico, the Moorish slave.

CLICK-LEARNING
> **Hernando De Soto**
> **Luis Moscoso**
> **Friar Marcos de Niza**
> **Seven Cities of Cíbola**

> Coronado's search for the Seven Cities

Based on Friar Marcos de Niza's report, the Viceroy sent an expedition in 1540 led by Francisco Vázquez de Coronado to find the Seven Cities of Gold and claim their wealth for Spain. Friar Marcos accompanied Coronado on the expedition. The Seven Cities turned out to be Zuni pueblos.

The role of Friar Marcos has been the source of much controversy. Some accuse him of lying and returning to Mexico as soon as word reached him of the fate of Estebanico. Others feel that the Friar was used by the Viceroy to justify sending an expedition to the North. Coronado was deeply disappointed at the failure of the expedition but went on to become the first to explore vast areas of New Mexico, Texas, and Kansas.

Still chasing "El Dorado", Coronado believed a story told by a native called Turk who claimed to know of other large cities where there was much gold. This new El Dorado was called Gran Quivira, and Coronado and his men wandered aimlessly for days before realizing that their guide was out to betray them. Turk was killed for his treachery.

With a new guide, the expedition reached Quivira in 1541. Once again, Coronado found only Wichita adobe pueblos and huts with the only precious metal being the copper collar worn by the chief.

Turk, the native guide leads Coronado and his expedition.

> **"pueblo"**
> A communal village built by Amerindians of the southwest, consisting of single and multistory buildings built of mud or stone.

> **"El Dorado"**
> An imaginary city or country said to be rich in gold and precious stones.

> **"adobe"**
> Building material found in hot and dry areas that is made from clay or mud that is sun dried and not fired.

Spanish crossbowman.

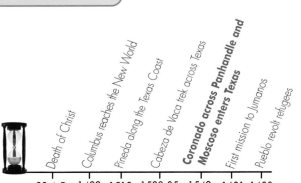

Death of Christ | Columbus reaches the New World | Pineda along the Texas Coast | Cabeza de Vaca trek across Texas | **Coronado across Panhandle and Moscoso enters Texas** | First mission to Jumanos | Pueblo revolt refugees

33 A.D. 1492 1519 1528-35 1542 1631 1680

> The Blessed Mother appears as an Indian woman

"apparition"
A sudden and dramatic appearance of a supernatural nature.

"tilma"
A rough, cape-like garment of ayate cloth, made from the fiber of the maguey cactus.

In 1531 the Blessed Virgin appeared on a hillside near Mexico City to Juan Diego, a Christian Indian. In the apparition, known as Our Lady of Guadalupe, Mary appeared as a dark-skinned Indian woman. The image that she left on the tilma of Juan Diego played an important role in combating the conquistadors' efforts to brand the natives as less than fully human.

In the Spanish lands of both North and South America, the conquistadors' treatment of the natives had been shameful. Cabeza de Vaca, who grew to respect and admire the Amerindians during his eight years of living among them, became a great champion of their rights. He urged King Carlos to act to end the exploitation and cruelty by many of the Spaniards. The king intervened, and priests were charged with protecting the natives and looking after their interests.

He mandated that Amerindians should not be removed from their villages, be overworked, be enslaved, be underfed or be under clothed. Similar provisions were included in the royal charters given to De Soto and other conquistadors. However, the history of the Spanish explorations is marked by repeated violations of the royal mandates.

Tapestry by Fr. B.G. Eades, a priest of the Diocese of Dallas, now displayed in the great hall of Dallas' Cathedral.

> Our Lady of Guadalupe

In 1525 an Aztec named Quauhtlatoatzin was baptized and took the Christian name of Juan Diego. In 1531, he began experiencing a series of apparitions of the Blessed Virgin on a hillside near Mexico City. When he told his story to the bishop, he wasn't believed. So Mary told him to gather into his tilma the roses that were growing on the hillside and take them to the bishop so that he would believe him. When Juan Diego opened his tilma to present the roses to the bishop they were both amazed to find the image of Our Lady as an Indian woman mira-culously imprinted on the ayate cloth. Juan Diego told the bishop that Our Lady wished that a shrine be built on the site where she had appeared. The first one was built in 1533. Less than 20 years after Mary appeared, 9 million Aztecs had been converted to Christianity. Juan Diego died in 1548. Devotion to Our Lady of Guadalupe has spread throughout the hemisphere and the world. Many miracles have been attributed to her intervention. In 1945 Pope Pius XII declared Our Lady of Guadalupe "Queen of Mexico and Empress of the Americas." In 1990 Juan Diego was declared Blessed by Pope John Paul II, who canonized him a saint in 2002 after several miracles were attributed to his intervention.

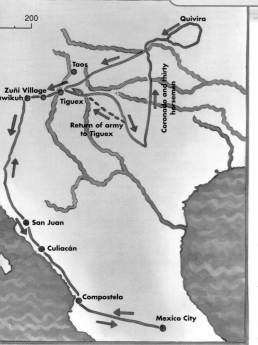

200

Quivira

Taos

Zuñi Village wikuh

Tiguex

Return of army to Tiguex

Coronado and thirty horsemen

San Juan

Culiacán

Compostela

Mexico City

Route followed by Coronado's expedition from New Spain to New Mexico, Texas and Kansas in his futile search for the Seven Cities of Gold.

19

> Souls to be won for Christ

With the failure of Coronado's expedition, the Spaniards began to regard the northern frontiers as empty and useless territory. They centered their interests on the valley of Mexico. Missionaries saw the northern territories as filled with souls to be won for Christ and the Church. Coronado's expedition provided the first opportunity to carry the Catholic faith to the frontier. Friar Marcos de Niza and three other Franciscans were among those accompanying Coronado. Their purpose was to carry the Gospel to the natives. Friar Juan de Padilla, the youngest, was a priest. Friar Luis de Escalona was a lay brother, and the aging Friar Juan de la Cruz was also a priest.

"lay brother"
A member of a religious order like the Franciscans, who chooses not to be ordained.

Friar de Padilla accompanied Coronado to Quivira where he was welcomed. When a dejected and disappointed Coronado began his return journey to Mexico, Friar De Padilla decided to go back to Quivira to minister and spread the Gospel.

He established a mission and was well received by the Wichitas. When he decided to move deeper into the frontier to evangelize another village, his companions and he encountered a hostile war party. At this time many natives saw the Spaniards as invaders of their land and destroyers of their culture. As the warriors attacked, Friar de Padilla told the others to flee to save themselves, then knelt in prayer. The war party descended upon the missionary and pierced him with arrows and threw his body in a pit. His companions were captured but later escaped to tell of the self-sacrifice. Many mistakenly believe that the place of his martyrdom was the Texas Panhandle.

"Wichitas"
An Indian nation found in Texas, Oklahoma and Kansas.

"evangelize"
To preach, teach and witness to the Gospel.

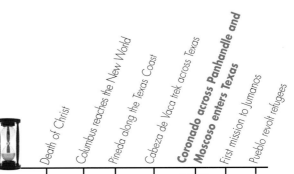

Death of Christ | Columbus reaches the New World | Pineda along the Texas Coast | Cabeza de Vaca trek across Texas | **Coronado across Panhandle and Moscoso enters Texas** | First mission to Jumanos | Pueblo revolt refugees

33 A.D. 1492 1519 1528-35 **1542** 1631 1680

Francisco Vásquez
de Coronado.

> Francisco Vásquez de Coronado

1510 > † 1544

One of the most famous and unsuccessful treasure hunters in history, Coronado was born of a noble family in Spain and came to the new world in 1535. He was appointed governor of New Galicia, a province in New Spain. He spent two years leading an expedition in a fruitless search for the legendary Seven Cities of Cibola. Disgraced by his failure, Coronado was later found guilty of corruption and died in Mexico, a dishonored man at the age of 34.

Friar Juan de Padilla kneels in prayer as he awaits martyrdom at the hands of a hostile war party, Nov. 30, 1544.

> First American martyrs

The other two Franciscans also were martyred. Friar De la Cruz was killed by the Tiguas, and jealous shamans murdered Friar De Escalona. Friar de Padilla is honored as the first martyr in what would become the United States.

It is difficult today to imagine the hardships these explorers and missionaries experienced. They had no protection from the weather. They were subject to various diseases. Their food was what they could take from the land. Their medicines were very primitive, and they were constantly attacked and harassed by those who saw them as invaders of their land.

In many cases, the explorers treated the natives as less than human. The missionaries struggled constantly, often unsuccessfully, to keep them from being slaughtered.

Sadly, the Spanish brought more than Christianity to the new land. They also brought diseases to which the Amerindians had never been exposed. Because they had no natural immunity to the European diseases such as small pox and cholera, thousands fell ill and died.

CLICK-LEARNING

> Quivira
> Friar Juan de Padilla
> Tiguas

"Tiguas"
A native group in New Mexico.

"martyr"
A person who willingly gives up his/her life as a witness to his/her faith in Christ.

"shaman"
A medicine man or Indian priest.

VENERABLE MADRE MARIA JESUS DE AGREDA
1620 **THE LADY IN BLUE** 1631

The mural of the Venerable Mother María de Jesús de Agreda presently hangs in St. Anne Church, Beaumont.

> The Woman in Blue

Among the missions founded in New Mexico was San Agustín de la Isleta established in 1613. It was there in 1629 that a group of Jumano Amerindians from Texas arrived and asked that missionaries be sent to instruct them in the Gospel. According to the Amerindians they had been told by a "Woman in Blue" to come and seek priests to teach them.

Amazed, two Franciscans, Friar Juan de Salas and Friar Diego López, accompanied the Jumanos to a spot near present-day San Angelo. There they found many other Amerindians who told of being instructed by the mysterious woman in blue who said that the missionaries were coming. The Franciscans spent several days among the Amerindians before returning to their mission in New Mexico.

A number of the Jumanos returned with the Franciscans to the Isleta mission where a separate mission, called San Isidro, was established for them. The mission closed when most of the Jumanos returned to Texas.

Two years later, Friar Salas and Friar Juan de Ortega returned with a Spanish expedition to revisit the Jumanos who welcomed them. Friar Salas returned to New Mexico, but Friar Ortega remained with the Indians for six months. In 1684 Franciscans with another Spanish expedition from New Mexico spent a month among Indians, temporarily gathered at a site on the Colorado River, which they called the San Clemente.

"Jumano"

An Indian nation located in west and southwest Texas.

"juncture"

A place where things come together.

22

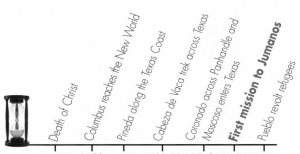

Death of Christ
Columbus reaches the New World
Pineda along the Texas Coast
Cabeza de Vaca trek across Texas
Coronado across Panhandle and Moscoso across Texas
First mission to Jumanos
Pueblo revolt refugees

33 A.D. 1492 1519 1528-35 1542 **1631** 1680

> Who was she?

Prior to the arrival of the Jumanos, the Archbishop of Mexico had received inquiries about the claims of a nun in Spain, who told of being transported in dreams to Eastern New Mexico and Western Texas where she instructed several Amerindian groups about Christianity.

Friar Alonso de Benavides, who had served as religious superior in New Mexico, went to Spain to visit the nun who claimed to have made the visits. She was Mother María de Jesús de Agreda, who belonged to a Franciscan convent whose order wore a brown habit with a blue cloak. According to Mother Maria de Jesús her apparitions ended in 1632. Stories of the woman in blue continued to surface among Amerindians in Texas for years after her death in 1665.

"venerable"
A step on the way to be canonized a saint.

"Poor Clare"
A member of a cloistered Franciscan order of women religious named for St. Clare of Assisi.

Jumano missionary activities ■

Map showing location of missionary activities among the Jumanos in 1600s.

CLICK-LEARNING

> Jumanos
> convent

> Mother María de Jesús de Agreda The Woman in Blue
1602 > † 1665

*Venerable **Mother María de Jesús (Maria Coronel) never left her native Spain and spent most of her life as a cloistered nun. Yet she is honored as an apostle to the natives of Texas and New Mexico.***

María was the oldest surviving child of a noble family in Spain. In 1618, her home was converted into a convent and she, along with her mother and sister, became a member of the Poor Clare Order.

In 1621 she experienced visions in which she was taken to Texas and New Mexico where she taught about Jesus and the Gospel.

Her apparitions ended in 1632.

An ancient woodcut print of Mother María de Jesús de Agreda.

This carving on the San[...]
Cathedral door d[...]
refugees fl[...]
the Indian r[...]

> A prelude to Texas missions

Territory that was to become Texas remained largely ignored by the Spaniards, except for the limited expeditions of Moscoso and Coronado. All their attention had been focused on New Mexico in the search for gold.

Wealth and religion continued to be the two forces driving Spanish expansion. In 1598 the Crown granted a charter to Juan de Oñate to pacify and to Christianize the natives. This meant converting them to Christianity. Forcing a "heathen" to become a Christian was not only acceptable, it was considered a virtuous act. To the Pueblo nations, this meant the destruction of centuries-old traditions and subjection to intolerable conditions.

Oñate, a man of great wealth, was appointed the first governor of New Mexico and established the original capital at San Gabriel. The Pueblo Indians did not welcome the Spaniards. Some revolted and killed members of the first expedition; the revolt was brutally put down by the Spanish.

Excessive cruelty resulted in the revolt of the Pueblo people against the Spanish in New Mexico as depicted in this old print.

"Pueblo nations"

Spanish name for town-dwelling Indian groups in New Mexico.

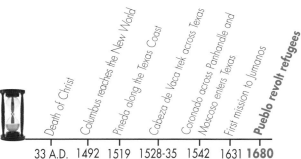

Death of Christ
Columbus reaches the New World
Pineda along the Texas Coast
Cabeza de Vaca trek across Texas
Coronado across Panhandle and
Moscoso enters Texas
First mission to Jumanos
Pueblo revolt refugees

33 A.D.   1492   1519   1528-35   1542   1631   **1680**

> Revolt of the Pueblo Indians

Settlements were founded, and missions were established in the pueblos and villages. The pacification and Christianization efforts continued. Spanish officials made excessive labor and tribute demands on the pueblos, and the missionaries sought to eliminate the native religion.

Opposition to the efforts of the missionaries remained, particularly on the part of the shamans or medicine men. Because of their continued resistance, the Spanish punished them often with great brutality. One of the medicine men, who was called Popé, organized a revolt among the Pueblo Indians to drive out the Spanish. Plans for the revolt were kept secret. However some members of the Tewa nation warned the governor. Learning that the secret was out, Popé ordered the revolt to begin earlier than planned.

On August 10, 1680, Spanish soldiers were besieged in the new capital of Santa Fe. Throughout New Mexico missions and settlements were attacked and sacked. In all, over 400 Spaniards were killed, including the brutal deaths of 21 of the 33 Franciscans serving in New Mexico. Those who could, escaped south to the El Paso area.

It was 16 years before Spain regained stable control of New Mexico. In the meantime the Spaniards' attention turned toward Texas.

"Tewa nation"
One of the Pueblo language groups friendly to the Spanish.

"besieged"
means surrounded or under heavy attack.

"sack"
To plunder, steal and destroy.

"Moctezuma"
Emperor of the Aztecs when Cortés conquered Mexico.

GLICK-LEARNING

> Pueblo Revolt
> Juan de Oñate
> Moctezuma

> Juan de Oñate

1550 > † 1626

Sometimes referred to as "the last Conquistador", Oñate was born in Mexico. He was married to a descendant of Hernán Cortés and Moctezuma.

He professed to be a deeply religious man committed to spreading the Christian faith among the native population. However under his direction the Acoma Pueblo was brutally subdued in retaliation for killing Spaniards. Many blame Oñate's actions for the bloody Pueblo revolt. He was reprimanded for using excessive force against the Pueblos and was banished from New Mexico and Mexico City.

Juan de Oñate, the first governor of New Mexico.

2 Missions and settlements

> La Salle and the French incursion

France, a long time rival of Spain in the New World, was responsible for Spain's sudden new interest in New Spain's largely neglected northeastern frontier.

French explorer and adventurer René Robert Cavelier, Sieur de La Salle heard stories of the Orient with its riches and wondered if it could be reached through the great interior waterways and rivers and lakes of North America.

With a commission from the King of France, he explored the Mississippi River and claimed it and all the territory to the west (including New Spain) for France. He first believed that the Mississippi River would provide that magic pathway to the Pacific, but soon discovered that the system drained into the Gulf of Mexico. La Salle then won a Royal Charter to establish a French colony where the Mississippi River flowed into the Gulf.

In 1684 he set sail with a fleet of four ships from France. From the beginning the expedition was beset by problems. Pirates captured one of his ships; a number of his men deserted, and his navigation was off by more than 400 miles. Instead of finding the mouth of the Mississippi, he landed at Matagorda Bay northeast of Corpus Christi.

His problems were far from over. A second ship was wrecked attempting to navigate the narrow channel at the mouth of Matagorda Bay, and a third ship decided to return to France.

Ships from La Salle's expedition stand off shore as a landing party heads for Matagorda Island.

"incursion"

A hostile entrance into another's territory.

"pirates"

Sea raiders who preyed upon ships of all nations.

Catholic missions at Socorro and Ysleta	La Junta mission attempt	**La Salle establishes Fort St. Louis**	First East Texas mission Attempt	La Junta missions	East Texas missions	San Antonio, mission, fort and settlement	La Bahia fort and mission	Three East Texas missions to San Antonio and San Fernando Parish in San Antonio	Lower Rio Grande Settlements	Comanches destroy San Saba mission	East Texas Missions abandoned	Nacogdoches parish founded	San Elizario parish founded	Refugio mission founded	Secularization of missions
1682	1683	**1685**	1690	1715	1716	1718	1722	1731	1749	1758	1773	1779	1789	1793	1793

"Jesuit"
A member of the Society of Jesus religious community.

> René Robert Cavelier, Sieur de La Salle

1643 > † 1687

René Robert Cavelier was born in France and originally entered the Jesuit Society but was lured by adventure and wealth in the New World.
He became a fur trader in Canada and then traveled the length of the Mississippi by canoe.
He was commissioned by King Louis of France to establish a colony at the mouth of the Mississippi River.
His mission failed and after a series of disasters, he was murdered by one of his men.

René Robert Cavelier Sieur de La Salle.

> The establishment of Fort St. Louis

Undeterred by these misfortunes, La Salle, and his remaining soldiers and settlers, used the lumber from the wrecked ship to build a fort at Matagorda Bay. He named it Fort St. Louis and used it as his base for finding the mouth of the Mississippi, which he still believed to be nearby.

When word of the French expedition reached Mexico, the Spanish launched a frantic search for the colony. La Salle himself was doing some searching. A group of men and he traveled overland to the west as far as the Rio Grande in an unsuccessful search for the Mississippi. He then traveled eastward, but found no great river. While his men and he were away from the fort, a storm grounded and sank his only remaining ship, La Belle, and the colony was stranded.

Disease, drowning and raids by the hostile Karankawas had decimated the colony, and a desperate La Salle set out overland with a small group of men, hoping to reach the Illinois River and French settlements he had established earlier. On the journey, his men mutinied, and La Salle was murdered. A few, including his priest brother, survived and eventually reached French territory and returned to Canada.

"Karankawas"
Members of an Indian nation that lived along the Texas coast.

"mutinied"
Revolted against the leadership.

"massacre"
Killed in large numbers.

By the time the Spanish discovered Fort St. Louis's location in 1689, a raid by the Karankawas had destroyed it. All but the children and a few others who had been away from the Fort at the time were massacred.

"undeterred"
Not discouraged.

"grounded"
Run aground, stuck on the sandy bottom.

French attempts to establish settlements beyond the Mississippi failed, but the experience had been a wake up call for the Spanish, who realized that their undefended and uninhabited northeastern frontier was an open invitation to rival nations. This realization gave birth to the first Spanish settlements northeast of the Rio Grande, the East Texas Missions.

CLICK-LEARNING
> **La Belle**
> **René Robert Cavelier, Sieur de la Salle**
> **Karankawa**
> **Fort St. Louis**

> The First Texas missions

Texas' oldest missions were in West Texas, then a part of New Mexico, and Nueva Vizcaya (in Mexico). In 1682 Pueblo Indians who accompanied the Spanish survivors of the Pueblo Revolt to El Paso established Socorro and Ysleta along the banks of the Rio Grande below El Paso. In 1683 missions were established further down the Rio Grande at La Junta (today's Presidio). After a few years, the La Junta missions were abandoned, but were reestablished in 1715.

In 1690, the next missions founded in Texas were more than 700 miles east of El Paso deep in the forests of East Texas. Two factors were behind the founding of the East Texas missions. The first was that Spain realized, after the incursion of La Salle, that the northwest frontier might be the next target of French expansion. The second was the obsession of a Franciscan to respond to the call of the "Woman in Blue" for priests to minister to the Indians.

Friar Damián Massanet used the danger of French expansion as a means of convincing the Viceroy to establish a Spanish presence by founding missions on the northeastern frontier. Alonso de León was appointed by the Viceroy to accompany Friar Massanet on the expedition. Their journey took the party across what is now the San Antonio River. De León named the river the Arroyo De León to honor himself, but the name would be short-lived.

They arrived in East Texas in May and selected a site for the first mission near Augusta. The simple log building was erected by the Spaniards in four days and was given the name San Francisco de los Tejas.

"obsession"
A driving desire to achieve or accomplish something.

"frontier"
A region on the margin of a settled territory.

Franciscans spent much time preaching to the Indians and teaching them about Jesus and the Gospel.

"log building"
Missions were built from available material. In East Texas, they were built from plentiful logs.

Catholic missions at Socorro and Ysleta — 1682
La Junta mission attempt — 1683
La Salle establishes Fort St. Louis — 1685
First East Texas mission Attempt — **1690**
La Junta missions — 1715
East Texas missions — 1716
San Antonio, mission, fort and settlement — 1718
La Bahia fort and mission — 1722
Three East Texas missions to San Antonio and San Fernando Parish in San Antonio — 1731
Lower Rio Grande Settlements — 1749
Comanches destroy San Saba mission — 1758
East Texas Missions abandoned — 1773
Nacogdoches parish founded — 1779
San Elizario parish founded — 1789
Refugio mission founded — 1793
Secularization of missions begins — 1793

Angelina,
a Christian Indian woman
has been memorialized
by the naming of a county,
a river and a national forest after her.

> Mission San Francisco de los Tejas

The new church was blessed, and De León and Friar Massanet immediately began their return trip to Mexico. They left behind three priests and three Spanish soldiers. Friar Miguel de Fontcuberta was left in charge of the mission. De León had scouted the area and found that the French had made contact with the Indians. His report to the Viceroy resulted in both joy at the establishment of the mission and serious concern over the French presence.

In September a second mission, Santísimo Nombre de María, was established but a flood destroyed it in 1692. Many difficulties plagued the East Texas missions. Among them was the disenchantment with the Amerindians. Friar Massanet believed the Tejas were among the tribes reached by the Woman in Blue, but the missionaries found no trace of Christianity among them.

Of Texas' 254 counties, only one is named after a woman. That is Angelina County, and the woman for which it was named was indeed an extraordinary person for her time. She was a Christian Caddo named Angelina. Her parents were converts of the first missionaries to come to East Texas. When the missions were abandoned the family returned to Mexico with the Franciscans. Angelina lived with a Spanish family and acquired knowledge of the Spanish language and culture. Because of her experience , she was a sought after adviser to the missionaries and military officials. Angelina returned to the land of the Tejas where her bicultural skills proved extremely valuable. She served as an interpreter for the Spanish missionaries, soldiers, and Indian leaders in discussions about where the East Texas missions should be located. Her bi-cultural background and education enabled Angelina to become a key figure in Texas history. The work of this Christian Indian woman has been memorialized by the naming of a county, a river and a national forest after her.
A bronze statue of Angelina with a Franciscan and another Indian has been erected in Lufkin.

"converts"
people who become Catholic are referred to as "converts".

This statue of Angelina, a friar and an Indian brave was sculpted by Jim Knox and is located outside the Civic Center in Lufkin, Texas, in Angelina County.

CLICK-LEARNING

> Angelina
> Caddo

> A decision to abandon the East Texas missions

Friar Massanet returned to East Texas in 1691 with Domingo Terán de los Ríos, the governor of Coahuila y Texas. They were accompanied by several missionaries, among them Friar Francisco Hidalgo. They once more crossed the River De León which Friar Massanet renamed for San Antonio de Padua and noted that the site would be a fine location for a future mission. It was destined to be the site of San Antonio and its missions, the most successful in Texas.

When Friar Massanet and Terán arrived at the East Texas missions, they found that Friar Fontcuberta had died. The missionaries were discouraged. The earlier friendliness of the Amerindians had turned to hatred. Converts had been few. Many feared baptism, believing the diseases brought by the Spaniards had been caused by the ceremony. In addition, the Mission Nombre de María was destroyed by a flood.

Friar Massanet's plan to save the East Texas missions by forcing the Indians to live on or near the missions was rejected by the Viceroy. Internal problems in Mexico had distracted the Viceroy and the Northeast frontier was no longer a high priority.

In October, 1693, a discouraged Friar Massanet set fire to Mission San Francisco. The remaining priests returned to Mexico. Friar Massanet never came back, but Friar Hidalgo, convinced that they were abandoning their obligation to Christianize the natives, began planning how the missions could be reestablished. Continuing rivalry with France would give him his opportunity.

East Texas' first missions were not adobe buildings but were simple log churches like this picture of Mission San Francisco de Tejas.

Catholic missions at Socorro and Ysleta — 1682
La Junta mission attempt — 1683
La Salle establishes Fort St. Louis — 1685
First East Texas mission Attempt — **1690**
La Junta missions — 1715
East Texas missions — 1716
San Antonio, mission, fort and settlement — 1718
La Bahia fort and mission — 1722
Three East Texas missions to San Antonio and San Fernando Parish in San Antonio — 1731
Lower Rio Grande Settlements — 1749
Comanches destroy San Saba mission — 1758
East Texas Missions abandoned — 1773
Nacogdoches parish founded — 1779
San Elizario parish founded — 1789
Refugio mission founded — 1793
Secularization of missions begins — 1793

The French were traders and actively sought opportunities to trade and interact with the natives and the Spaniards. The Spanish attempted to isolate their colonies and forbade trade with foreigners as well as relationships with any non-Spaniard. Nevertheless, the French in Louisiana continued to attempt to establish trading relationships with the Spaniards in Texas.

CLICK-LEARNING
> **Domingo Terán de los Ríos**
> **San Antonio River**
> **Friar Francisco Hidalgo**

> Francisco Hidalgo

1659 > † 1726

Friar Francisco Hidalgo was a man with a cause which was to preach the Gospel to the Tejas. When the East Texas missions were first abandoned in 1693 by order of the Viceroy, he went back to Mexico but prayed for the day he could return to work among the Tejas. His obsession would lead him to take a dangerous treasonous action.

> A desperate and treasonous action

In 1711, Friar Hidalgo in frustration took the bold and potentially treasonous step of writing to the French governor of Louisiana to seek his help in reestablishing the East Texas missions. Seeing in the letter an opportunity to establish trade with the Spanish, Governor de Cadillac sent Louis Juchereau de St. Denis, a Canadian trader, to contact Friar Hidalgo.

Having crossed Texas, St. Denis arrived at San Juan Bautista on the Rio Grande to the surprise of the Spanish. He was placed under house arrest, and the Viceroy in Mexico City was asked for instructions as to what to do with St. Denis.

Meanwhile, St. Denis fell in love with the commandant's granddaughter whom he later married. When he was ordered to Mexico City, the Canadian, far from being punished, was made commissary for an expedition to reestablish the missions in East Texas.

Friar Antonio Margil de Jesús, the Franciscan Superior, decided to reestablish the missions personally, and planned to take Friar Hidalgo and other Franciscans with him.

Once again the missions would be used to counter French influence, but this time a more substantial Spanish presence would include a presidio with a garrison of 25 soldiers in addition to six new missions.

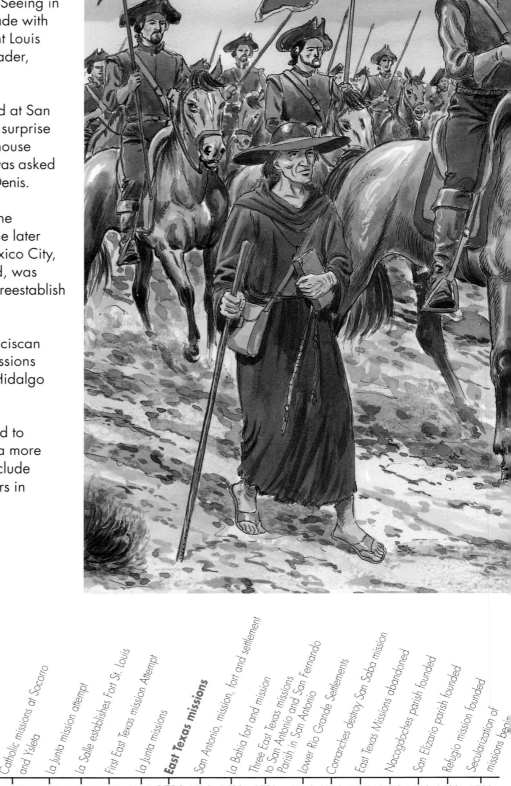

"commissary"

A person given a specific task or assignment.

"presidio"

A fort or military post.

"garrison"

The soldiers assigned to a presidio.

Catholic missions at Socorro and Ysleta	La Junta mission attempt	La Salle establishes Fort St. Louis	First East Texas mission Attempt	La Junta missions	**East Texas missions**	San Antonio, mission, fort and settlement	La Bahia fort and mission	Three East Texas missions to San Antonio and San Fernando Parish in San Antonio	Lower Rio Grande Settlements	Comanches destroy San Saba mission	East Texas Missions abandoned	Nacogdoches parish founded	San Elizario parish founded	Refugio mission founded	Secularization of missions begin	
1682	1683	1685	1690	1715	**1716**	1718	1722	1731	1749	1758	1773	1779	1789	1793	1793	

> Louis Juchereau de St. Denis

1674 > † 1744

Louis Juchereau de St. Denis was a Canadian who was educated in France. A real frontiersman, he recorded valuable information about Indians in Texas and Louisiana. He was involved in trade with the natives and the Spanish, much of which was illegal.

The French governor of Louisiana dispatched him to the Spanish Rio Grande outpost of San Juan Bautista.

He was taken prisoner there and sent to Mexico City, where he acquitted himself so well that he was appointed as part of the expedition to reestablish the East Texas Missions. He served both the French and the Spanish and played an important role on the northeastern frontier. He served as commandant of the French fort at Natchitoches, Louisiana, where he died in 1744.

Louis Juchereau de St. Denis.

> East Texas Missions reestablished

Friar Margil fell ill and was unable to accompany the expedition. In April, 1716 the expedition continued with Friar Hildago. It crossed the Rio Grande and began the journey to East Texas.

In June the entrada reached East Texas and was welcomed by the Indians. In July, Mission San Francisco de los Tejas was reestablished at a new location. It was renamed Nuestro Padre San Francisco de los Tejas with Friar Hidalgo as minister. Concepción Mission and Mission Guadalupe were established near Nacogdoches. Mission San José was set up among the Nazoni.

> **"entrada"**
> An expedition into a region or area.

Friar Margil arrived after the establishment of the four missions, but supervised the construction of Mission Dolores near the present city of St. Augustine and Mission San Miguel de los Adaes, in present-day Louisiana, in 1717. A presidio would later be erected nearby and serve as the first capital of Texas.

Supplying the East Texas missions from San Juan Bautista created many problems and the Spanish ban on trade with the French was still in effect. St. Denis was able to provide some food and provisions for the missions. By 1718 the situation was critical. It was obvious that a way station needed to be established from which the frontier missions could be supplied.

> **"provisions"**
> Supplies and materiel needed to support an activity.

Friar Francisco Hidalgo returns to his beloved East Texas missions with the expedition sent to strengthen the Spanish presence on the northeastern frontier with France.

CLICK-LEARNING
> **Nazoni**
> **missions**

> **"way station"**
> A stopping place or a resting place between the beginning and the end of the journey.

> San Antonio Mission, Presidio and Villa founded

A site near the San Antonio River had been identified as a desirable location for a future mission. It was decided by the Viceroy to relocate the Mission San Francisco Solano from the Rio Grande to the San Antonio River as a necessary way station. The mission would be renamed San Antonio de Valero in honor of the Viceroy. It would serve as a half-way point between Mission San Juan Bautista on the Rio Grande and the East Texas Missions.

Governor Martín de Alarcón, of Coahuila y Texas, was ordered by the Viceroy to lead an expedition to establish the mission at San Antonio and provide support for the struggling East Texas missions. Alarcón's entrada included not only families needed to establish the first permanent settlement in the eastern half of Texas, but also supplies and livestock.

In May, 1718, on the day he arrived in San Antonio, Friar Antonio Olivares established the mission. Four days later the Presidio San Antonio de Béxar was established by Alarcón, soon to be followed by Villa San Fernando de Béxar. The villa would become the City of San Antonio taking its name from the presidio. In 1731, the parish of San Fernando would be established to serve the citizens of the villa and the military. Its church, opened in 1755, was the first non-mission church in Texas and eventually San Fernando Cathedral. The pastor was the first of thousands of secular priests to serve the church in Texas.

Alarcón continued his journey to East Texas and arrived in October. His visit was a disappointment to the missionaries and the soldiers because he failed to bring either new settlers or additional soldiers for the presidio.

In 1719 the French invaded East Texas. The Spanish retreated to the Trinity River and awaited help from San Antonio. The East Texas Missions were abandoned for a second time.

> **"villa"**
> A town with a city council.
> **"retreat"**
> To withdraw.

The later Mission San Antonio de Valero (the Alamo) as it was originally planned. The roof and front façade were never completed.

> **CLICK-LEARNING**
> > **San Fernando de Béxar**
> > **San Antonio de Valero**

Catholic missions at Socorro and Ysleta	La Junta mission attempt	La Salle establishes Fort St. Louis	First East Texas mission Attempt	La Junta missions	East Texas missions	San Antonio, mission, fort and settlement	La Bahia fort and mission	Three East Texas missions to San Antonio and San Fernando Parish in San Antonio	lower Rio Grande Settlements	Comanches destroy San Saba mission	East Texas Missions abandoned	Nacogdoches parish founded	San Elizario parish founded	Refugio mission founded	Secularizati
1682	1683	1685	1690	1715	1716	**1718**	1722	1731	1749	1758	1773	1779	1789	1793	179

How would you like to walk from Nicaragua to East Texas? That is a 2000 mile hike; a pretty impressive stroll for anyone, but an amazing one for a sickly 60-year-old man. That is how Friar Antonio Margil de Jesús came to East Texas from Nicaragua; he walked. But then, Friar Margil walked everywhere. Strange? Not really. Franciscan missionaries walked nearly everyplace they went. It was part of the simplicity of life as a *mendicant* priest.

Friar Antonio Margil de Jesús spent five years in Texas and founded four missions, among them San José y San Miguel de Aguayo, known as the Queen of the Missions.

This astounding man was in Texas only five years. Yet he founded four missions, three in East Texas, and one in San Antonio. This was all after he was 60-years-old.

Friar Margil was born in Spain in 1657. While still a teen-ager he expressed a desire to become a missionary and joined the Franciscan Order. He was ordained at 25 and immediately left for New Spain (Mexico). During his missionary years he acquired a saintly reputation. He insisted upon walking in his bare feet wherever he went. On his trips, he would pray and sing hymns. He had not been idle before that time having already founded three colleges, two in Mexico and one in Guatemala. He served as a missionary in Mexico, Honduras, Nicaragua and Guatemala.

In 1722 he was recalled to Mexico, where he died four years later. His *epitaph* contains the words: "He was famous for his *virtues* and celebrated for his miracles." The process of *canonization* to sainthood has begun for this heroic "Apostle of Texas."

"virtue"
A moral quality that makes for goodness.

"mendicant"
One who owns neither personal nor community property. Who begs for his living.

"epitaph"
A statement commemorating a deceased person.

"canonization"
The process by which a person's life is examined before adding them to the list (canon) of saints.

35

> Retreat to San Antonio

After waiting three months at the Trinity River, Friar Margil received word that no military support was on the way, and the entire party headed for San Antonio. Both the King of Spain and the Viceroy recognized the danger of the war in Europe spilling over to the Americas. The importance of the northeastern frontier as a buffer against France had once more been recognized. The Marqués de Aguayo was named the new governor of Coahuila y Texas. He offered to personally finance an entrada to drive the French from Texas.

"buffer"
Something that separates.

While in San Antonio, Friar Margil received permission to establish a second mission. On February 23, 1720, the Mission San José de Aguayo (honoring the new governor) was founded. It would become the "Queen of Texas missions" and the one that most closely realized the ideal envisioned by the Franciscans.

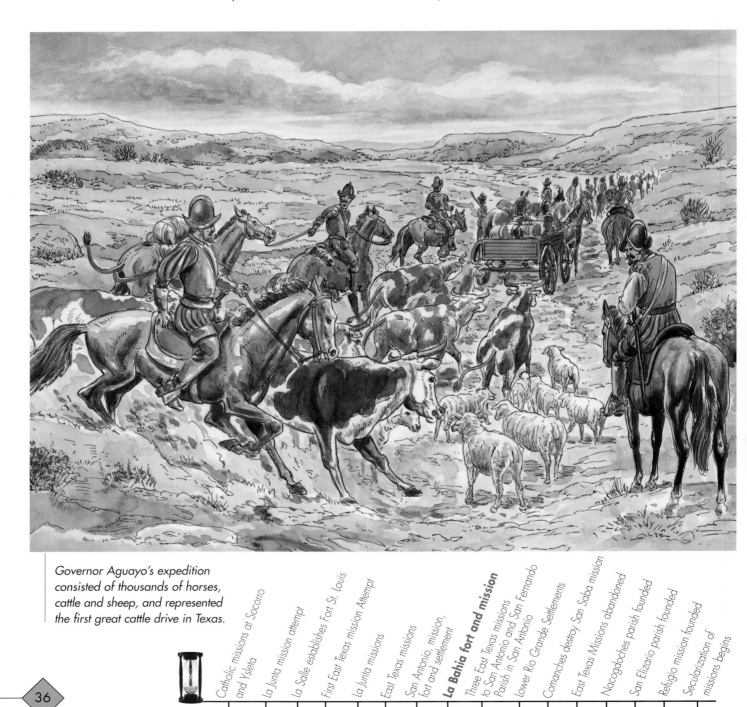

Governor Aguayo's expedition consisted of thousands of horses, cattle and sheep, and represented the first great cattle drive in Texas.

Catholic missions at Socorro and Ysleta	La Junta mission attempt	La Salle establishes Fort St. Louis	First East Texas mission Attempt	La Junta missions	East Texas missions	San Antonio, mission, fort and settlement	**La Bahia fort and mission**	Three East Texas missions to San Antonio and San Fernando Parish in San Antonio	Lower Rio Grande Settlements	Comanches destroy San Saba mission	East Texas Missions abandoned	Nacogdoches parish founded	San Elizario parish founded	Refugio mission founded	Secularization of missions begins
1682	1683	1685	1690	1715	1716	1718	**1722**	1731	1749	1758	1773	1779	1789	1793	1793

San Fernando church in San Antonio served the Spanish settlers and soldiers as the first parish church in Texas.

> East Texas Missions Regained

When Governor Aguayo marched to East Texas with a strong military force, the French retreated to Natchitoches, and the six missions were returned to the control of the Franciscans.
The Presidio de los Tejas near Mission Dolores was reactivated. Another presidio, with a complement of 100 soldiers, was established near the Los Adaes Mission, and Los Adaes was designated the capital of Texas. Aguayo then returned to San Antonio. He then sent an expedition to Matagorda Bay to establish a presidio at the exact location of La Salle's Fort St. Louis and supervised the establishment of Mission Espiritu Santo de Zúñiga nearby. This new foundation was known as "La Bahia," Spanish for "the bay," even when it was later relocated further inland.

Upon his return to Mexico, the Marqués de Aguayo resigned the governorship and returned to private life. Historian Donald Chipman describes his accomplishments as having "anchored Spanish Texas at three vital points: Los Adaes, Matagorda Bay and San Antonio. At the first, French activities at Natchitoches were monitored and the further ambitions of St. Denis checkmated.
The second defended the coast from French incursions at the exact location of La Salle's ill-fated colony.
The third, San Antonio, secured a vital way station with the newly reconstructed presidio at Béxar."

> Marqués de San Miguel de Aguayo

Unknown > † 1734

Born in Spain of Spanish nobility, the Marqués title and wealth came from his wife, the Marquésa de San Miguel de Aguayo. They were among the largest landholders in Mexico.

As governor and captain general of Coahuila y Tejas, Aguayo used his wife's wealth to finance an expedition to drive the French from East Texas. It consisted of thousands of horses, cattle and sheep, and represented the first great cattle drive in Texas. Some say this was the beginning of the cattle industry in Texas. Spain and France signed a peace treaty before he reached East Texas. The presence of Aguayo's 500 soldiers was enough to cause the French to withdraw from all territories they had taken from Spain.
The new governor reestablished all six East Texas missions and increased the military presence with new presidios. However, Aguayo's efforts in Texas were largely undone after his resignation. Spain was no longer at war with France, and once again the ebb and flow of relations with the French resulted in a reduction in the Spanish presence in East Texas. Within a decade three of the missions were relocated to San Antonio, where they still function as parish churches. Forty years later the remaining three were closed.

CLICK-LEARNING
> Marques
> Marquesa

> Were the Missions successful?

Missions established by the Franciscans were much more than a church. They had four goals. Their first goal was to evangelize, to preach and teach the Gospel. Their "civilizing" goal was to convert the Indians not only to Christianity but to the culture of Spain. Their political goal was to provide a religious and cultural presence at the outposts of the Spanish empire. Finally, they served a very important role of tempering the harsh and brutal ways of the conquistadors.

"autonomous"
Independent, self-governing.

"communal":
Belonging to the community not to individuals.

Oblate Father Robert E. Wright, writing in the "*Handbook of Texas,*" describes the ideal of the mission movement. The goal, he says, was "to establish autonomous Christian towns with communal property, labor, worship, political life and social relations, all supervised by the missionaries and insulated from the possible negative influences of other Indian groups and Spaniards themselves." Ideally if the Christianizing and socializing ministry succeeded and the surrounding areas had become populated with Spanish settlers, the missions would be "secularized."

Based on Father Wright's description, did they succeed? The answer is yes and no. Better yet, sometimes. For the most part the missions in the San Antonio and El Paso areas were successful, and many exist as active Catholic parishes today. San Antonio missions succeeded largely because they provided a safe refuge for smaller and weaker groups of Indians from their hostile, warlike neighbors to the north and south. The El Paso missions succeeded because they provided a haven for the already Christianized refugees from the Pueblo Revolt. Many others were unsuccessful. Those who attempted to serve nomadic groups like the Apaches generally failed. The East Texas missions failed partially because the small pox and cholera epidemics that took many lives were attributed to Catholic rites, particularly Baptism. Their failure was also due to the constantly changing relations between Spain and France.

Socorro and Ysleta in the El Paso area were the first missions established in Texas in 1682. The last established was Refugio in 1793, founded to serve the Karankawas on the Texas Gulf Coast. From 1745 to 1775 was the "Golden Age" of Texas missions. Secularization of the missions began in 1793, and the last was secularized in the eastern half of Texas in 1830 after Mexican Independence. It was not until 1852 that Socorro and Ysleta were officially secularized, although they had long since become mixed Indian-Spanish towns.

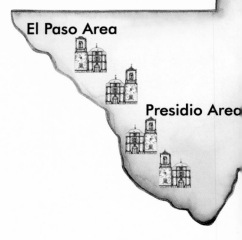

El Paso Area

Presidio Area

"secularized"
Missions were secularized when they became parish churches, that is no longer institutions dedicated to preparing native Americans for life in the regular community and church.

"rites"
Religious ceremonies.

"Apache"
A name of nomadic frequently hostile Indians.

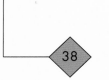
38

Catholic missions at Socorro and Ysleta — 1682
La Junta mission attempt — 1683
La Salle establishes Fort St. Louis — 1685
First East Texas mission Attempt — 1690
La Junta missions — 1715
East Texas missions — 1716
San Antonio, mission, fort and settlement — 1718
La Bahia fort and mission — 1722
Three East Texas missions to San Antonio and San Fernando Parish in San Antonio — 1731
Lower Rio Grande Settlements — 1749
Comanches destroy San Saba mission — 1758
East Texas Missions abandoned — 1773
Nacogdoches parish founded — 1779
San Elizario parish founded — 1789
Refugio mission founded — 1793
Secularization of missions begins — 1793

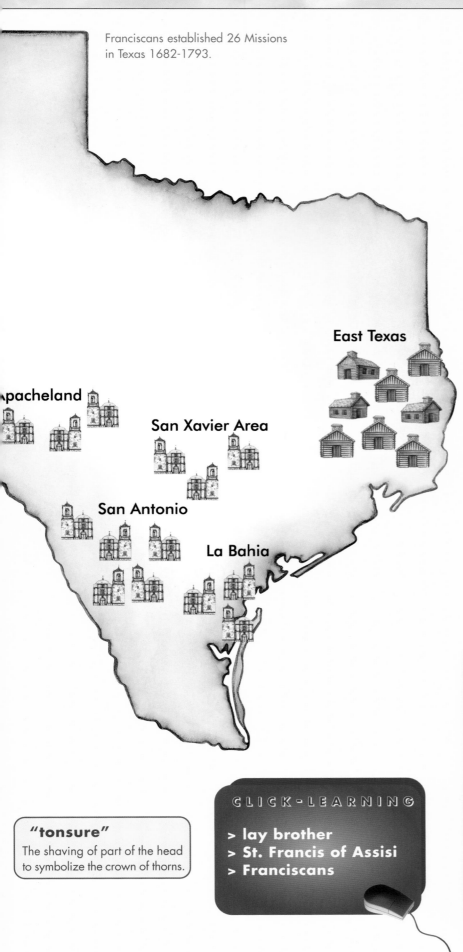

Franciscans established 26 Missions in Texas 1682-1793.

East Texas

Apacheland

San Xavier Area

San Antonio

La Bahia

> Franciscan Missionaries

We have already spoken of the Franciscan missionaries who played an important role in planting the Catholic Faith in the New World. Franciscans take their name from their founder, St. Francis of Assisi, a deacon, who established the Order of Friars Minor in 1209, nearly three hundred years before Columbus's first voyage. The name friar means brother and so Order of Friars Minor is another way of saying Community of Little Brothers.

St. Francis founded the community as mendicant; that is, the Franciscans owned no personal property and depended upon the generosity of others for their support. Francis felt that a simple life was an important witness to the Gospel, and that the ownership of personal property was a distraction from the important work of preaching.

Friars also had the top of their heads shaved in a ceremony called tonsure.

Among the Franciscans there were both priests and lay brothers. The Indios or Indians of the New World were seen as a field of souls to be harvested for Christ, and the Franciscans' zeal for their ministry was great.

St Francis of Assisi.

"tonsure"
The shaving of part of the head to symbolize the crown of thorns.

CLICK-LEARNING

> lay brother
> St. Francis of Assisi
> Franciscans

39

> Hispanic settlements

History is true but historians are limited. Historical research and writing tends to reflect the personal interests and attitudes of the historians and their cultures. As a result, many important and interesting aspects of history go largely unrecognized.

In the history of Catholicism in Texas, one such area is the growth of the church among Hispanic settlers and the contribution of secular or diocesan priests. The era of the missions is well known and even romanticized, as is the contribution of the Franciscan missionaries who labored among the Indians. The missions were a very important part of our Catholic history, as was the work of the Franciscan missionaries. But, other important things were also occurring alongside the mission efforts.

An example would be the situation in San Antonio. Thousands of people each year visit the Alamo and the river missions and learn about the work of missionaries among the Indians. Relatively few people visit San Fernando Cathedral (the actual center point of San Antonio, from which mileage is calculated to other towns) which was the first parish church in Texas. Even fewer know of the Spanish presidio or fort that was constructed there and of the settlers from Mexico and the Canary Islands who comprised the first official town in Texas.

Oblate Father Robert Wright, a widely-recognized Catholic historian in Texas, wrote recently that "in order to come to a greater appreciation of what Catholics, specifically Hispanic Catholics, have contributed to the Texas heritage, one must recognize their presence in early Texas not only in the missions, but also and more permanently in their military garrisons and towns." He then continues "thus, for example, San Antonio does not derive its name from the (San Antonio de) Valero mission, but rather from the San Antonio de Bexar garrison and civilian settlement that were begun at the same time as the mission in 1718."

While many mission efforts in Texas failed to Christianize and Hispanicize the Indians, a few succeeded.

This map by Oblate Father Robert Wright shows in yellow the area along the Rio Grande and other locations where non-mission parishes served Hispanic communities.

"Historian"
One who researches historical data to determine, as closely as possible, what really occurred during an earlier era.

"Romanticized"
Depicted as better or more significant than the reality. Exaggerated.

Catholic missions at Socorro and Ysleta — 1682
La Junta mission attempt — 1683
La Salle establishes Fort St. Louis — 1685
First East Texas mission Attempt — 1690
La Junta missions — 1715
East Texas missions — 1716
San Antonio, mission, fort and settlement — **1718**
La Bahia fort and mission — **1722**
Three East Texas missions to San Antonio and San Fernando Parish in San Antonio — 1731
Lower Rio Grande settlements — **1749**
Comanches destroy San Saba mission — 1758
East Texas Missions abandoned — 1773
Nacogdoches parish founded — **1779**
San Elizario parish founded — **1789**
Refugio mission founded — 1793
Secularization of missions begins — 1793

The Socorro Church, begun as a mission in 1682. It has evolved into an Hispanic parish by the 1800s.

As Catholics we always have a bishop as our shepherd though sometimes he may be very far away. Our Catholic faith reached North America in 1519; in 1530 the first bishop was appointed in New Spain with the establishment of the Diocese of Mexico City.

You may now be in the Diocese of Amarillo or the Archdiocese of San Antonio, but where you live was once part of New Spain. When Texas began to be settled by Hispanics in the later 1600s, South and East Texas became the northernmost section of the Diocese of Guadalajara, established in 1548. In far West Texas the Franciscan missionaries successfully held off the efforts of the Diocese of Durango, established in 1620, to claim jurisdiction there until the later 1700s.

In 1777 South and East Texas came under the new Diocese of Linares-Monterrey. Sections of Texas first began to be detached from these Mexican dioceses with the creation in 1839 of the Prefecture Apostolic of Texas, which covered central and east Texas. In 1849 the Diocese of Galveston was enlarged to incorporate all of today's Texas, but geographical misunderstandings, local resistance and lack of priests kept the Presidio and El Paso districts under the Diocese of Durango until 1872.

This was the case in Ysleta and Socorro in West Texas, as well as to some degree in the San Antonio missions. But the Catholic church was also firmly and permanently established in Texas in parishes dating back to the Spanish and Mexican periods in the El Paso vicinity, San Antonio, Goliad, Laredo, Nacogdoches, Refugio, Victoria, and San Patricio. By the 1830's most were ministered to by diocesan clergy from the Mexican dioceses of Linares (Monterrey) and Durango.

Permanent Hispanic Catholic foundations were also being established in New Mexico, Arizona, and California. When the first bishop was appointed in the United States in 1790 to lead 35,000 Catholics (including over 3000 slaves), there were some 23,000 Hispanic Catholics in what would become the future U.S. Southwest.

Both Mexico's war of independence against Spain and Texas' war of independence from Mexico took their toll on many of the Catholic parishes. They bounced back and provided the basis for the strong Hispanic Catholic presence that exists today in South Texas and beyond.

The first Texas bishop was pastor for the entire state. Today, in Texas we have one archbishop and fourteen bishops. That is more than any other state and many countries.

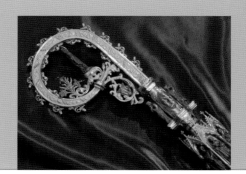

The bishop's crozier (shepherd's staff) is a symbol of his pastoral office. Other symbols of the bishop's office are his pectoral cross (on a chain around his neck), a ring on his right hand and the miter or special head piece he wears on formal occasions.

CLICK-LEARNING

> **Map of San Antonio de Bexar**

> **Presidio de Béxar**

3 Independence, statehood and civil war

"turmoil"
Confusion and unrest following an unexpected event.

> Mexican Independence

Spanish control of Texas ended in 1821 with Mexican Independence. Turmoil and instability preceded and followed Mexico's independence from Spain. Infighting continued between those who wanted a Mexican monarchy and those who wanted a republic. Struggles between royalists, who were loyal to the Spanish throne, and rebels, who wanted an independent Mexico, overflowed into Texas.

During this time of instability following Mexican Independance, the seeds of Texas' Independence were sown. Before the end of Spanish control, the United States had acquired Florida by treaty from Spain. One of the treaty's provisions required the U.S. to renounce any claim to Texas. This decision was to be both regretted and challenged.

For Spain, and later for Mexico, threats to their borders now came from the American pioneers who were moving westward in search of fertile land on the frontier.

Colonization of Texas was limited to Catholics, or to those who agreed to become Catholic. In the eyes of Spain and Mexico, the United States was viewed as a Protestant nation, and U.S. citizens were considered as aggressive and troublesome. Efforts to recruit Catholic colonists from Mexico and Ireland were only moderately successful.

"treaty"
An agreement between two nations.

Equestrian portrait of General Santa Anna, engraved by W. H. Dodd, University of Texas Hand-tinted Engraving, Prints and Photographs Collection

Mexican Independance	First Land Titles Issued to Austin Colony	Catholic colonies established	Battle of the Alamo, Texas Declaration of Independence	Texas made a Prefecture Apostolic by Rome, first Mass in Galveston & Houston	Texas Congress returns confiscated lands to Catholic Church	Texas made a Vicariate Apostolic, Jean Marie Odin, CM, named first Vicar	Texas annexed by the United States	United States / Mexican War	Diocese of Galveston, established, Bishop Odin first Bishop	Ursulines establish first Catholic school in Galveston	St. Mary's College founded in Galveston	St. Mary's Cathedral dedicated in San Antonio, St. Mary's Seminary in Galveston	Civil War begins, Texas secedes from the Union, Sam Houston deposed as Governor	Bishop Claude Dubuis named Second Bishop of Galveston	Civil War ends – Federal troops occupy Galveston	Reconstruction	St. Mary's Infirmary opens in Galveston
1821	1823	1824	1836	1839	1841	1841	1845	1846 1847	1847	1847	1848	1852	1861	1862	1865	1866 1874	1867

Some illegal colonists had slipped into Texas from Louisiana and Arkansas, but the first charter for an Anglo-American colony would go to Moses Austin, a Connecticut Yankee and a nominal Catholic. Austin's success was due in great part to assistance of Baron de Bastrop, a knowledgeable and respected Catholic citizen of San Antonio. Moses would die before he could complete his plans for the new colony. Leadership fell to his son, Stephen F. Austin, who is known as the "Father of Texas".

In *Shamrock and Cactus: The Story of the Catholic Heroes of Texas Independence*, author W. M. Ryan describes Moses Austin as the Grandfather of Texas and Baron de Bastrop as its Godfather. Bastrop continued to assist the younger Austin to navigate the bureaucratic red tape of the unstable Mexican government.

Texas was part of the Mexican state of Coahuila y Texas. Bastrop was elected to the state legislature and did much to advance the cause of the Anglo-American colonies.

In 1823 Bastrop issued the first land titles to Austin's colonists. By 1828 the number of colonists was 2,021. The colony had grown to 5,655 by 1831. The Anglicization of Texas had begun and would continue for 150 years.

...mmigrants from the United States (some legal colonists, some illegal), moved into Texas in a steady stream in the final years of Mexican control of Texas.

"charter"
An instrument issued by a country or state granting privileges.

CLICK-LEARNING

> **Mexican Independence**
> **Treaty of 1819**

> The Baron de Bastrop "Godfather of Texas"

1759 > † 1827

Phillip Hendrick Nering Bogel, The Baron de Bastrop

One of the most interesting and mysterious figures in Texas history was the man known as Baron de Bastrop. This seven-foot-tall Dutchman was a scoundrel turned hero. Many frontiersmen tried to hide their past and true identities. Bastrop was one of them. Born in Dutch Guiana as Philip Hendrick Nering Bogel, he became a tax collector in Holland. He was charged with embezzlement of tax funds and fled the country. Bogel turned up in Louisiana in 1795 with a price on his head. He assumed the new name of Philip Enrique Neri and the title of Baron de Bastrop. He moved to Spanish Texas in 1803 where he quickly won the respect and friendship of the Spanish authorities. He was elected second alcalde (deputy mayor) of San Antonio in 1810, but the governor refused to approve his election.

In spite of his questionable past, Bastrop served Texas well. He is credited with reversing the Spanish governor's decision to turn down Moses Austin's request for a charter to establish the first Anglo-American colony in Texas.

He later served as Land Commissioner for the Mexican government in Texas and as Texas' representative in the legislature of the State of Coahuila y Texas.

Several of the business enterprises that he started, failed. When he died in 1827, he was penniless.

His fellow legislators donated funds for his funeral.

Only within the past 50 years did Baron de Bastrop's true identity become known. Stephen F. Austin named the city and county of Bastrop after him because of his contributions to Texas.

Cover of the Mexican Constitution of 1824

> The Catholic colonies

Mexico, continuing the Spanish policy, required immigrants to Texas to be Catholic. But there were actually few Catholics among the immigrants after 1821. The great majority of the immigrants were not required to demonstrate their Catholicity, or they went through the certification process insincerely. One of the factors which facilitated this was the absence of priests in the areas occupied by most Anglo-American colonies

In 1831-32 a Father Michael Muldoon was appointed Vicar for the new immigrant colonies by the Diocese of Linares-Monterrey, which was in charge of eastern Texas. Although the Austin colonists did not build a church for him or provide him his own residence. However, he befriended them and baptized many of them who went through the ceremony only at the urging of their leaders in order to show compliance with the colonization laws. Many of those who were thus baptized later became known as "Muldoon Catholics," meaning one who received Catholic baptism only as a legal requirement and not as a sincere declaration of Catholic faith.

Aside from the Austin Colony there were many Catholics in Texas, not only from Mexico but also from other Catholic countries such as Ireland and France. Among the Catholic empresarios were Martin de Leon, James McGloin, John McMullen, James Power, Lorenzo de Zavala, James Hewitson and Ben Milam. Some of their colonies were successful; others were not. De Leon established a colony at the site of the present city of Victoria in 1824. His colony was established for Mexicans but included a number of Irish who were fleeing persecution by the English. One of them was John J. Linn, who was a delegate to the convention that declared Texas' independence. His attendance was blocked by the Mexican invasion. He later served in the Congress of the Republic of Texas.

James Power and James Hewitson, both natives of Ireland, established Refugio, which was populated with many Catholic Irish and Mexicans (who already lived in the area). The town was named after Mission Nuestra Señora de Refugio, which had been established in 1793. John McMullen and James McGloin founded another Irish and Mexican Catholic colony at San Patricio (St. Patrick).

These three Irish and Mexican colonies—Victoria, Refugio, and San Patricio – were on the frontier during Texas' war for independence. Both Irish and Mexicans divided their allegiances during the war for independence.

"immigrants "
A person who comes to a new country to live.

"empresarios"
One who obtains the right to establish a colony in an area and works to find people willing to move to the colony.

Timeline:

- Mexican Independence — 1821
- First Land Titles issued to Austin Colony — 1823
- **Catholic colonies established** — **1824**
- Battle of the Alamo, Texas Declaration of Independence — 1836
- Texas made a Prefecture Apostolic by Rome, first Mass in Galveston & Houston — 1839
- Texas Congress returns confiscated lands to Catholic Church — 1841
- Texas made a Vicariate Apostolic Jean Marie Odin, CM, named first Vicar — 1841
- Texas annexed by the United States — 1845
- United States / Mexican War — 1846/1847
- Diocese of Galveston established, Bishop Odin first Bishop — 1847
- Ursulines establish first Catholic school in Galveston — 1847
- St. Mary's Cathedral dedicated in Galveston — 1848
- St. Mary's College founded in San Antonio, St. Mary's Seminary in Galveston — 1852
- Civil War begins, Texas secedes from the Union, Sam Houston deposed as Governor — 1861
- Bishop Claude Dubuis named Second Bishop of Galveston — 1862
- Civil War ends – Federal troops occupy Galveston — 1865
- Reconstruction — 1866/1874
- St. Mary's Infirmary opens in Galveston — 1867

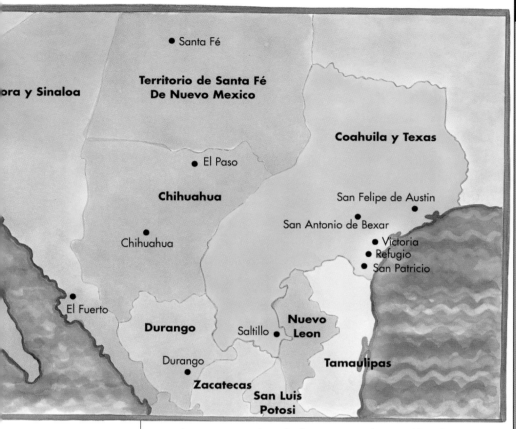

Map showing State of Coahuila y Texas in the Republic of Mexico.

> **Michael Muldoon**

1789 > †18(?)

It is difficult to separate legend from fact in the story of Father Michael (Miguel) Muldoon. Born about 1780 in Ireland at a time when it was a crime to teach the Catholic religion, Muldoon was educated in a seminary in Spain set up for Irish refugees. He came to Mexico with Juan O'Donoju, the last Spanish Viceroy to Mexico. He was assigned to the Diocese of Linares-Monterrey, of which Texas was a part. In early 1831 he arrived in the diocese of Linares-Monterrey (Nuevo León) and was assigned as pastor of the Austin colony.

Father Muldoon came to Texas and worked among the Anglo-American colonists in 1831-32. His name came to be associated with "Muldoon Catholics" because of the number of people he baptized to enable them to become colonists. He also performed numerous marriages. Legally, if a Catholic priest was available the only civilly recognized marriage was a Catholic ceremony.

After his return to Mexico he was the only visitor to Stephen F. Austin during his imprisonment in Mexico City. In 1837 he helped an American escape from prison at Matamoros, and he served as unofficial interpreter for a Republic of Texas mission to Mexico in 1839. He was imprisoned by Mexico for his pro-Texas views. In 1842 he received a letter from the Republic of Texas recognizing his service, and a monument was erected in his honor near Hostyn, Texas, South of La Grange.

Some opted for independence while others chose to stay with Mexico. Large numbers of both groups perished or were dislocated during the struggle.

Lorenzo de Zavala was given a grant, with David Burnet and Joseph Vehlin, to establish a colony of 800 families east of Galveston. The company was able to bring 300 settlers to the colony but never was completely successful. The City of Beaumont is located on a portion of Zavala's colony. While he failed as an empresario he went on to become a hero of Texas and the first vice-president of the Republic of Texas. Ben Milam, another unsuccessful Catholic entrepreneur, went on to become a hero of the Texas War of Independence leading the successful attack on San Antonio in December, 1835. This led to the defeat of the Mexican garrison under General Martin Perfecto de Cos, brother-in-law of General Santa Anna. Milam was killed by a sniper during the assault.

"entrepreneur"

A risk taker. One, like an empresario, who begins a venture whose outcome may not be favorable.

CLICK-LEARNING
> **Father Michael Muldoon**
> **Irish colonies**
> **Ben Milam**

> Indecision on Independence

"constitution"

The basic document establishing a nation or an organization that set forth the rights and obligations of citizens or members.

Many Texans did not support independence from Mexico. They were loyal to their adopted country but opposed to the dictatorial regime of General Santa Anna who revoked the Mexican Constitution of 1824. Early in the revolution, many Texans were espousing the Constitution of 1824, and calling themselves "Federalists". Some say that the flag flown during the siege of the Alamo was the "1824" flag. It was the red, white and green flag of Mexico with the date "1824" on the white field.

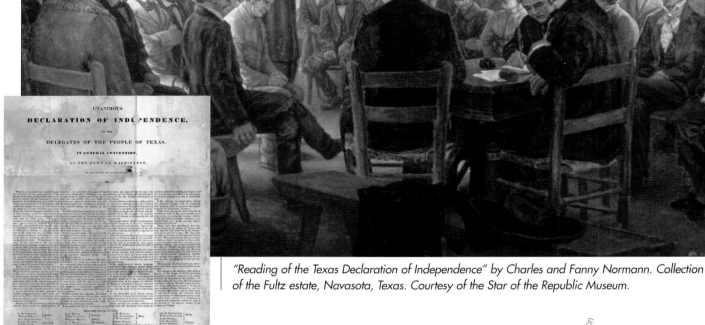

"Reading of the Texas Declaration of Independence" by Charles and Fanny Normann. Collection of the Fultz estate, Navasota, Texas. Courtesy of the Star of the Republic Museum.

UNANIMOUS
DECLARATION OF INDEPENDENCE,
BY THE
DELEGATES OF THE PEOPLE OF TEXAS,
IN GENERAL CONVENTION,
AT THE TOWN OF WASHINGTON.

The Texas Declaration of Independence. Eight Catholics were among the signers.

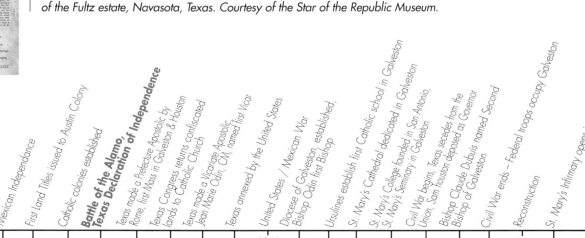

Mexican Independence — 1821
First Land Titles issued to Austin Colony — 1823
Catholic colonies established — 1824
Battle of the Alamo, Texas Declaration of Independence — **1836**
Texas made a Prefecture Apostolic by Rome, first Mass in Galveston & Houston — 1839
Texas Congress returns confiscated lands to Catholic Church — 1841
Texas made a Vicariate Apostolic Jean Marie Odin, CM, named first Vicar — 1841
Texas annexed by the United States — 1845
United States / Mexican War — 1846 1847
Diocese of Galveston established, Bishop Odin first Bishop — 1847
Ursulines establish first Catholic school in Galveston — 1847
St. Mary's Cathedral dedicated in Galveston — 1848
St. Mary's College founded in San Antonio, St. Mary's Seminary in Galveston — 1852
Civil War begins, Texas secedes from the Union, Sam Houston deposed as Governor — 1861
Bishop Claude Dubuis named Second Bishop of Galveston — 1862
Civil War ends – Federal troops occupy Galveston — 1865
Reconstruction — 1866 1874
St. Mary's Infirmary opens in Galveston — 1867

> **José Antonio Navarro**
1795 > †1870

José Antonio Navarro

José Antonio Navarro and his uncle Francisco Ruiz, both born in San Antonio, were the only two native Texans who signed the Texas Declaration of Independence. All of the others were immigrants. Navarro was descended from an original Canary Island family who had settled in Texas. He served as a member of the legislature of the State of Coahuila and Texas and was elected to the Congress of Mexico. When Santa Anna rejected the Constitution of 1824, Navarro refused to take his seat in Congress and allied himself with the cause of Texas. Although a fall from a horse left him handicapped and unable to serve in the army, he served Texas brilliantly as a member of the House of the Republic of Texas.

On an expedition to Santa Fe, Navarro was captured by the Mexicans and confined in a dungeon at Vera Cruz. Santa Anna offered him the rank of Brigadier General in the Mexican Army if he would renounce his Texan citizenship which he refused to do. He escaped and returned to Galveston by ship. Upon his arrival, the entire population turned out to welcome and to honor him. After Texas was annexed to the United States in 1845, Navarro continued to serve as a member of the State Senate.

"dungeon"
A dungeon is a prison cell, usually dark and often underground.

"declaration"
A document declaring an action to be taken and the reasons for it.

The decision for independence was not easily made. Sam Houston, Lorenzo de Zavala and Stephen Austin opposed a Declaration of Independence. Their hope was for Texas to be separated from the Mexican state of Coahuila y Texas, but, it was not to be.

The first unofficial declaration of independence was drawn up by a group of Irish Catholics from Refugio, Victoria and Matagorda in December, 1835, at Goliad. Philip Dimmit led the group's effort. Immediately afterward, Nicholas Fagan, an enthusiastic Catholic patriot , ran a flag up the flagpole. It bore a red arm which held a drawn sword, a symbol of armed revolt. Dimmit and 46 other Catholics, mostly Irish, signed the Goliad Declaration.

Nearly three months later, while the Alamo was under siege, the official Declaration of Independence was signed on March 2 at Washington-on-the-Brazos. Eight Catholics were among the signers: Lorenzo de Zavala, James Power, Michel B. Menard, Jose Antonio Navarro, Francisco Ruiz, Charles S. Taylor, John White Bower and Edwin Conrad. John J. Linn, Juan Antonio Padilla, John Joseph Powers and Dr. James Kerr were scheduled to be among the signers, but did not arrive in time.

On March 6, the Alamo fell, two days after Sam Houston had been named "Commander of all the land forces of the Texas army." On March 13, Houston ordered the evacuation of the troops at Gonzalez and Goliad. The fall of the Alamo and Houston's decision to retreat caused great panic. The government was moved first to Harrisburg, then to Galveston.

Before leaving Washington-on-the-Brazos, David Burnet was elected President of the provisional government. Houston blamed the government's retreat for demoralizing the army. Burnet told Houston that because of the army's retreat "the enemy are laughing you to scorn." The situation was critical because it was in political and military chaos. The totally unexpected victory at San Jacinto brought new hope to the new government of Texas.

"siege"
The act of surrounding and cutting off a place or a group from outside help

"provisional"
Provisional refers to something that is temporary that is to be replaced by something permanent.

CLICK-LEARNING
> **Texas Declaration of Independence**
> **Goliad**

47

> Catholic heroes of the War of Independance

This painting by artist Judy Courtwright shows Father Michael Muldoon (standing in the middle of the circle incorrectly dressed as a Franciscan), performing multiple marriages during one of his visits to Austin's Colony. Courtesy of the Brazoria County Museum

There were many Catholic heroes in Texas' war for independence. Catholics played an important role in every encounter with Mexican troops. It should also be remembered that most of the Mexican troops were also Catholic.

Three of the better known Texans have counties named after them. They are Jim Bowie, Ben Milam and Erastus "Deaf" Smith. Bowie died at the Alamo; Milam died in the Storming of Bexar (San Antonio).
Smith was at Bexar and the Alamo and played a key role in the Battle of San Jacinto. The city of Seguin bears the name of a fourth hero, Colonel Juan Seguin, who was also at Bexar, the Alamo and San Jacinto.

"speculation"

Speculation in land involves trying to determine what land will be valuable in the future and buying it at a low price in hopes of reselling it at a profit.

Bowie was born in Kentucky but moved with his family to Spanish Missouri and then to southeastern Louisiana.

Mexican Independence	First Land Titles issued to Austin Colony	Catholic colonies established	**Battle of the Alamo, Texas Declaration of Independence**	Texas made a Prefecture Apostolic by Rome, first Mass in Galveston & Houston	Texas Congress returns confiscated lands to Catholic Church	Texas made a Vicariate Apostolic, Jean Marie Odin, CM, named first Vicar	Texas annexed by the United States	United States / Mexican War	Diocese of Galveston established, Bishop Odin first Bishop	Ursulines establish first Catholic school in Galveston	St. Mary's Cathedral dedicated in Galveston	St. Mary's College founded in San Antonio, St. Mary's Seminary in Galveston	Civil War begins, Texas secedes from the Union; Sam Houston deposed as Governor	Bishop Claude Dubuis named Second Bishop of Galveston	Civil War ends – Federal troops occupy Galveston	Reconstruction	St. Mary's Infirmary opens in Galveston
1821	1823	1824	**1836**	1839	1841	1841	1845	1846 1847	1847	1847	1848	1852	1861	1862	1865	1866 1874	1867

As a young man he was a gambler, involved in land speculation and slave trading.

When he moved to San Antonio, he became a Catholic and married Ursula Veramendi, daughter of the governor of the Mexican province of Texas. She and their baby died in the cholera epidemic of 1833.

When Mexican General Martin de Cos was driven out of San Antonio at the Storming of Bexar, Bowie was sent by Sam Houston with orders to evacuate and dismantle the Alamo. In fact, he urged that Bexar not be evacuated because of its strategic position. The small garrison was reinforced by the arrival of Lt. Colonel William Travis on February 3 with regular troops, and Davy Crockett and his Tennessee volunteers on February 11.

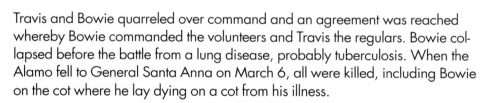

> Erastus "Deaf" Smith
1795 › †1837

A skilled scout and tracker, this native New Yorker lost most of his hearing as a result of a childhood illness. Smith moved to San Antonio in 1821 and married a Tejano widow, Guadalupe Ruiz Durán. He tried to remain neutral in the Texas revolution. When prevented from returning to his family in San Antonio by the Mexicans, he joined the Texans' army.

He proved invaluable in the armies of Stephen F. Austin and Sam Houston. At the Storming of Bexar, Smith spotted a Mexican supply train. The Texans attacked the mule train hoping to capture much needed supplies. Instead of supplies, the mules were carrying only grass to feed the army's animals. The incident became known as the "grass fight."

Smith guided the Texans into San Antonio where he was seriously wounded in the same firefight that took the life of Ben Milam. He served as a courier at the Alamo and brought out Travis' famous appeal for help. At San Jacinto he destroyed Vince's Bridge, cutting off Santa Anna's means of escape.

After Texas' independence he briefly commanded a company of Texas Rangers, but died in 1837. Houston wrote of him: "A man more brave and honest never lived."

Travis and Bowie quarreled over command and an agreement was reached whereby Bowie commanded the volunteers and Travis the regulars. Bowie collapsed before the battle from a lung disease, probably tuberculosis. When the Alamo fell to General Santa Anna on March 6, all were killed, including Bowie on the cot where he lay dying on a cot from his illness.

Benjamin Rush Milam was also a Kentuckian. He fought against the British in the War of 1812 and in Mexico's revolution against Spain. He volunteered in the taking of the Goliad Presidio in October 1835, and was leading a contingent of volunteers in house-to-house fighting in the Storming of Bexar in December when he was killed by a rifle shot.

Juan Seguin was born in San Antonio to a well-to-do family. His father was alcalde (mayor). In 1835 he recruited a company of Tejanos and fought in the Storming of Bexar. He was at the Alamo, but was sent for reinforcements and left before the siege. He fought bravely at San Jacinto and later served as the only Tejano in the Republic of Texas Senate.

Deaf Smith appeared on the Republic of Texas five dollar bill.

"Tejanos"
A term referring to Texans of Mexican descent, first used in the Mexican Constitution of 1824 to refer to Mexicans residing in Texas.

While serving as mayor of San Antonio, he was accused of treason on trumped-up charges and fled to Mexico with his family. He was later recognized as a Texas patriot.

CLICK-LEARNING
> **Juan Seguin**

> **Storming of Bexar**

> **Tejano heroes**

> Independence leaves Catholic Church with many challenges

After the Texas War of Independence, the Catholic Church was faced with many problems. Although Texas under Spain and Mexico had never extended south or west of the Nueces River, the new Republic of Texas claimed to reach all the way to the Rio Grande River. But Mexico remained firmly in control of the Rio Grande country. The Revolution had devastated the Church in what became the actual Republic of Texas. Several Catholic towns (San Patricio, Refugio, and Goliad) were especially hard hit and occasionally abandoned due to ongoing insecurity for several years.

The only parish that remained with a resident priest was San Fernando Church at San Antonio. There were still nine parishes with resident priests along the Rio Grande, beyond the Republic of Texas. They included Laredo, Ysleta, and San Elizario (the latter both near El Paso), all three with their administrative centers on the future Texas side of the river, and six parishes (mostly in the Lower Rio Grande Valley) whose centers were located just across the river in Mexico.

There were about 12,000 Catholics in the future state, counting the "Muldoon Catholics." Most of them were Mexican, more than half living along the Rio Grande. There were also some Spaniards and the recent Irish colonists in the new Republic. Joining them were an increasing number of French, German, American and English Catholic immigrants.

The Republic of Texas was still nominally under the authority of the Diocese of Linares-Monterrey, which had been without a bishop from 1821 until 1831. When a bishop was named he was forced to flee his diocese because of persecution. Recognizing the plight of Catholics in the new Republic, in 1838 the Vatican asked Bishop Antoine Blanc of New Orleans to report back to Rome on the situation in Texas. Bishop Blanc chose Father John Timon, the American-born leader of the Vincentian community in the United States, to survey the situation of the church in Texas.

Father Timon took a steamboat to New Orleans where Father Juan Llebaria joined him. They took a ship to Galveston arriving the day after Christmas. Strangers in a bustling new town, Father Timon recognized two cousins he had known as a missionary in Illinois.

> **" Vincentian "**
> A member of the Congregation of the Missions, a religious community founded by St. Vincent de Paul.

Vincentian Father John Timon, future prefect apostolic for the Republic of Texas, preached at the first public Mass celebrated in Galveston in a warehouse owned by Michael and Peter Menard.

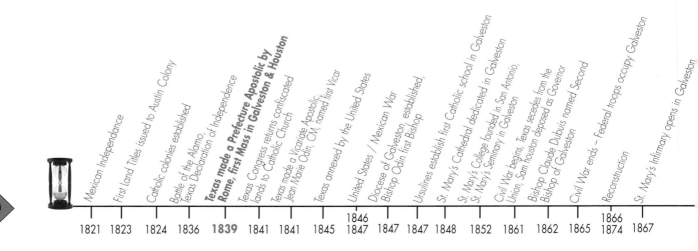

Mexican Independence	1821	
First Land Titles issued to Austin Colony	1823	
Catholic colonies established	1824	
Battle of the Alamo, Texas Declaration of Independence	1836	
Texas made a Prefecture Apostolic by Rome, first Mass in Galveston & Houston	**1839**	
Texas Congress returns confiscated lands to Catholic Church	1841	
Texas made a Vicariate Apostolic, Jean Marie Odin, CM, named first Vicar	1841	
Texas annexed by the United States	1845	
United States / Mexican War	1846 1847	
Diocese of Galveston established, Bishop Odin first Bishop	1847	
Ursulines establish first Catholic school in Galveston	1847	
St. Mary's Cathedral dedicated in Galveston	1848	
St. Mary's College founded in San Antonio, St. Mary's Seminary in Galveston	1852	
Civil War begins, Texas secedes from the Union, Sam Houston deposed as Governor	1861	
Bishop Claude Dubuis named Second Bishop of Galveston	1862	
Civil War ends – Federal troops occupy Galveston	1865	
Reconstruction	1866 1874	
St. Mary's Infirmary opens in Galveston	1867	

> **Michael Menard**

1805 > †1856

Michael Menard, who played a major role in the Catholic history in Texas, led an adventurous life that started as a youth who could neither read nor write and ended as the major founder of Galveston, Texas. Menard was born near Montreal, Canada, and became a fur trader as a young man. He later moved to Illinois where his uncle was a trader.
He traded with the Shawnee Indians in Illinois and Missouri and was made a Shawnee chief. It was at this time that he learned to read and write both French and English. He also met a young missionary priest by the name of John Timon.

Moving with the Shawnee tribe to Arkansas Territory, he then migrated to Nacogdoches and became a Spanish citizen. He continued to trade in Texas and Mexico. In 1836 he became one of the Catholic signers of the Texas Declaration of Independence and served as a member of the Congress of the Republic of Texas.

It was after he had led a group of businessmen who founded the City of Galveston, that he again met Father Timon on the latter's first trip to Texas.

Michael Menard, Catholic entrepreneur and principal founder of Galveston.

They were Michael and Peter Menard, leading citizens and founders of Galveston. Michael had been among the signers of the Declaration of Independence and a member of the Texas Constitutional Convention. The Menards insisted the two priests stay at their home, and it was there on the following day that Father Timon celebrated the first Mass in Galveston. The next Sunday a public Mass was celebrated in one of the Menards' warehouses by Father Llebaria with Father Timon preaching. Large numbers of Catholics and Protestants were present.

Two days later the Vincentians left by steamboat for Houston, but not before organizing a group of Galveston Catholics to construct a church. In Houston the priests stayed in a borrowed cabin where they celebrated Mass. During their visit they met a number of Catholic leaders of the new nation including Senators Juan Seguin of San Antonio and John Dunn from the Irish colonies. They also met Representatives José Antonio Navarro, James Kerr and John Linn from whom they gathered valuable information about the situation of Catholics. They also met the new president, Mirabeau B. Lamar, and the former president, Sam Houston, who told them that he considered himself a Catholic.

On January 9 they began their return trip to New Orleans. In his report to Rome and Bishop Blanc, Father Timon estimated that there were about 12,000 Catholics in the new Republic, but half of them were colonists who were Catholic in name only. He reported that the Church was in great difficulty in Texas. He recommended that priests be sent to the republic to counteract the increase of Protestant preachers and that Texas be immediately established as a diocese temporarily administered by the Bishop of New Orleans.

CLICK-LEARNING

> **Michael Menard**
> **Juan Seguin**

> An official Catholic presence in the Republic of Texas

Father John Timon was not the only person interested in an official Catholic presence in the Republic of Texas. William Henry Daingerfield, a diplomatic agent of the republic in New York, was urging the establishment of an archdiocese in Texas. Daingerfield was a Catholic layman and former Secretary of the Treasury, Senator and Mayor of San Antonio. In addition, Bishop Simon Bruté of Vincennes, Indiana, had written to Bishop Blanc urging the establishment of a Texas diocese with Father Timon in charge. Bishop Blanc, however, rejected the idea of a separate diocese for Texas until things had settled down politically.

New Orleans was the busiest port on the Gulf coast. Early Texas missionaries arrived in New Orleans from Europe and Missouri by ship or steamboat and took coastal boats to Galveston or Linnville.

1821	Mexican Independance
1823	First Land Titles issued to Austin Colony
1824	Catholic colonies established
1836	Battle of the Alamo, Texas Declaration of Independence
1839	**Texas made a Prefecture Apostolic by Rome, first Mass in Galveston & Houston**
1841	Texas Congress returns confiscated lands to Catholic Church
1841	Texas made a Vicariate Apostolic, Jean Marie Odin, CM, named first Vicar
1845	Texas annexed by the United States
1846 1847	United States / Mexican War
1847	Diocese of Galveston, established, Bishop Odin first Bishop
1847	Ursulines establish first Catholic school in Galveston
1848	St. Mary's Cathedral dedicated in Galveston
1852	St. Mary's College founded in San Antonio, St. Mary's Seminary in Galveston
1861	Civil War begins, Texas secedes from the Union, Sam houston deposed as Governor
1862	Bishop Claude Dubuis named Second Bishop of Galveston
1865	Civil War ends – Federal troops occupy Galveston
1866 1874	Reconstruction
1867	St. Mary's Infirmary opens in Galveston

Father John Timon, CM, Prefect Apostolic of Texas, later Bishop of Buffalo, New York.

"vice-prefect"

One who assists the prefect, and represents him when the prefect is not able to be present. He is the associate prefect.

> Vincentian Father John Timon

1797 > †1867

John Timon was a rarity on the frontier, an American-born priest. He was born in 1797 in Pennsylvania to Irish parents, the third of twelve children. The family lived in Baltimore before moving to Missouri when John was 19. The failure of his father's business freed him to follow his desire to enter the priesthood. At 25 he was accepted at St. Mary of the Barrens Seminary. He was ordained a Vincentian priest at 29.

He immediately began teaching at the seminary, acting as treasurer, serving in a parish and visiting missions in Missouri and Illinois. Bishop Joseph Rosati of St. Louis wrote to a Vatican official that Father Timon had accomplished more in winning converts and bringing back lapsed Catholics than all the other priests of the diocese combined. In 1835 he was named provincial superior of Vincentian priests in the United States. Although he turned down his first appointment as a bishop to serve as prefect apostolic of Texas, he subsequently became the Bishop of Buffalo, New York.

Instead he recommended, and the Vatican concurred, that the Republic of Texas be made a "prefecture apostolic", a church division that frequently precedes the establishment of a diocese. A priest who has many of the powers of a bishop heads it. Bishop Blanc's choice for prefect was Father Timon.

Still the head of the Vincentians in the United States, Father Timon had also been named to be coadjutor bishop of St. Louis, an appointment which he rejected. Because he retained his Vincentian duties in Missouri, he was allowed to appoint a vice-prefect to reside in Texas. He chose a fellow Vincentian, Father Jean Marie Odin.

In a world where all transportation was by horse, wagon or boat, things moved slowly. While the new prefecture was established in fall of 1839, Father Timon's appointment was not received until April of 1840, and Father Odin did not leave Missouri for Texas until May 2. Three Vincentians who had volunteered to serve in Texas accompanied Father Odin. The three priests and one Brother, traveling down the Mississippi on the steamboat *Meteor*, narrowly missed being struck by a tornado near Natchez, Mississippi.

"coadjutor bishop"

A bishop assigned to assist another bishop who heads a diocese. When the other Bishop becomes ill, retires or dies a coadjutor bishop automatically succeeds him.

Upon their arrival in Natchez, they found that the town had been devastated by the tornado. There were injured and dead everywhere. Two steamboats at the Natchez wharf had been destroyed, one was sunk. The priests ministered to the dead and dying and saw the hand of God in their captain's decision to halt the *Meteor* upstream from Natchez because of the ferocity of the storm. The band of Vincentians arrived in Louisiana May 9 and remained there until July 1, when they boarded the steamship *Henry* for Texas. Their destination was not Galveston, but Linnville, on Lavaca Bay, named after the Catholic statesman John Linn, whom Father Timon had met in Houston.

CLICK-LEARNING

> **William Henry Daingerfield**
> **Steamboat**
> **Tornado**

With the arrival of Father Odin and his companions on July 12, 1840, a new chapter in the Catholic history of Texas had begun as the sons of St. Vincent de Paul took up the work started by the sons of St. Francis of Assisi.

> Restoring church property

The Catholic Church faced many challenges in the new Republic of Texas. Among them was the lack of priests to minister to the scattered Catholics and the recognition of all church property by the government. Priests and brothers of the Vincentian congregation helped address the need for ministers. Two priests from Kentucky had already arrived in Texas to work with immigrants. Restoration of the church lands was more difficult but was achieved through the efforts of Catholic legislators, a French diplomat and a letter from the Vatican to President Mirabeau B. Lamar.

Father John Timon asked Cardinal James Fransoni at the Vatican to send a letter requesting that the Republic of Texas recognize all former Church properties. Father Timon traveled to Texas to present the letter personally to the president. He then joined Father Odin in Austin to await developments.

The letter was well received by President Lamar and the Texas government, which looked upon it as an official recognition of the Republic by the Vatican. Lamar promised his assistance in restoring church property, but the Texas Congress had to act upon it. Alphonse Dubois de Saligny, who extended the hospitality of his home to the two Vincentians during their stay, headed the French legation in Austin. He used his considerable political influence to win the support of members of the legislature for recognition of the church lands.

With the support of Catholic legislators and others influenced by De Saligny and Sam Houston, the former president, the restoration bill was passed by a wide margin. It was, in effect, a compromise because it recognized only the lots on which the churches were standing, not to exceed 15 acres. This meant that the extensive farmlands of the former missions, if not already sold by the Spanish or Mexican governments, were lost.

In addition, a last minute amendment excluded the Alamo from the restoration bill. A few days later the Senate passed the bill. Later, the Alamo was also returned, but it was never again used as a church because of its proximity to San Fernando. Pleased with the outcome, the prefect and vice-prefect began a tour of East Texas to determine the situation of Catholics and churches in that area.

What has been referred to as "the Catholic re-occupation of Texas", actually of the Republic of Texas, since the Rio Grande country was still occupied by the Mexican church, seemed to be on track, but a letter from the Vatican appeared to cause a setback. Father Odin had been appointed by Rome as the coadjutor Bishop of Detroit.

"restoration"
To restore to a previous condition. In this case, to return to the Church control of the lands that had been taken away after the War of Independence.

"Vatican"
The residence of the Pope. Today it is an independent state completely surrounded by the city of Rome, Italy.

ST.
STOCKADE
8TH STREET
SHOWING LOCATION OF CAPITOL AND STOCKADE
CONGRESS AVE.
CAPITOL BUILDING REPUBLIC OF TEXAS 1839-1853

"proximity"
Proximity refers to a person or a thing being close to another person or thing.

Mexican Independence — 1821
First Land Titles issued to Austin Colony — 1823
Catholic colonies established — 1824
Battle of the Alamo, Texas Declaration of Independence — 1836
Texas made a Prefecture Apostolic by Rome, first Mass in Galveston & Houston — 1839
Texas Congress returns confiscated lands to Catholic Church — 1841
Texas made a Vicariate Apostolic, Jean Marie Odin, CM, named first Vicar — 1841
Texas annexed by the United States — 1845
United States / Mexican War — 1846 1847
Diocese of Galveston established, Bishop Odin first Bishop — 1847
Ursulines establish first Catholic school in Galveston — 1847
St. Mary's Cathedral dedicated in Galveston — 1848
St. Mary's College founded in San Antonio, St. Mary's Seminary in Galveston — 1852
Civil War begins, Texas secedes from the Union, Sam Houston deposed as Governor — 1861
Bishop Claude DuBuis named Second Bishop of Galveston — 1862
Civil War ends – Federal troops occupy Galveston — 1865
Reconstruction — 1866 1874
St. Mary's Infirmary opens in Galveston — 1867

CLICK-LEARNING
> **French legation + Texas**
> **Alphonse Dubois de Saligny**

> Alphonse Dubois de Saligny

1809 > † 1888

Recognition of the new Republic of Texas by other nations was very important to acceptance of the new nation. Alphonse Dubois de Saligny, a junior diplomat at the French Legation in Washington, was sent to Texas to determine whether France should extend diplomatic recognition to Texas.

French chargé d'affaires for the Republic of Texas

In his report De Saligny wrote: "The recognition of the independence of Texas by the Government of the King (Louis Philippe) will bring great advantages to France for many years to come." Recognition was granted, and De Saligny became the chargé d'affaires in Austin. He successfully used his influence to assist in the return of church lands taken over by the Republic after independence. He also was instrumental in obtaining property for the first Catholic church in Austin.

The haughty French diplomat brought continental culture to the frontier capital but spent more time in New Orleans than in Texas. He was recalled when Texas came into the union and later became French minister to Mexico.

> **"chargé d'affaires"**
>
> A diplomat who looks after the affairs of his nation in another country where no ambassador is present.

AS THE CAPITOL BUILDING LOOKED FROM THE SOUTH EAST

COMMITTEE ROOMS

HOUSE SENATE PLAN

PORCH

This simple frame building served as the Capital of the Republic of Texas when Fathers John Timon and Jean Marie Odin sought the restoration of Church lands. It continued to serve as the capital after Texas became a state until 1858.

> **"amendment"**
>
> An amendement is something that is added to a document and becomes part of the original document

This pen and ink sketch of the French Legation from 1896 is part of the Rosenberg Library collection in Galveston.

> A bishop for Texas

In July of 1841 Father Odin was named Vicar Apostolic for Texas, and Father Timon turned over responsibilities to the new Bishop. Father Odin became Bishop Odin in ceremonies at St. Louis Cathedral in New Orleans on March 6, 1842.

On the eve of his consecration, Mexican forces invaded Texas and occupied Goliad, Victoria and San Antonio, proclaiming Mexican sovereignty. Having made a show of force, they retreated back across the Rio Grande two days later. Some renegade Texas troops invaded Mexico but were defeated and taken prisoner.

On his return to Texas, the new bishop had to deal with the fact that the situation in Texas and his vicariate was desperate. The country was near bankruptcy; crop failure had caused widespread famine and a storm struck Galveston destroying the recently completed St. Mary Church.

Bishop Odin's new title made little difference in his ministry. He still covered his large diocese by horseback, frequently traveling by night to avoid Indian attacks. On occasion he was isolated for days by floods and once was near death from a sudden fever. He was invited to be an observer at the Plenary Council of American Bishops in Baltimore, but illness kept him confined to his bed during most of the meeting.

Father Timon urged Bishop Odin to go to Europe to recruit more priests for Texas. When he arrived in New Orleans in March, 1845, word was that Texas had been annexed by the United States, a change desperately needed by the struggling republic. The question was, "How would Mexico react to the annexation?" The United States was expected to push for the surrender by Mexico of much of the nation's northern territory including New Mexico, Arizona and northern California.

Bishop Odin took the train to New York where he would leave for France wondering what changes were instore for Catholics in Texas and for him.

"consecration"

The dedication of a person or an object to the service of God; in this case, the ceremony that consecrated a priest to the service of God as a bishop.

"renegade"

A renegade is a person who abandons a cause or a principle for another.

"famine"

A time where there is not enough food to feed everybody.

"Plenary Council"

A meeting of all the archbishops and bishops of the United States.

CLICK-LEARNING

> John Marie Odin

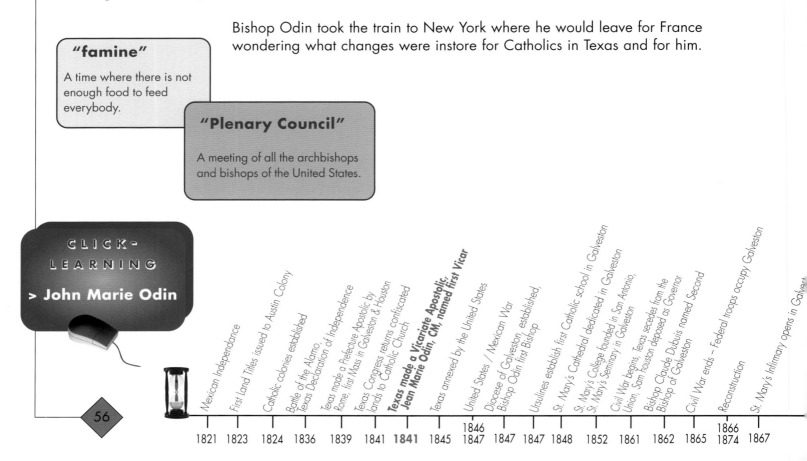

Mexican Independence — 1821
First Land Titles issued to Austin Colony — 1823
Catholic colonies established — 1824
Battle of the Alamo, Texas Declaration of Independence — 1836
Texas made a Prefecture Apostolic by Rome, first Mass in Galveston & Houston — 1839
Texas Congress returns confiscated lands to Catholic Church — 1841
Texas made a Vicariate Apostolic; Jean Marie Odin, CM, named first Vicar — **1841**
Texas annexed by the United States — 1845
United States / Mexican War — 1846 1847
Diocese of Galveston established, Bishop Odin first Bishop — 1847
Ursulines establish first Catholic school in Galveston — 1847
St. Mary's Cathedral dedicated in Galveston — 1848
St. Mary's College founded in San Antonio, St. Mary's Seminary in Galveston — 1852
Civil War begins, Texas secedes from the Union, Sam Houston deposed as Governor — 1861
Bishop Claude Dubuis named Second Bishop of Galveston — 1862
Civil War ends – Federal troops occupy Galveston — 1865
Reconstruction — 1866 1874
St. Mary's Infirmary opens in Galveston — 1867

St. Louis Cathedral in New Orleans as it appeared when Bishop Odin was consecrated. Before he became Archbishop of New Orleans in 1861, the cathedral had undergone extensive renovation and assumed its present appearance.

John Marie Odin, C.M.
First Bishop of Galveston

> Bishop Jean Marie Odin

1800 > † 1870

Jean Marie Odin volunteered to serve as a missionary in the United States while a seminarian for the Diocese of Lyon, France. When he arrived in the U.S. he was sent to the Vincentian seminary at St. Mary of the Barrens in Missouri, where he was ordained to the priesthood in May, 1823.

Father Odin served the Church in Texas first as a priest, then as a bishop. When the Diocese of Galveston was established in 1847, he was named the first *ordinary*.

He traveled continuously and encountered many dangers. In a letter to his sister in France he once wrote: "God watches over us with such paternal care and goodness, that no accident has yet occurred; frequently my horse has fallen; the branches of trees could many times have endangered my life; serpents, which abound every-where, are often between the legs of my horse; bears have fled before me, and amidst all these perils, nothing serious has befallen me."

In 1861 he was appointed Archbishop of New Orleans where he served until 1870. He died in Europe where he was participating in the First Vatican Council.

"ordinary"

A term used for the presiding bishop of a diocese.

57

> A new state, a new diocese, defining the boundaries

This map shows the area claimed by the Republic of Texas and that portion sold to the United States that later became parts of the states of New Mexico, Oklahoma, Kansas, Colorado and Wyoming.

On February 19, 1846, the Republic of Texas became the State of Texas and on May 4, 1847 the Vicariate Apostolic of Texas became the Diocese of Galveston with Jean Marie Odin as its first bishop. Surprisingly, Bishop Odin did not know how much territory his diocese covered. The papal bull that established it stated that the boundaries would be the same as the state and that was as yet undecided.

"papal bull"
An official document from the Pope. Papal bulls are used in establishing a new diocese or appointing a bishop.

"slave-holding state"
Before the Civil War, individual states were permitted to decide whether or not their citizens could own slaves. A slave-holding state was one permitting the owning of slaves.

The United States war against Mexico in 1846-47 was based upon the land claims of the newly annexed Republic of Texas. The Republic believed that its territory extended to the Rio Grande along its entire course, from that river's source in Colorado down through the middle of the Mexican jurisdictions of New Mexico, Chihuahua, Coahuila, and finally, to Tamaulipas, where the river emptied into the Gulf of Mexico.

New Mexico was a very old and populated political unit that had never been a part of Texas. Strong political interests in the United States were against allowing Texas, a slave-holding state, to have such a large territory that might later become divided into additional slave-holding states.

While the Texas state boundaries were being negotiated, Bishop Odin wrote to Rome for clarification as to the territorial extent of his diocese. In the Spring of 1849, just as he was about to leave for a council of the United States bishops in Baltimore, the bishop received the reply from Rome that the diocese was to include all the area claimed by Texas.

Mexican Independence — 1821
First Land Titles issued to Austin Colony — 1823
Catholic colonies established — 1824
Battle of the Alamo, Texas Declaration of Independence — 1836
Texas made a Prefecture Apostolic by Rome, first Mass in Galveston & Houston — 1839
Texas Congress returns confiscated lands to Catholic Church — 1841
Texas made a Vicariate Apostolic, Jean Marie Odin, CM, named first Vicar — 1841
Texas annexed by the United States — **1845**
United States / Mexican War — 1846 1847
Diocese of Galveston established, Bishop Odin first Bishop — **1847**
Ursulines establish first Catholic school in Galveston — 1847
St. Mary's Cathedral dedicated in Galveston — 1848
St. Mary's College founded in San Antonio, St. Mary's Seminary in Galveston — 1852
Civil War begins, Texas secedes from the Union, Sam Houston deposed as Governor — 1861
Bishop Claude Dubuis named Second Bishop of Galveston — 1862
Civil War ends – Federal troops occupy Galveston — 1865 1866
Reconstruction — 1874
St. Mary's Infirmary opens in Galveston — 1867

Anson Jones, the last president of the Republic of Texas, lowers the Republic flag upon annexation to the United States.

It took a rugged man to serve as a priest or a bishop on the frontier. Here is what Oblate Father P. F. Parisot, a missionary priest in the early 1850s, wrote of the men who were the first bishops of Texas: "Monsignor (Bishop) Odin chooses poverty and strictness and is only rich and lavish towards the poor."
He quotes the Bishop as admitting that he lived upon a dollar a week.
"Sometimes discouragement almost seizes me, when I know not what means to adopt to procure even the most indispensable provisions; but God is a good father and always comes to my help."

He continues the story: Abbé (Bishop) Dubuis wrote a letter from Castroville, which concluded with these words:
"To this hour I have never known one moment of disgust or regret, and, if I were still in France, I would quit it immediately for the missions of Texas, which I shall only abandon when strength and life are taken from me."

Another of Father Parisot's stories relates that "one day, when traveling through Texas, (Aug. 4, 1855), I met Father (Bishop) Neraz all alone in the woods 100 miles from Nacogdoches, ...we camped on the road and he prepared some coffee for me.
When I tasted it I exclaimed: "Eh! There is no sugar in your coffee." "Sugar in my coffee," said he, "how could I afford such a luxury, when I received only $92 during the whole of last year?"

The Baltimore Council realized that this would be an unmanageably huge diocese and requested that New Mexico be made a separate church unit. That is what happened in 1850. This was the same year that the face-saving 1850 Compromise of the U.S. Congress established the southern and western boundary of Texas as the Rio Grande River all the way up to El Paso. This gave Texas 10 million dollars for its supposed "loss" of New Mexico above that point. The state of Texas, and thus the Diocese of Galveston, finally had definite limits.

Communication being what it was in those days, however, the El Paso district in far West Texas did not come under the jurisdiction of a United States diocese until 1872! Since the El Paso district was nearer to the settled part of New Mexico than to other Texas settlements that ended at Fredericksburg near San Antonio in 1850, Bishop Odin asked the new bishop of New Mexico to take care of the El Paso district for him.

When Bishop John B. Lamy of Santa Fe tried to take over jurisdiction in the El Paso district, the Mexican priests there and their bishop in Durango, Mexico, refused to transfer control. The district was finally transferred to the jurisdiction of the Vicariate Apostolic of Arizona in 1872. Twenty years later, in 1892, the El Paso district finally became part of a Texas diocese when it was added to the recently created north Texas Diocese of Dallas.

CLICK-LEARNING

> **Treaty of Guadalupe-Hidalgo**

> **annexation of Texas**

"abbé"
The French word for Father, when referring to a priest Abbé John is the same as Father John.

> New Colonists, Help Wanted!

St. Mary's Cathedral Basilica in Galveston has been the mother church of Catholicism in Texas since the time of Independence. The present structure was built in 1847 but has had extensive remodeling.

More new colonists poured into the state overland and by ship, many of them Catholic. Bishop Odin recruited more priests and seminarians from Europe, especially France, and brought in the first group of women religious. He now had German priests to minister to the German Catholics in the area around New Braunfels. Ursuline postulants recruited in France with other nuns from the New Orleans convent opened Ursuline Academy in Galveston with 70 students. Galveston's Ursulines were the vanguard of the thousands of nuns and sisters who would serve the church in Texas.

> **"postulants"**
> Men or women living with a community of religious before being accepted for membership.

> **"vanguard"**
> Those in the vanguard are the first arrivals, ones who are the first of many to come later.

St. Mary's Church, which had been under re-construction only two months, was designated the Cathedral for the new diocese. It was completed in the fall of 1848, and Bishop Blanc of New Orleans and Father John Timon, who had been appointed Bishop of Buffalo, New York, assisted Bishop Odin in the consecration ceremonies.

In the new diocese, the bishop and his missionaries suffered many hardships in reaching out to the widely scattered settlements of colonists. Their three greatest problems were the weather, hostile Indians and disease. Springtime floods and summertime heat often exceeding 100 degrees plagued the missionaries traveling by horseback or wagon. It was not unusual for the missionaries to come across scalped victims of hostile Indian bands on their journeys. Cholera and yellow fever frequently struck and claimed hundreds of lives, including many priests and sisters.

> **"cholera"**
> An infectious intestinal disease that caused many deaths in Texas during the 19th century.

> **"yellow fever"**
> A mosquite-borne tropical disease that caused many deaths in the coastal area of Texas in the 18th and 19th centuries.

- Mexican Independence — 1821
- First Land Titles issued to Austin Colony — 1823
- Catholic colonies established — 1824
- Battle of the Alamo, Texas Declaration of Independence — 1836
- Texas made a Prefecture Apostolic by Rome, first Mass in Galveston & Houston — 1839
- Texas Congress returns confiscated lands to Catholic Church — 1841
- Texas made a Vicariate Apostolic Jean Marie Odin, CM, named first Vicar — 1841
- Texas annexed by the United States — 1845
- United States / Mexican War — 1846 1847
- Diocese of Galveston established, Bishop Odin first Bishop — 1847 1847
- Ursulines establish first Catholic school in Galveston — 1847
- **St. Mary's Cathedral dedicated in Galveston** — **1848**
- St. Mary's College founded in San Antonio, St. Mary's Seminary in Galveston — 1852
- Civil War begins, Texas secedes from the Union, Sam Houston deposed as Governor — 1861
- Bishop Claude Dubuis named Second Bishop of Galveston — 1862
- Civil War ends – Federal troops occupy Galveston — 1865
- Reconstruction — 1866 1874
- St. Mary's Infirmary opens in Galveston — 1867

Thousands of Hispanic Catholics along the lower and middle Rio Grande were now part of the Diocese of Galveston. Bishop Odin looked north to Canada for assistance in ministering to their needs. As a result of his visit to Montreal, two Ursuline nuns and five Oblates

of Mary Immaculate (three priests, a Brother, and a seminarian) agreed to come to Texas. The Oblates began a ministry to the lower Rio Grande Valley and other places in Texas that continues to this day. Bishop Odin was constantly amazed by the enthusiasm and self-sacrificing spirit of the men and women assisting him in his work as chief pastor.

Religious communities of men and women showed an amazing flexibility and willingness to adapt to the constantly changing conditions of the new state. While diocesan structures developed slowly, the religious communities can draw resources from throughout the country, and indeed the world, to provide personnel and expertise that would otherwise be lacking by a new and struggling diocese.

Catholicism in Texas is firmly rooted in the work of the diocesan priests and religious sisters, brothers and priests who responded so unselfishly to the call of Bishop Odin to establish churches, schools, hospitals and orphanages in the frontier villages and towns of Texas.

Growth continued at a rapid rate with Catholic colonists arriving daily from Europe and the northeast. Many changes were in store for both the Diocese of Galveston and its bishop.

> St. Mary's Cathedral Basilica

Most cathedrals don't serve as lighthouses, but ship captains entering Galveston harbor in the old days used the lighted crown on the statue of the Blessed Virgin atop St. Mary's Cathedral to guide them into port. The 15-foot high statue was placed on the top of the cathedral's tower in 1878 and became the highest structure in the Gulf-side city.

The present structure dates to 1847. Bishop Jean Marie Odin began construction in March, two weeks before Pope Pius IX established the Diocese of Galveston. The original frame church built in 1842 was blown down by a storm seven months after it was built. Temporary repairs were made and it served has the cathedral until the present one was dedicated in 1848.

The tower with the statue of Mary was added 30 years later by Texas architect and Catholic layman Nicholas Clayton. Clayton redesigned and heightened the front towers in 1884. St. Mary's has withstood several hurricanes including the great storm of 1900. The exterior is essentially the same as in 1884, but many interior renovations have been made. In 1979 Pope John Paul II raised the cathedral to the status of minor basilica, a special honor reserved for churches of historical importance.

CLICK-LEARNING

> **Oblates of Mary Immaculate**

> **Ursuline**

Panna Maria, Texas, was established by colonists from Poland. Most schools in immigrant colonies like St. Joseph School in Panna Maria taught classes in both English and their native language. Bilingual classes are still taught in some Texas schools.

> God's Cavalry

Oblate priests who traveled south Texas on horseback in the 19th Century were called God's Cavalry.

Pioneer priests often served many communities great distances apart. They would visit their mission stations or "circuit" on horseback. They were, in effect, God's cavalry. In most communities, the priest might visit once a month or so. In others, it would be only three or four times a year.

Of course, there were many stories of these rugged clergymen. One that is especially interesting is about Father Thomas Hennessy. It is taken from a history of Immaculate Conception Church in Jefferson, Texas, written by Father John O'Rourke.

"Father Hennessy without a doubt is the most colorful of all the Jefferson pastors, for of him a Baptist minister said: 'Of all my son-in-laws, my favorite is Father Hennessy.' As a very young man Thomas Hennessy met, fell in love and was married. The young Irishman and his wife lived in Powderhorne, where their two children were born. In the late 1850s an epidemic of yellow fever, one of the many which swept Texas in those days, visited the home of Mr. and Mrs. Thomas Hennessy. Tom lost both his wife and his two children. It was then that he decided to devote the rest of his life to the service of his fellowmen by becoming a priest of the Catholic Church.

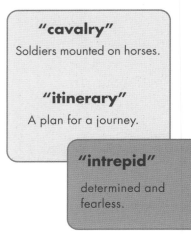

"cavalry"
Soldiers mounted on horses.

"itinerary"
A plan for a journey.

"intrepid"
determined and fearless.

Mexican Independence — 1821
First Land Titles issued to Austin Colony — 1823
Catholic colonies established — 1824
Battle of the Alamo, Texas Declaration of Independence — 1836
Texas made a Prefecture Apostolic by Rome, first Mass in Galveston & Houston — 1839
Texas Congress returns confiscated lands to Catholic Church — 1841
Texas made a Vicariate Apostolic, Jean Marie Odin, CM, named first Vicar — 1841
Texas annexed by the United States — 1845
United States / Mexican War — 1846 1847
Diocese of Galveston, established, Bishop Odin first Bishop — 1847
Ursulines establish first Catholic school in Galveston — 1847
St. Mary's Cathedral dedicated in Galveston — 1848
St. Mary's College founded in San Antonio, St. Mary's Seminary in Galveston — **1852**
Civil War begins, Texas secedes from the Union, Sam Houston deposed as Governor — 1861
Bishop Claude Dubuis named Second Bishop of Galveston — 1862
Civil War ends — Federal troops occupy Galveston — 1865
Reconstruction — 1866 1874
St. Mary's Infirmary opens in Galveston — 1867

> Father Pierre Parisot, O.M.I.

1827 > † 1903

When Pierre Parisot left his home in France to come to Texas as a missionary, he never thought one of his first challenges would be to break a wild mustang...quickly.

Parisot was a newly ordained Oblate missionary priest when, in 1852, he was given $2 by his bishop to take the ferry from Galveston Island and to search out and minister to Catholics in East Texas. When he stepped off the ferry he had no money, only the clothes on his back and a saddlebag with a few personal items and what he needed to celebrate Mass.

His journey, which he recounted 50 years later in "Reminiscences of a Texas Missionary," was literally made on God's providence. Providence caused him to stumble upon several dying people who were praying for a priest in their last hours. Providence provided him with the opportunity to visit Catholics who had not seen a priest for years and to provide them with the Eucharist, reconciliation and Baptism.

Providence also provided him with the wild mustang that had never been ridden. The wild pony was saddled and bridled for the first time and was held while the missionary mounted him. The horse was then released. After a wild ride through the woods, Father Parisot outlasted the mustang, which became his friend and in his words, "gentle as a lamb."

In his 50 years as a missionary he served all over Texas and in Louisiana and Mexico. Some would say only a fool would do that.

He would agree that he was a fool for God, and only God knows how many people came to God through his labors.

Father Pierre Parisot, OMI, was a pioneer missionary priest and circuit rider in early Texas.

One of the French missionary priests introduced him to Bishop Claude Dubuis, the second Bishop of Galveston, who sent him to the seminary and then ordained him on June 21, 1863."
Father Hennessy, like all the early priests of Texas, kept moving all the time. Though his headquarters was Jefferson, he had a vast territory to visit. Minus roads and modern cars, these early padres traveled by horseback from one group of Catholics to the next, baptizing, preaching, validating marriages and celebrating Mass.

As a letter of an old Nacogdoches parishioner states, "We never saw a priest oftener than twice a year, possibly not so often, as Father Hennessy's itinerary included Liberty, Jefferson, Orange, Polk, Angelina, Nacogdoches, San Augustine and Smith Counties."

These missionary priests carried all they needed for their priestly ministry in the saddlebags: vestments, chalice, wine, hosts and candles. When crossing streams on horseback, they placed their saddlebags on their heads to keep their "mass kits" dry. At least one pioneer priest, Father M. Perrier, first pastor in Dallas, was of such a size that he could not get on a horse. He rode his circuit in a buckboard wagon. These intrepid men brought the joy and consolation of the sacraments to the scattered Catholics carving a state out of the wilderness.

CLICK-LEARNING

> **Bishop Claude Dubuis**

> **buckboard wagon**

> Religious communities of men.

Religious communities of men might be called the Church's "special forces," because of their mobility and ability to provide many types of ministry in many different areas. Unlike diocesan or secular priests who commit themselves to service of a particular place, religious priests and brothers serve many dioceses and many nations. For this reason, many serve as missionaries, as many have in Texas.

Evangelization of Texas was greatly aided by religious communities of men. Franciscan priests and brothers had ministered to the Indians, as well as to the explorers and pioneers, who carved Texas out of the wilderness. With the appointment of Father John Timon as prefect apostolic in 1839, Vincentian priests of the Congregation of the Mission took over pastoral responsibility for the Republic of Texas. Fellow Vincentian Jean Marie Odin was later named vicar apostolic and first Bishop of Galveston. Both Timon and Odin spent much effort in recruiting priests for Texas, both secular and religious.

St. Mary's University in San Antonio was alone in the countryside when this picture was made in 1892.

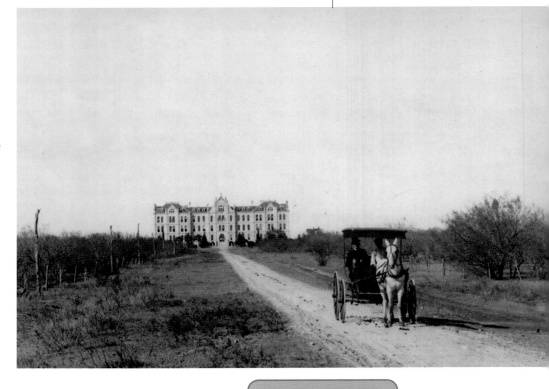

In 1849 the Oblates of Mary Immaculate came from French Canada to establish the Oblates' first permanent American foundation at Brownsville. The Oblates and members of other communities chose to abandon their home countries to preach on the frontiers of Texas. They underwent incredible hardships to foster the seeds of Faith in south Texas where it still blossoms today.

"incredible"
Unbelievable.

GLICK-LEARNING

> **Congregation of the Mission**
> **Society of Jesus**

64

Mexican Independance — 1821
First Land Titles issued to Austin Colony — 1823
Catholic colonies established — 1824
Battle of the Alamo, Texas Declaration of Independence — 1836
Texas made a Prefecture Apostolic by Rome, first Mass in Galveston & Houston — 1839
Texas Congress returns confiscated lands to Catholic Church — 1841
Texas made a Vicariate Apostolic Jean Marie Odin, CM, named first Vicar — 1841
Texas annexed by the United States — 1845
United States / Mexican War — 1846/1847
Diocese of Galveston established, Bishop Odin first Bishop — 1847
Ursulines establish first Catholic school in Galveston — 1847
St. Mary's Cathedral dedicated in Galveston — 1848
St. Mary's College founded in San Antonio, St. Mary's Seminary in Galveston — **1852**
Civil War begins, Texas secedes from the Union, Sam Houston deposed as Governor — 1861
Bishop Claude Dubuis named Second Bishop of Galveston — 1862
Civil War ends – Federal troops occupy Galveston — 1865
Reconstruction — 1866/1874
St. Mary's Infirmary opens in Galveston — 1867

Another French congregation that responded to Bishop Odin's plea was the Society of Mary (Marianists) who opened St. Mary's College in San Antonio in 1852 and have served in Texas continuously since that time. In addition to the university and a high school in San Antonio, Marianists are in parish and educational ministries in the dioceses of Galveston-Houston and Fort Worth.

Members of the Congregation of Holy Cross first came to Galveston in 1870 to take over the troubled St. Mary's College and seminary. The Galveston institution failed in 1879, but the Holy Cross brothers had taken on another foundation in 1872, St. Edward's College in Austin. Like St. Mary's in San Antonio, St. Edward's has provided a strong Catholic educational presence to the present time.

Jesuits, members of the Society of Jesus, have had a presence in Texas since 1874, but their first permanent foundation came in 1881 when the society assumed the major pastoral responsibilities for El Paso and the surrounding area, where they are still in active ministry. In addition, Jesuits continue to have a strong educational presence in Dallas and Houston.

Other religious communities of men who responded to the call to the frontier were the German Conventual Franciscans and the German Benedictines. Polish Resurrectionist Fathers gave strong leadership to Polish communities in the later 1800s. In far west Texas, the Carmelite Fathers established parishes in the Permian Basin and Davis Mountain area.

> **Apostle to El Paso**

1841 > † 1919

Jesuit Father Carlos Pinto, the Apostle of El Paso

Jesuit Father Carlos Pinto was born to wealth but chose to give his life to others as a priest. Forced to leave his native Italy by a revolution, he came to the United States and later was assigned to El Paso in 1892. That same year El Paso became part of the new Diocese of Dallas, whose bishop resided nearly 650 miles to the east. Until a bishop was appointed for El Paso in 1914, the Jesuit was the principal vicar for the Church in far west Texas.

Father Pinto set about planting the Catholic faith firmly along the borderlands. He worked tirelessly on both sides of the border for 27 years. No church existed in El Paso when the Italian priest arrived. When he died in November, 1919, burned out from his labors in the Lord's vineyard, he left behind five churches in El Paso and one in Ciudad Juarez, and as many schools. He was a priest wholly given to God's people and is remembered to this day as the "Apostle to El Paso."

St. Mary's College was established in San Antonio in 1852 by the Society of Mary (Marianists) one of the religious communities of men who responded to Bishop Jean Marie Odin's call for assistance.

> Religious Communities of Women.

Members of religious communities of women came early to the Texas frontier where they served as nurses, cared for orphans, opened schools and witnessed mightily to the Gospel. Women religious, nuns and sisters, arrived in Texas in 1847. Bishop Jean Marie Odin had invited Ursuline nuns from France and New Orleans to assist him in building up the church in his new Diocese of Galveston. They opened the first non-parochial Catholic school in Texas and the first public hospital in response to the yellow fever epidemic. The order rapidly spread to San Antonio (1851), Laredo (1868), and Dallas (1874).

Women religious established many of the first hospitals in Texas. Shown here is an early operating room at St. Mary's Infirmary in Galveston operated by the Sisters of Charity of the Incarnate Word.

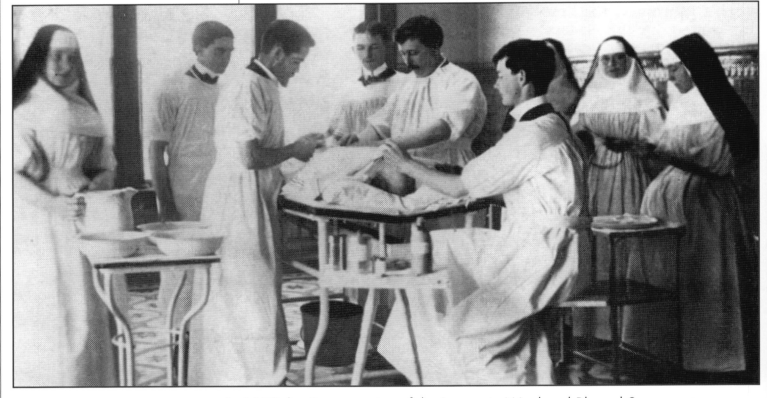

In 1852 the Congregation of the Incarnate Word and Blessed Sacrament came from their convent in Lyon, France, to Brownsville in response to Bishop Odin's request. They soon established houses in Victoria (1866) Corpus Christi (1871), Houston (1873), Shiner (1879) and Halletsville (1882).

"Epidemic"
A particularly serious outbreak and spread of an infectious disease.

"Mentor"
A coach, a guide or trusted counselor.

Mexican Independence — 1821
First Land Titles issued to Austin Colony — 1823
Catholic colonies established — 1824
Battle of the Alamo, Texas Declaration of Independence — 1836
Texas made a Prefecture Apostolic by Rome, first Mass in Galveston & Houston — 1839
Texas Congress returns confiscated lands to Catholic Church — 1841
Texas made a Vicariate Apostolic Jean Marie Odin, CM, named first Vicar — 1841
Texas annexed by the United States — 1845
United States / Mexican War — 1846 1847
Diocese of Galveston, Bishop Odin first Bishop — 1847
Ursulines establish first Catholic school in Galveston — **1847**
St. Mary's Cathedral dedicated in Galveston — 1848
St. Mary's College founded in San Antonio, St. Mary's Seminary in Galveston — 1852
Civil War begins, Texas secedes from the Union, Sam Houston deposed as Governor — 1861
Bishop Claude Dubuis named Second Bishop of Galveston — 1862
Civil War ends – Federal troops occupy Galveston — 1865
Reconstruction — 1866 1874
St. Mary's Infirmary opens in Galveston — 1867

Bishop John Timon of Buffalo, Bishop Odin's friend and mentor, brought a Belgian community, the Sisters of St. Mary Namur, to the U.S. They soon came to Texas in 1863 and established academies in North Central Texas at Waco, Dallas, Fort Worth, Sherman, Denison and Wichita Falls. Another French community, the Congregation of the Sisters of Divine Providence came first to Austin in 1866 at the invitation of Bishop Claude Dubuis. They soon established a permanent foundation in Castroville. The American community became independent in 1883 and moved the motherhouse to San Antonio in 1896, where the cornerstone for Our Lady of the Lake College had been laid the previous year.

In 1866 Bishop Dubuis founded the Sisters of Charity of the Incarnate Word to establish Catholic hospitals in the state. The first was St. Mary's Infirmary in Galveston, soon to be followed by Santa Rosa Infirmary in San Antonio in 1869. Bishop Dubuis convinced the Sisters of the Congregation of the Holy Cross to come to Texas in 1870, where they eventually established a successful academy in Austin in 1874.

In 1875, the Daughters of Charity from France established a school and hospital at the thriving East Texas river port of Jefferson. Both were short lived, but the Daughters returned to Texas in 1892 to open a hospital in El Paso, followed in 1896 by St. Paul Sanitarium in Dallas.

A number of other communities of women brought their charisms to Texas in the 19th century, including the Sisters of Mercy, the Sisters of Loretto, the Dominican Sisters, the Olivetan Benedictine Sisters, and the Sisters of the Holy Family. Special mention should be made of the Sisters Servants of the Holy Ghost and Mary Immaculate, a congregation established in San Antonio in 1893 by a wealthy Irish widow, Margaret Mary Healy-Murphy. The community was dedicated to teaching African-American children. The early communities of women religious willingly endured many difficulties in order to bring the teaching and compassion of Christ to thousands of children and adults.

CLICK-LEARNING
> **Sisters of Charity of the Incarnate Word**
> **Sisters of Divine Providence**
> **Sisters of St. Mary Namur**

> Margaret Mary Healy-Murphy

1833 > † 1907

Margaret Mary Healy-Murphy was a widow who established the Sisters of the Holy Ghost and Mary Immaculate

Margaret Mary Healy was born in Ireland in 1833, the daughter of a doctor who practiced primarily among the poor. When her father was widowed in 1839, he brought Margaret Mary and two brothers to America, where they first settled in West Virginia, but then soon moved on to Texas. Her father died on the journey, and she lived with relatives in Matamoros, Mexico. In 1849 she met and married John B. Murphy, a volunteer in the American army. The Murphys moved to Corpus Christi where John became a successful lawyer and mayor. Margaret Mary had inherited her father's compassion for the poor. She nursed yellow fever victims and adopted three children orphaned by the epidemic. In 1875 Margaret Mary and three friends purchased a homeless center that became known as

*"Mrs. Murphy's Hospital for the Poor." After her husband*s death in 1884, she was inspired by the sermon of an Oblate priest in San Antonio to commit herself to work among the African-Americans. She used her wealth to build a church, convent and school in San Antonio. Unable to obtain teachers, she founded a religious community of women, the Congregation of the Holy Ghost and Mary Immaculate, to minister to African-Americans. She returned to her native Ireland to recruit new members, and her community grew rapidly throughout Texas and the United States. Reverend Mother Margaret Mary died in 1907 in the convent she had founded in San Antonio. The convent continues to exist today as the Healy-Murphy Center, an accredited, alternative high school, child development center, and health clinic.*

> What Catholic schools were like in early Texas

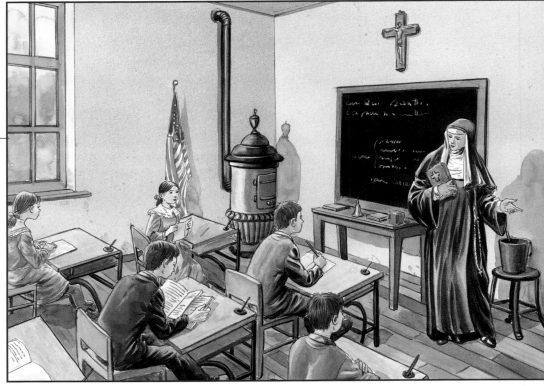

Catholic school children in early Texas, like those in this class picture, wore very different clothes and had very few of the comforts and conveniences that students enjoy today.

It is natural to believe that things were always the way they are or at least close to it. Of course, that is not the case. Take your school for instance. You probably have a clean and comfortable classroom that is warm when the weather is cold and cool when the weather is hot. You have plenty of paper, pens and pencils with lots of light in your room, and you probably regularly use the computer and view videos or special television programs.

Let's take a look backward. Education has always been of number one importance to the Catholic church. Every bishop is told he has three responsibilities to his people: "to teach, to sanctify and to govern" in that order. Catholic education recognizes that knowledge of the arts and sciences must be based upon Christian values and they must be integrated into the curriculum.

Catholic education in Texas first occurred in the mission era when Indian children were taught to read, write and add until they were nine. From then on their subjects were vocational, that is, they learned skills like making pottery,

farming or carpentry. Their classrooms were usually outdoors or perhaps under a shelter made from branches. The early Catholic parishes in Texas under Spain and Mexico also often provided basic education in religion, reading, and writing to the Mexican and immigrant children of the community. In 1847 the Ursuline nuns founded the first non-parochial Catholic school in Galveston. It was for girls.

By 1856 there were six Catholic schools for boys, three academies for young ladies and one college in Texas. Colleges were not just for university students in the mid-19th century, but were like our middle school and high school, and they often took in elementary level pupils. Students at this time were referred to as "scholars."

"rhetoric"
The art of using words effectively to influence or persuade others.

"scholar"
A student, one attending a school.

Mexican Independence — 1821
First Land Titles issued to Austin Colony — 1823
Catholic colonies established — 1824
Battle of the Alamo, Texas Declaration of Independence — 1836
Texas made a Prefecture Apostolic by Rome, first Mass in Galveston & Houston — 1839
Texas Congress returns confiscated lands to Catholic Church — 1841
Texas made a Vicariate Apostolic, Jean Marie Odin, CM, named first Vicar — 1841
Texas annexed by the United States — 1845
United States / Mexican War — 1846 1847
Diocese of Galveston, established, Bishop Odin first Bishop — 1847
Ursulines establish first Catholic school in Galveston — 1847
St. Mary's Cathedral dedicated in Galveston — 1848
St. Mary's College founded in San Antonio, St. Mary's Seminary in Galveston — **1852**
Civil War begins, Texas secedes from the Union, Sam Houston deposed as Governor — 1861
Bishop Claude Dubuis named Second Bishop of Galveston — 1862
Civil War ends – Federal troops occupy Galveston — 1865
Reconstruction — 1866 1874
St. Mary's Infirmary opens in Galveston — 1867

Our Lady of Good Counsel Academy in Dallas was established by the Sisters of St. Mary of Namur. It was typical of academies for young ladies established by religious communities in Texas.

> **Higher Education**

You probably realize by now that things were very different when Texas was a young state. There were no public schools in many places and very few private schools. Schools that were roughly the equivalent of today's senior high schools were called colleges. Some schools, often called academies, started at first grade and continued through high school. Many schools for young ladies taught only the subjects that would be needed to be a wife and mother and offered few if any academic classes.

Catholic religious orders were the pioneers of education in Texas beginning with the schools operated by Spanish missionaries. Communities of sisters like the Ursulines, Incarnate Word and Blessed Sacrament, Divine Providence and Sisters of St. Mary of Namur established academies and colleges. Communities of religious established some of the earliest colleges for boys. The Marianists established St. Mary's in San Antonio in 1852 and the Congregation of Holy Cross founded St. Edwards in Austin in 1878. Public schools were rare and transportation very slow, so many families sent their children to the academies in the larger cities where they stayed during the school term. As more parochial schools were established throughout the state, there was less need for boarding, schools and many of them changed to regular schools or were closed.

The school year began on the first of October and ended on the first of August. An advertisement for Immaculate Conception school in Galveston noted that "the regular course of study comprises the Latin, Greek, English and French languages, reading, writing, grammar, geography, mathematics, history, rhetoric, poetry, mythology, astronomy, chemistry, surveying, botany, English composition, bookkeeping and natural and moral philosophy."

Such schools only existed in the larger towns. In the small rural communities there were often no schools, or a one-room school with students from all elementary grades who shared a single teacher. The course of studies was much simpler because the teacher often had only a 10th grade education. Country schools would frequently close down during harvest time to free the children to help bring in the crops. Of course, there was no air conditioning or central heat. School buildings were built with high ceilings and tall windows that opened from both the top and the bottom to allow circulation of the air. Heat usually came from a wood or coal stove in the classroom.

Early Catholic schools were normally taught by Sisters or religious priests and Brothers; Most of them were missionaries from France, Ireland or Germany, who had left their homes to teach in America. Paper was often very scarce, and lessons were done on a slate with a slate pencil. Many students never went beyond elementary school. Wealthy families frequently hired a tutor or teacher who taught the children

"slate"

A thin piece of rock used as a writing surface with chalk. A small blackboard.

at home if no good school was available. Many children of wealthy families were sent to boarding schools in the East or in Europe for their education. Education as we know it today only began to take shape in the 20th Century.

CLICK-LEARNING

> **St. Mary's University**

> **St. Edward's University**

CLICK-LEARNING

> **yellow fever**

> **Ursuline nuns**

> Ursuline Nuns

Life on the Texas frontier was hard. It was a constant struggle for survival in the days of the Republic and early statehood. The frontier attracts tough people who have little time for the niceties of life. Galveston was a rough-and-tumble port city on the Gulf of Mexico when the first Ursuline nuns arrived in 1847 at the invitation of Bishop Jean Marie Odin.

Bishop Odin first met the Ursulines in New Orleans in 1841. They provided him with hospitality during the retreat he made prior to his consecration as bishop and vicar apostolic for Texas.

His admiration for the work of the nuns resulted in a determination to have them establish a foundation in Galveston. He believed that the Ursulines would bring not only an educational excellence and a strong Catholic witness to the growing, young port city, but also a much needed touch of culture.

On Monday, January 18, 1847, eight nuns arrived in Galveston on the coastal steamer Palmétto. Less than two weeks later, on February 8, 1847, they opened a school with 23 young ladies as students. Within a week the number had increased to 42 of which 15 were Catholic.

Shortly after the arrival of the Ursuline nuns in Galveston in 1847, the first convent and school were built near the Gulf of Mexico.

"retreat"

A quiet time away from normal activities to listen to the voice of God in our lives and be renewed spiritually.

"witness"

The way we live is a witness of our values to others. As Catholic Christians we are called to witness Gospel values in our lives.

Mexican Independence — 1821
First Land Titles issued to Austin Colony — 1823
Catholic colonies established — 1824
Battle of the Alamo, Texas Declaration of Independence — 1836
Texas made a Prefecture Apostolic by Rome, first Mass in Galveston & Houston — 1839
Texas Congress returns confiscated lands to Catholic Church — 1841
Texas made a Vicariate Apostolic, Jean Marie Odin, CM, named first Vicar — 1841
Texas annexed by the United States — 1845
United States / Mexican War — 1846 1847
Diocese of Galveston established, Bishop Odin first Bishop — 1847
Ursulines establish first Catholic school in Galveston — **1847**
St. Mary's Cathedral dedicated in Galveston — 1848
St. Mary's College founded in San Antonio, St. Mary's Seminary in Galveston — 1852
Civil War begins, Texas secedes from the Union, Sam Houston deposed as Governor — 1861
Bishop Claude Dubuis named Second Bishop of Galveston — 1862
Civil War ends — Federal troops occupy Galveston — 1865
Reconstruction — 1866 1874
St. Mary's Infirmary opens in Galveston — 1867

Two Ursuline nuns sit with their students for a class picture at Ursuline Academy in Dallas. The photograph was made about 1880 on the steps of the Academy building.

> Austrian Orphans

It was a promising beginning for an educational institution that would serve Galveston and Texas for 130 years before being consolidated. During those 130 years, the Galveston Ursuline foundation provided leadership for Ursuline schools in San Antonio, Laredo, Dallas and Bryan, Texas. In 1851, with only $30 in the treasury, Galveston sent nuns to establish a San Antonio foundation.

The history of the Galveston Ursulines is a record of dedication and stamina in the face of unbelievable hardships. Their buildings were damaged or destroyed by eight hurricanes in 1853,1875,1891, 1900, 1909, 1915, 1943 and 1961. Buildings were gutted twice by fire. Yellow fever, "the plague of the South," struck repeatedly in the 19th Century requiring the school to close. During the Civil War one building was turned into a hospital that cared for both Confederate and Union soldiers. Eight nuns became battlefield nurses.

No disaster compared to the 1900 hurricane when the convent and academy became a refuge for nearly 1,000 victims of the storm. The hurricane left in its wake 10,000 homeless, more than 5,000 dead and a city devastated beyond belief. For more than a month, the Ursulines cared for the victims.

Hurricane Carla hit Galveston and Ursuline Academy in 1961. The buildings were again rebuilt. In 1967 Ursuline was consolidated with other Catholic schools.

There are no Ursulines in Galveston today, but the spirit lives on in Dallas where Ursuline Academy, founded in 1874 by the Galveston motherhouse, maintains a proud heritage and presence. Even though it is the only remaining Ursuline school in Texas, Ursuline nuns minister in a number of dioceses. They continue to bring educational excellence and "a touch of culture" to Texas as well as strong Catholic witness in a variety of ministries.

In 1854 a German priest arrived at Ursuline Academy in Galveston with three young Austrian girls orphaned by the yellow fever epidemic that had struck Houston. Teresa Holly was thirteen, and her little sister, Catherine, was only four, a third sister, Barbara, was only a toddler. The nuns took in the foundlings. Ursuline became their home.

Both Teresa and Catherine chose to become Ursuline nuns as they grew in wisdom and grace. Teresa became Sister Joseph Holly, and Catherine became Sister Mary Evangelist. Their home and family had been Ursuline Academy in Galveston, but both were destined to serve their order and the Church in other places. Barbara changed her name to Teresa, after her older sister entered the convent. She later married and moved to San Patricio, Texas.

Sister Joseph Holly was chosen to be the superior of a group of sisters who were sent to Dallas in 1874 to establish that city's first Catholic school, Ursuline Academy. They arrived in Dallas with $146 and a commitment to found a parochial school and an academy for young ladies. Mother Joseph died in 1884, but in ten years she had accomplished her mission of establishing Sacred Heart parish school and Ursuline Academy. Sister Mary Evangelist was assigned to Dallas the following year. Like her Sister, she was chosen to be superior of the Dallas Ursulines and became Mother Mary Evangelist.

> **"superior"**
> Another term used to designate the person in charge of a group. The one to whom others are accountable are their superiors.

When several Ursuline communities were combined into the Roman Union, Mother Mary Evangelist was called to Rome to be assistant general for the English-speaking Ursulines throughout the world. After 17 years she returned to Dallas where in 1942 she died at the age of 90.

The monuments to the Holly sisters' dedication to the Catholic education of young ladies are not carved in stone, but are imprinted on the lives of the religious sisters and students touched and enriched by their love and service.

> Civil War and new Bishop

"boom times"
Times of great growth and prosperity

"condoned"
Permitted something to take place or be done

Boom times for the Diocese of Galveston ended abruptly in 1861 when a double blow struck: the Civil War began, and Texas was left without a bishop.

Many hardships were brought on by the war. All Texans were not sympathetic with the secessionists. Sam Houston was deposed as governor because he refused to take the oath of allegiance to the Confederate government. Many of the Polish and German Catholic immigrants were union sympathizers, and the Hispanic Catholics were divided over the issue of slavery.

Because the influence of the "old south" had been strong in Texas, it had become a slave state. Many Texas Catholics owned slaves, including Bishop Odin himself. Bishop Odin, like most southern bishops, condoned the institution of slavery, even if some of them tried to mitigate its evils or even hoped for its gradual disappearance.

Texas seceded from the union on March 5, 1861. Less than a year earlier, Archbishop Antoine Blanc of New Orleans had died leaving the See vacant. Bishop Odin was named to succeed him and Texas lost its first bishop. Bishop Odin accepted the new appointment reluctantly because of his age (60) but more because of his love for Texas.

Bishop Claude Dubuis, front row center, is shown with a group of priests he recruited in France to serve as missionaries in Texas.

In October, 1862, the pope named Father Claude Marie Dubuis the second bishop of Galveston. The bishop-elect was a veteran of the Texas frontier having served in Castroville and as pastor of San Fernando in San Antonio. At the time of his appointment he was in France and faced the problem of returning to his diocese through the blockade of Galveston by the Union navy. He decided to return by the back door. He sailed to Matamoros, Mexico, and crossed the border into Brownsville.

"deposed"

Removed from office

Mexican Independence / First Land Titles Issued to Austin Colony / Catholic colonies established / Battle of the Alamo, Texas Declaration of Independence / Texas made a Prefecture Apostolic by Rome, first Mass in Galveston & Houston / Texas Congress returns confiscated lands to Catholic Church / Texas made a Vicariate Apostolic, Jean Marie Odin, CM, named first Vicar / Texas annexed by the United States / United States / Mexican War / Diocese of Galveston, established, Bishop Odin first Bishop / Ursulines establish first Catholic school in Galveston / St. Mary's Cathedral dedicated in Galveston / St. Mary's College founded in San Antonio, St. Mary's Seminary in Galveston / Civil War begins, Texas secedes from the Union, Sam Houston deposed as Governor / **Bishop Claude Dubuis named Second Bishop of Galveston** / Civil War ends – Federal troops occupy Galveston / Reconstruction / St. Mary's Infirmary opens in Galveston

1821 1823 1824 1836 1839 1841 1841 1845 1846/1847 1847 1847 1848 1852 1861 **1862** 1865 1866/1874 1867

1819 > † 1895

The Diocese of Galveston was larger than many nations in Europe when it was established in 1847. Texas' first bishop, Jean Marie Odin, spent much of his time in Europe recruiting priests and sisters to help spread the faith in his vast diocese. On one of his early trips, while Texas was still only a Vicariate Apostolic, Bishop Odin met a young priest in Lyon, France, who had only been ordained two years. The priest was Claude Marie Dubuis.

Won over by Bishop Odin's plea for help, Dubuis joined others in a five-week voyage from France to New Orleans. When he arrived, his first assignment was to learn English. However, when he was assigned to Castroville he used French as much as English since most of the settlers were from Alsace and spoke French.
He was later made rector of San Fernando in San Antonio, the oldest church in Texas, and Vicar General for the western part of the diocese.

In 1862 Father Dubuis became Bishop Dubuis and succeeded Bishop Odin. Always the promoter of the Texas missions, before he returned to Texas he recruited 59 priests, seminarians and sisters, who made the long return voyage with him.

He returned to his native France in 1880 because of ill health. Bishop Nicholas Gallagher administered the Diocese of Galveston (reduced in size by the creation of other dioceses in Texas) until 1892. At this time Bishop Gallagher became third Bishop of Galveston when Bishop Dubuis resigned that title. Bishop Dubuis died in France in 1895.

Since the departure of Bishop Odin, Father Louis Chambodut, Odin's vicar general, had served as administrator. During the interim period Galveston had been taken by Union troops, then was retaken by the Confederates. In the battle to retake the island on January 1, 1863, the Ursuline Convent had served as a hospital, treating wounded from both the Union and Confederate forces.

Fortifications at Sabine Pass had also fallen into Union hands but had been retaken. A second attack by Union forces was thwarted by a Texas force under the command of Lieutenant Dick Dowling, an Irish-Catholic. His small force blocked the attempt by sinking a boat in the channel. Port Isabel and Brownsville were both occupied by Union forces, but the Confederates retook Brownsville.

Statue of Catholic Civil War Hero Lieutenant Dick Dowling, who commanded the Confederate defenders in the Battle of Sabine Pass at which the Union forces were defeated.
(Photo by Sherry Thorup is at the Dick Dowling Battlefield Park at Sabine Pass)

CLICK-LEARNING

> **Battle of Sabine Pass**

> **Lieutenant Dick Dowling**

Colonel Santos Benavides, a prominent Laredo Catholic, was an important Confederate military leader in South Texas. Other Hispanics such as Captain Octaviano Zapata fought on the Union side.

After Lee's surrender at Appomattox the local and state governments lost control in Texas, and there was a brief period of anarchy before the Federal troops arrived in Galveston on June 19, 1865. There the Emancipation Proclamation was read, giving rise to the Black Texan celebration of "Juneteenth," and slavery in Texas ended.

> Reconstruction and growth

Reconstruction following the war was a time of turmoil, but it was also a time of expansion. Thousands of settlers from the older southern states flooded into Texas seeking both stability and land. Many new Catholic immigrants of German, Polish, Czech, French and Irish extraction also arrived.

Healing came slowly after the war. Vigilante groups harassed Hispanics as well as German and Polish Catholic immigrants who had remained loyal to the Union. James Talmadge Moore in "Through Fire and Flood" tells of incidents at Panna Maria that included gunfights and attacks on women and children. Resurrectionist Father Adolph Bakanowski once dispersed a crowd of troublemakers by firing his pistol over their heads from a second-story window.

> **"extraction"**
> Having to do with your ancestry. If your ancestors came from another part of the world you would be of that extraction. European extraction, African extraction, Irish extraction, Mexican extraction.

Former supporters of the Confederate cause also suffered reprisals. Among them was Father Louis Chambodut who was publicly turned away from a voting place on the grounds that he had been a well-known supporter of the Confederacy. The French-born priest declared that he "was sorry for the effect, but did not regret the cause."

Bishop Dubuis made frequent trips to Europe to recruit priests and religious for his diocese. In 1866 he literally "built from scratch" a new nursing order of sisters called the Congregation of the Sisters of Charity of the Incarnate Word. They arrived in Galveston in October to find a partially completed hospital on the eastern end of the island.

The hospital opened in April of 1867. In July the island city was struck by a yellow fever epidemic, and the hospital received hundreds of victims. By the time the disease abated in November, 1,150 had died, including Mother Mary Blandine, the hospital's superior. Hundreds more died in Houston, among them Dick Dowling, the Catholic hero of the Battle of Sabine Pass. Three hundred died in Corpus Christi including two priests.

> **"tidal wave"**
> A very large and dangerous wave that can accompany a hurricane or be caused by an earthquake. Such waves can wipe out a community and cause many deaths.

In October, 1867, the lower Rio Grande Valley was devastated by a hurricane that literally washed away three towns. The hurricane brought a giant tidal wave that leveled three-quarters of the city of Brownsville and destroyed the convent and school of the Sisters of the Incarnate Word and Blessed Sacrament.

74

Mexican Independence — 1821
First Land Titles issued to Austin Colony — 1823
Catholic colonies established — 1824
Battle of the Alamo, Texas Declaration of Independence — 1836
Texas made a Prefecture Apostolic by Rome, first Mass in Galveston & Houston — 1839
Texas Congress returns confiscated lands to Catholic Church — 1841
Texas made a Vicariate Apostolic, Jean Marie Odin, CM, named first Vicar — 1841
Texas annexed by the United States — 1845
United States / Mexican War — 1846 1847
Diocese of Galveston established, Bishop Odin first Bishop — 1847
Ursulines establish first Catholic school in Galveston — 1847
St. Mary's Cathedral dedicated in Galveston — 1848
St. Mary's College founded in San Antonio, St. Mary's Seminary in Galveston — 1852
Civil War begins, Texas secedes from the Union, Sam Houston deposed as Governor — 1861
Bishop Claude Dubuis named Second Bishop of Galveston — 1862
Civil War ends – Federal troops occupy Galveston — 1865
Reconstruction — **1866 1874**
St. Mary's Infirmary opens in Galveston — 1867

The Alamo shown in this photograph has the familiar look of today, but the other buildings had not been restored and were in danger of destruction. The present front of the Alamo was added by the United States Army after annexation. It was used as a quartermaster depot.

> **Adina Zavala**

1861 > †1955

She locked herself inside the Alamo for three days to keep it from being sold. They called her the "Alamo Crusader" and the "Lady Who Saved the Alamo".
She was Adina Emilia de Zavala whose grandfather was the first vice-president of the Republic of Texas.

Adina was born in Harris County within sight of the San Jacinto Battlefield. After attending Ursuline Academy in Galveston and Sam Houston Normal (University) in Huntsville, she taught school in Terrell and San Antonio.

Adina organized a group of determined women who later affiliated with the Daughters of the Republic of Texas. Her passion to preserve Texas history included saving the Alamo convent from being torn down to build a wholesale grocery store. When it was proposed to rent out part of the Alamo, Adina went to the Alamo to stage a sit-in and refused to leave for three days. The sheriff tried to prevent her from receiving food and water. He was unsuccessful in removing her.

She is credited with originating the phrase "Six Flags Over Texas" and with saving the Spanish Governor's Palace and other historic sites.

Fr. Louis Chambodut
Confederate Supporter

In spite of the disasters that struck the state during this time, the church continued to grow. Many Mexicans fled to Texas to avoid the war between the forces of Emperor Maximilian and Benito Juarez. Bishop Dubuis continued to recruit priests and religious to serve his burgeoning flock.

The Sisters of St. Mary of Namur established an academy in Waco. The Sisters of Charity of the Incarnate Word began an orphanage in Galveston and sent sisters to San Antonio to establish what was to become Santa Rosa Hospital. The Holy Cross fathers, sisters and brothers came to Texas to work in Galveston and Brownsville and eventually established St. Edward's University in Austin.

Reconstruction ended in Texas in 1874, the year Bishop Dubuis petitioned Pope Pius IX to divide his large diocese. On August 27, a papal decree established the Diocese of San Antonio. Three weeks later, the pope established the Vicariate Apostolic of Brownsville.

CLICK-LEARNING

> **Civil War Reconstruction + Texas**

> **Daughters of the Republic of Texas**

4 Expansion and growth
> The Great 1900 Storm

"hurricane"

A powerful storm that originates in the ocean and contains winds up to more than 100 miles an hour and is accompanied by a great surge of water when it comes to shore.

That day, September 8, 1900, everybody knew that there was a hurricane in the Gulf, but Galveston had experienced many hurricanes before. Hurricanes were a part of life for residents of the Gulf coast. Telegraph messages had advised the weather bureau that the storm had crossed Cuba, touched Florida and was moving parallel to the coastline somewhere west of New Orleans. The ten Sisters of Charity of the Incarnate Word and their 93 wards could see the high waves from their beachfront orphanage.

"orphanage"

An institution for the care of children who have no parents or family or whose parents and family are unable to care for them.

As usual, two of the sisters from St. Mary's Orphanage drove with two of the older boys in their horse-drawn wagon to their order's nearby infirmary to pick up the evening meal for the children. That day, Mother Gabriel, the assistant superior at the infirmary, begged the orphanage sisters and the boys to take shelter at the infirmary because the storm was building rapidly. But they insisted that if they didn't return with the food there would be no dinner for the children. Reluctantly, Mother Gabriel waved them off with a prayer. The four never made it back; they were swept away by the waves and the wind.

At the orphanage, the remaining sisters and children watched the sand dunes on the beach front begin to disappear as the water rose, and the waves grew higher. Soon the waters of the storm surge reached the two frame dormitory buildings facing the Gulf. All of the children were brought to the girls' dormitory, the newer and stronger of the two buildings.

They all gathered in the first floor chapel, praying and singing the hymn, "Queen of the Waves."

No picture can show the horror and destruction of the Galveston Storm, but this painting gives some idea of the extent of the tragedy.

Diocese of San Antonio, Vicariate of Brownsville established
St. Edward's College founded in Austin
Diocese of Dallas established
Great Galveston storm destroys St. Mary's Orphanage
Persecution of Catholic Church in Mexico, Mexican refugees migrate to Texas
Brownsville Vicariate made Diocese of Corpus Christi
Diocese of El Paso established
World War I
Ku Klux Klan and Know-Nothings attacks on Catholics, Blacks and Jews
Diocese of Amarillo established
San Antonio made an Archdiocese
Texas Centennial Celebrated in Dallas
World War II

1874 1878 1890 1900 1910 1940 1912 1914 1914 1918 1920 1926 1926 1936 1939 1945

Ninety children and ten sisters from St. Mary's Orphanage were killed by the Galveston Hurricane of 1900. Only three boys survived. This photograph shows the children and the sisters before the storm.

St. Mary's Orphanage was built directly on the Gulf of Mexico in Galveston. It was literally blown away by the 1900 Galveston Hurricane.

Disaster often brings out the best in people, and they rise to the occasion to become heroes. That was the case with Father James M. Kirwin who emerged as one of the heroes of the 1900 Galveston Hurricane.

Father Kirwin had been ordained less than a year when he was appointed rector of Galveston's St. Mary's Cathedral in 1896. When the hurricane struck, the cathedral was one of the few buildings left standing on Galveston Island.

Sacred Heart Church was in ruins; St. Patrick Church was destroyed and St. Joseph Church suffered severe damage. Ursuline Academy sustained significant damage, but St. Mary's Orphanage was literally blown away.

In the midst of the chaos following the storm, Father Kirwin organized a committee of public safety to restore order and prevent looting. He took over the task of the recovery and disposal of the bodies of more than 6,000 people killed in the storm. Among the dead were about 1,000 Catholics including the ten sisters and 90 orphans at the orphanage.

Father Kirwin served on the Central Relief Committee that cared for the survivors and was the prime mover in the building of a seawall to prevent a repetition of the tragedy. His heroism did not end there. A year later he severely damaged his eyes rescuing people from a fire that swept the island city.

St. Mary's Cathedral still stands as an historic landmark and can be visited today.

The water continued to rise and the eight sisters herded the children to the second floor. As the howl of the wind grew deafening, the sisters took clothesline and tied the children to their own bodies to prevent them from being blown away.

Buildings were lifted from their foundations by the power of the water as it swept across the island. At the weather station the wind reached 85 miles per hour before the wind gauge blew away.

The frame building shook, the windows shattered and finally, the building was lifted up from its foundation. The roof collapsed, and it was carried away as so much flotsam. Three boys found themselves caught in a tree uprooted by the water. Desperately the three clung to the branches for more than a day before they were able to climb to dry ground. They were the only survivors of 93 children and ten nuns. Nothing was left of the orphanage. The bodies of two of the nuns were found at Texas City, across the bay. Other bodies were discovered as far away as Virginia Point on the mainland.

One sister's body was found still holding two tiny bodies in her arms.

The island was devastated by the storm. 6,000 people died in the worst natural disaster in the history of the United States. Two other Catholic institutions, Ursuline Academy and Sacred Heart Academy, sheltered refugees and survivors.

The three boys told the story of the sisters' heroic efforts to save the children. There were many examples of heroism that day and in the days following. The story of the ten heroic sisters is just one of them.

CLICK-LEARNING

> **Great Storm + Galveston**

> **Great Storm + St. Mary's Orphanage**

Members of the Ku Klux Klan, who wore white hoods and robes, were responsible for fanning the flames of prejudice against Catholics, African-Americans and Jews in Texas and throughout the nation.

> Growth and Anti-Catholicism

Have you ever been made fun of because of who you are? Most of us have at one time or another. Chances are that if this happened to you, your reaction was a feeling that if they really knew you, they would not treat you that way. What you experienced was prejudice. The word means to pre-judge or to form an opinion about something before we have the facts. So, we can say that prejudice is the result of a lack of understanding.

Most prejudice today is because of race or religion or economics. When people are different than we are, it is very easy to be uncomfortable around them and to be suspicious of them. That is why it is easy to make fun of a person or people who are different from us. In the history of our state and our country there have been many times that people were mistreated because they were Catholic or Jewish or Muslim, or because they were Irish or Polish or African-American, especially when their numbers were increasing.

When railroads began to be built all across Texas in the decades following the Civil War, the formerly less developed northern, western, and southern sections of the state experienced significant growth. The new transportation system opened up lands to farming, ranching, and mining and led to the rapid growth of urban centers. This not only promoted continued European and Mexican Catholic immigration, but also brought many Catholic farmers from the Midwest. To serve these new areas, four new dioceses were created between 1890 and 1947: Dallas stretching across north Texas, El Paso in far west Texas, Amarillo in the

Diocese of San Antonio, Vicariate of Brownsville established
St. Edward's College founded in Austin
Diocese of Dallas established
Great Galveston storm destroys St. Mary's Orphanage
Persecution of Catholic Church in Mexico, Mexican refugees migrate to Texas
Brownsville Vicariate made Diocese of Corpus Christi
Diocese of El Paso established
World War I
Ku Klux Klan and Know-Nothings attacks on Catholics, Blacks and Jews
Diocese of Amarillo established
San Antonio made an Archdiocese
Texas Centennial Celebrated in Dallas
World War II

1874 1878 1890 1900 1910 1940 1912 1914 1914 1918 1920 1926 1926 1936 1939 1945

Panhandle, and Austin in the center of the state. In 1926 San Antonio was made an Archdiocese.

This noticeably increasing and often 'foreign' Catholic presence in Texas alarmed some Anglo-American Protestants who already had a long-standing prejudice against Catholics and Mexicans. We have already noted how Mexicans such as Juan Seguin in San Antonio and the Polish along the lower San Antonio River were harassed and ill treated. The secretive Know-Nothing party championed anti-Catholic and anti-foreign politics in the 1850s. The Carmelites were badly treated in Stanton in 1890.

Early in the twentieth century, another wave of prejudice against Catholics swept the country and the state. In Texas in the 1920s priests were abducted and beaten by the Ku Klux Klan. There were threats to blow up Catholic churches, and an attempt was made to burn the Ursuline convent in Galveston. The Klan successfully forced the closing of a Catholic school, St. Dominic's Villa in Lampasas.

The Knights of Columbus and the Catholic Truth Society were leaders in confronting the prejudice against Catholics which surfaced in Texas from time-to-time. Both organizations published tracts and advertisements explaining the Catholic Faith, and the Knights of Columbus on occasion physically protected Catholic institutions. Knowledge and understanding are always the most powerful weapons against prejudice.

"Ku Klux Klan"

An organization opposed to Catholics, African-Americans and Jews that has been responsible for racial and anti-religious violence and prejudice in Texas.

"Know-Nothings"

A political movement of the mid-nineteenth century directed against the Catholic Church. It was a reaction to the great migration of foreign Catholics to the United States following 1846. Members feared a dilution of the Protestant, Anglo-American society of colonial times.

> **Father Max Murphy**

1902 > †1973

Father Max Murphy, a native of Dallas, was the first African-American priest from Texas. He was ordained in 1934.

Father Max Murphy was the first African-American priest born in Texas, but because of the racial discrimination present at the time, his lifetime of priestly ministry was spent on the island of Trinidad in the Caribbean.

Born Malcolm Ed Max Murphy in 1902, he was one of three brothers who was raised by Mary Jordan, a family friend after the death of his mother. He attended St. Peter School in Dallas, which was founded by his foster mother.

He was educated at St. Patrick Seminary in Menlo Park, California and the German Theological School in Prague, Czechoslovakia, where he was ordained to the priesthood in 1934. He went immediately to Trinidad where he served in the Archdiocese of Port of Spain.

In 1952, because of his knowledge of German he was chosen to undertake a special assignment in Germany for the State Department among the refugees dislocated by the Second World War. It was a mission of extreme delicacy and of great importance in easing the strained relations between Americans and Germans in Western Germany.

Father Murphy returned frequently to Dallas to visit his family and his old school. He died in 1973 during a trip to Washington after a life of missionary service to his church and diplomatic service to his country.

> Black Catholics arrived with the Spanish

Fellow bishops applaud as Bishop Curtis J. Guillory takes his place in the bishop's chair (cathedra) at his installation in 2000 as Bishop of Beaumont. Bishop Guillory, a native of Louisiana, is Texas' first African-American bishop.

Black or African-American Catholics have been part of Texas Catholic history from the time of the first Spanish exploration. Estéban the Moor, one of the few survivors of Cabeza de Vaca's eight-year odyssey was a slave who became an explorer.

The long shadow of slavery falls upon the history of the Church in Texas, whose members and clergy condoned the evil practice. Father James Talmadge Moore in "Through File and Flood" writes that "the cook and servants for Bishop Odin at his residence in Galveston were legally slaves." Catholic slaveholders were bound to see that their slaves were trained in the Faith and were to hold slave marriages inviolate.

Plantation owner Malcolm Spain brought a large group of slaves to Washington County in 1840. A mission was established for them in 1849 that still exists today as the Mission of the Blessed Virgin Mary at Old Washington-on-the-Brazos. Many German and Mexican Catholics were against slavery and suffered mistreatment before and especially during the Civil War because of their anti-slavery attitude.

In the late 1880s Bishop Nicholas Gallagher of Galveston established Holy Rosary parish in Galveston for Black Catholics. The first pastors were diocesan priests, but it was later turned over to the Josephite Fathers. In 1898 the Sisters of the Holy Family, a community of Black Sisters founded in New Orleans sixty years earlier by Henriette Delille, replaced the Dominican Sisters in the school at this parish. Father Tom Hennessy started St. Nicholas School in Houston, taught by the Sisters of the Incarnate Word, who were replaced by the Sisters of the Holy Family in 1905.

"inviolate"
Sacred, not to be violated or disrupted.

"condoned"
To allow to happen without interference or objection.

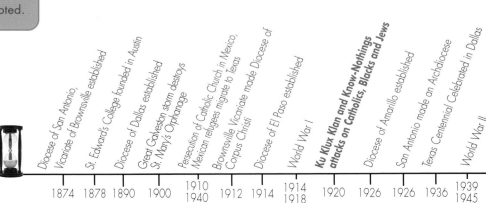

1874	1878	1890	1900	1910 1940	1912	1914	1914 1918	1920	1926	1926	1936	1939 1945

"cathedra"
A bishop's official chair or throne. A cathedral is the place where the bishop's cathedra is located.

In 1888, Margaret Mary Healy-Murphy, a wealthy Irish widow built St. Peter Claver church, school and convent for Black Catholics in San Antonio St. Peter's parish was established in Dallas in 1905, staffed by the Josephites. Holy Cross parish was established in Austin in 1936. Particularly significant was the fact that the parish included not only a school, but a hospital, which offered the opportunity for nurses training to young Black women.

Most Catholic parishes are integrated today but there still are predominantly African-American congregations. The Beaumont-Port Arthur-Orange area has one of the largest concentrations of African-American Catholics.

Many Catholics from Nigeria have migrated to Texas in recent years, adding a new dimension to the already lively worship experiences of African-American Catholics.

In 1987 Texas received its first African-American bishop, when Bishop Curtis J. Guillory, SVD, was named auxiliary bishop of Galveston-Houston. In 2000, Bishop Guillory was appointed Bishop of Beaumont.

In Dallas, a courthouse is named in honor of former Catholic city councilman and judge George L. Allen, Sr., the first African-American to be elected to the city council in that city.

First communicants from St. Peter's Church, Dallas

Miss Mary C. Muse, long-time kindergarten teacher at St. Peters was among the many African-American teachers who served the school prior to its closing in 1987. In this 1970 photo, she checks the height of one of her students.

CLICK-LEARNING

> **Henriette Delille**

> **Black Catholics + Texas**

> **Josephite Fathers**

> **St. Katharine Drexel**

St. Peter's School in Dallas was not Texas' first Catholic school for African-American children, but it is unique in that the establishment of the school and the parish by Dallas Bishop Edward Joseph Dunne in 1905 was due to the efforts of a Baptist woman who was a former slave. Her name was Mary Jordan. Mary's husband, Valentine, was a carpenter and a contractor on the construction of Ursuline Academy in Dallas. He was so impressed with the work of the Ursuline nuns that he and his wife believed that a Catholic church and school would be a wonderful thing for the black community.

They went to Bishop Dunne who, in response to urgings by the Jordans, agreed to dismantle the old Cathedral and rebuild it as a church for African-American Catholics. He turned to the Josephites, or Society of St. Joseph, a spin-off of the English Mill Hill Missionaries, who were committed to the service of African-Americans.

Josephite Father John J. Ferdinand, with the assistance of a gift from St. Katharine Drexel, established St. Peter's School in 1908. It was first known as the Sisters Institute, and was staffed by the Sisters of the Holy Ghost and Mary Immaculate. St. Peter's School closed in 1987.

Texas' first African-American priestly vocation, Father Max Murphy, a foster son of Mary Jordan, was a graduate of the school. Mary Jordan became a Catholic in 1927.

> Explaining the faith

Ignorance dies in the face of truth. The misunder-standings of the Catholic Faith that were at the root of anti-Catholic activity in Texas were addressed in several different and effective ways. The work of the Knights of Columbus and the Catholic Truth Society has already been mentioned. Their efforts in confronting the evil of bigotry were truly noteworthy. But other efforts were also underway.

In San Antonio the Know-Nothings circulated truly appalling stories about the Ursuline nuns who operated an Academy in the city. Father Pierre Parisot, an Oblate priest who was acting rector of St. Mary's church, suggested that the sisters invite a group of visitors in to meet the sisters and examine the convent. The group visited with the sisters and was given a tour of every nook and cranny of the convent.

They left content that the convent contained no secret passages, dark dungeons and no supply of weapons awaiting word from the Pope to begin an uprising. After the visit they described the nuns as "very amiable and highly educated ladies."

Father Patrick Brannan of Weatherford used his gift of preaching to spread the truth about the gospel and the Catholic Church. Father Brannan, a native of Georgia and a Confederate veteran, was a successful lawyer whose wife died after their children were grown. The former mayor of Weatherford became a priest and a much sought-after missionary preacher. He didn't preach in church, but would give a week's series of talks on Catholicism in the local opera house or hall.

In most of the places he preached the audience was made up primarily of Protestants. He preached successfully in Texas, Arkansas, Missouri and Indiana doing much to dispel the ignorance and misunderstanding about the Catholic Church.

** OREGON CATHOLIC HISTORY NEWSLETTER**

Vol. 6   198-

The interiors of chapel cars looked like a small chapel, with pews and an altar. Behind the altar were sleeping quarters for the missionary priest.

"bigotry"

Discrimination or prejudice based on race, religion or ethnic origin

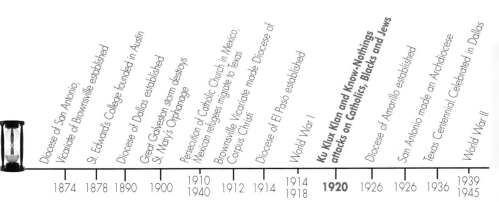

Diocese of San Antonio, Vicariate of Brownsville established — 1874

St. Edward's College founded in Austin — 1878

Diocese of Dallas established — 1890

Great Galveston storm destroys St. Mary's Orphanage — 1900

Persecution of Catholic Church in Mexico, Mexican refugees migrate to Texas — 1910 1940

Brownsville Vicariate made Diocese of Corpus Christi — 1912

Diocese of El Paso established — 1914

World War I — 1914 1918

Ku Klux Klan and Know-Nothings attacks on Catholics, Blacks and Jews — **1920**

Diocese of Amarillo established — 1926

San Antonio made an Archdiocese — 1926

Texas Centennial Celebrated in Dallas — 1936

World War II — 1939 1945

Chapel cars like this one were a means of taking Catholic worship and preaching to many Texas towns where there was no Catholic church.

The chapel car was another innovation that aided missionaries in reaching many parts of Texas where there were few or no Catholics. Chapel cars were railway cars that had been equipped with an altar, pulpit and pews, together with sleeping quarters for a priest.

At the height of the railroad expansion, there was rail service to many more towns than there is today. The chapel car would be attached to the end of a scheduled train and then parked at a siding for several days or a week. The priest would announce lectures on the Catholic Church around town and invite people to come to the chapel car. In good weather, several hundred people would gather around the observation platform at the back of the car and the priest would lecture from there.

The chapel cars were provided by the Catholic Church Extension Society, an organization dedicated to providing a Catholic presence in small towns and rural areas. Later motor chapel cars, similar to today's motor homes, were developed and enabled preachers to reach areas not served by the railroads.

Many people first learned of the Catholic Church from chapel cars and experienced their first Catholic Mass at their altars.

> Missionary Preachers

Father Patrick Brannan
Missionary preacher

Catholic evangelists, like Father Patrick Brannan, helped to dispel bigotry and anti-Catholic prejudice in Texas. Their work contributed much to the understanding of Catholicism. Other Catholic missionary-evangelists included Father S. R. Brockbank, an Irish Dominican, who, like Fr. Brannan, was more dedicated to spreading truth than making converts. Oblate Father Charles Haas preached in the small communities of northeast Texas and frequently drew large crowds. Bishop Stephen Leven had been a well-known street preacher before becoming the first auxiliary bishop of San Antonio and later Bishop of San Angelo. These missionary-preachers would frequently be on the same platform with Protestant ministers.

It would be untrue to give the impression that the preaching of these evangelists was always welcome. On occasion they were threatened and "invited" to leave town, but in most cases they were treated with respect. Father Brannan gave much credit to the fairness of the Protestant editors of small town newspapers. He said of them "as a rule they are not bigoted and could not treat me with more consideration were I a Protestant minister."

CLICK-LEARNING

> Extension Society

Thousands of refugees fled the civil war and religious persecution in Mexico early in the 20th Century. Many, like the women shown, were dependent upon relief agencies for food, clothing and shelter.

> Hope of Refuge

The effects of the civil discord and religious persecution that occurred in Mexico in the early 20th Century permanently changed Texas and the Catholic Church in the state. Discrimination against Catholics and the Church in Texas were minor in comparison to the unspeakable sufferings of Mexican Catholics for more than two decades.

Shortly after the Mexican Revolution began in 1910 priests and religious from Mexico began fleeing to Texas in large numbers. The revolutionary movement in Mexico had become strongly anti-clerical. Mexico first justified the expulsions on the grounds that it was cleaning out the last vestiges of colonialism by ordering all foreign-born priests and religious out of the country.

It soon became apparent that what was occurring was a full-blown persecution of the Catholic Church. Three Mexican archbishops, including Mexican-born Archbishop José Mora y del Rio of Mexico City, the chief bishop of the Mexican Church, arrived in San Antonio as refugees.

Diocese of San Antonio, Vicariate of Brownsville established
St. Edward's College founded in Austin
Diocese of Dallas established
Great Galveston storm destroys St. Mary's Orphanage
Persecution of Catholic Church in Mexico, Mexican refugees migrate to Texas
Brownsville Vicariate made Diocese of Corpus Christi
Diocese of El Paso established
World War I
Ku Klux Klan and Know-Nothings attacks on Catholics, Blacks and Jews
Diocese of Amarillo established
San Antonio made an Archdiocese
Texas Centennial Celebrated in Dallas
World War II

1874 1878 1890 1900 **1910 1940** 1912 1914 1914 1918 1920 1926 1926 1936 1939 1945

Clergy and religious were not the only ones seeking refuge in Texas. Thousands of their fellow-countrymen fled northward to escape the fighting in their homeland. Many of the priests and religious continued their ministry in Texas among the Spanish-speaking and other refugees.

A seminary for the training of refugee seminarians was established in San Antonio. It was staffed by refugee priests and bishops. Attempts were made by bishops in Texas and the U.S., to influence the American government to take action to bring an end to the persecution that was causing such devastation South of the Border. Sadly, both the American government and the press were largely indifferent to the situation.

At a meeting of the archbishops of the United States a letter was drafted against the new Mexican constitutions. In his book *Acts of Faith*, James Talmadge Moore writes that the letter protested the constitution that called for "nationalizing all church property and forbidding the church from obtaining any future property, outlawing all religious orders and forbidding the church to establish its own primary schools." Priests were forbidden to speak on any political issue and all services outside church buildings were forbidden. Violators were not entitled to a trial by jury.

Some of the constitution's provisions were liberalized. During the early 1920s the persecution subsided for a while but resumed in 1924. Once again bishops, priests and religious, who had returned, were exiled. It was during this time that Jesuit Father Miguel Pro was executed by a firing squad in Mexico City. Expecting the priest to beg for his life, the press was invited to the execution. Instead Father Pro knelt in prayer, then stood and faced his executioners refusing a blindfold. Seconds before the firing squad loosed its volley, he thrust his arms out in the shape of a cross and shouted "Viva Cristo Rey," (long live Christ the King). First steps have been taken to declare him a saint. He is now Blessed Miguel Pro.

Our Lady of Guadalupe Church in Dallas was one of many established by and for refugees from persecution and civil war in Mexico. The Dallas church was established by a refugee Vincentian priest and later was turned over to refugee Carmelite Fathers.

Persecutions did not subside until the 1940s. Thousands who fled to the United States remained here and continued to enliven, same line, the Catholic Faith first brought to Texas by their forebears.

> Seeds of the persecution

The seeds of persecution in Mexico resulted in many refugees migrating to the northern portions of the state in greater numbers. Among those seeking refuge in Texas were many priests, brothers and sisters, who had been expelled by the Mexican government. The result was the establishment of institutions to minister to the increasing Hispanic population.

One example is Dallas, where the exiled Spanish Vincentian Manuel de Francisco established the first Mexican parish in 1914, Our Lady of Guadalupe. It was in a storefront, but was later moved to a simple building in 1916. In 1923, a substantial building was built in the area known as Little Mexico.

The following year Father Francisco was moved from Dallas and the parish was taken over by another community of priests, expelled from Mexico in 1914, the Discalced Carmelite Fathers, who had been expelled from Mexico in 1914. Our Lady of Guadalupe thrived and the Carmelite Fathers served many parishes and missions.

In 1975 Our Lady of Guadalupe was merged with Sacred Heart Cathedral parish and renamed Cathedral Santuario de Guadalupe. The Carmelite Fathers continued to staff the Cathedral until 1988, when diocesan clergy took over administration. More than 11,000 people attend Sunday Mass at Our Lady of Guadalupe. Today the only cathedral in the United States with a higher Sunday Mass attendance is St. Patrick Cathedral in New York City.

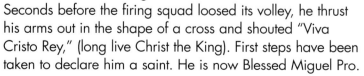

CLICK-LEARNING

> **Mexican religious persecution**
> **Father Miguel Pro**

"nationalizing"

The act of the government taking control of a company or an organization.

"persecution"

Attempts to suppress or destroy a group of people because of religious or racial bigotry.

> Centennial

Everybody loves a party, and Texas celebrated its 100th birthday party in 1936. The Catholic Church played a major role in the celebration. An article in *The Dallas Evening Journal* at the time explained that, "The Catholic Church, whose name and deeds are so closely interwoven with the history of Texas that it is impossible to mention one without the other, is responsible for the replica of Socorro Church on the lagoon at the Texas Centennial Exhibition."

The Socorro Church was a replica of one of the earliest missions in Texas, the Mission Nuestra Señora de la Concepción del Pueblo de Socorro, which was established near El Paso in 1682. The mission replica faced the lagoon at the Centennial Exhibition at Fair Park in Dallas. Catholics and Catholic institutions from all over the state planned and financed the Catholic exhibit.

Monsignor Joseph O'Donohoe, then pastor of St. Mary Church in Sherman, was appointed by the Texas bishops to organize the Catholic exhibit.

"Texas Centennial"
A centennial is a 100th anniversary. The Texas Centennial marked the 100th anniversary of the Texas Declaration of Independence from Mexico.

"replica"
A replica is a very close copy of an original.

The Cavalcade of Texas presented during the Texas Centennial Exhibition depicted the history of Texas from the coming of the Spaniards until 1936. Horses, stage coaches, covered wagons and a full-size replica of Sieur de La Salle's ship were part of the stage props. The photograph shows the arrival of La Salle's ship, the *La Belle*, in 1684.

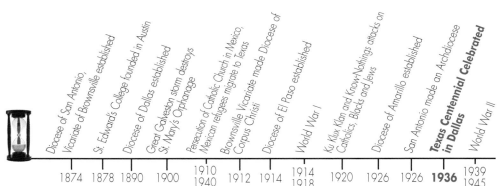

Diocese of San Antonio, Vicariate of Brownsville established — 1874
St. Edward's College founded in Austin — 1878
Diocese of Dallas established — 1890
Great Galveston storm destroys St. Mary's Orphanage — 1900
Persecution of Catholic Church in Mexico, Mexican refugees migrate to Texas — 1910 / 1940
Brownsville Vicariate made Diocese of Corpus Christi — 1912
Diocese of El Paso established — 1914
World War I — 1914 / 1918
Ku Klux Klan and Know-Nothings attacks on Catholics, Blacks and Jews — 1920
Diocese of Amarillo established — 1926
San Antonio made an Archdiocese — 1926
Texas Centennial Celebrated in Dallas — **1936**
World War II — 1939 / 1945

A Pontifical High Mass was celebrated in the Amphitheater by Dallas Bishop Joseph P. Lynch on October 11, 1936, a special Catholic Day. More than 25,000 persons attended the field Mass at which one archbishop, ten bishops and one abbot were present.

"Pontifical High Mass"
A sung Mass celebrated by a bishop or archbishop.

A full-scale replica of the Socorro Mission near El Paso constructed to house the Catholic exhibits at the Texas Centennial. The Socorro Mission was one of the first Catholic churches established in Texas in 1682.

It included historic artifacts, murals, models and other contributions of the Catholic Church to the history of Texas.

Among the items included was the desk that belonged to James Bowie and the original mission bells from both San Antonio de Valero (the Alamo) and Nuestra Señora del Refugio. Part of the exhibit featured a chapel with its original furnishings which included a hand-carved crucifix from the Socorro Mission above the altar. Many chalices, manuscripts and other vessels from the time of independence and early statehood were on display. Murals on the walls, provided by Incarnate Word College in San Antonio, pictured important moments in the Catholic Church history of Texas. Two exhibits drew particular interest. They were a tiny chapel depicting a Pontifical Mass and dolls dressed in the habits of the 36 orders of sisters who served in Texas.

While the Catholic Exhibit was a highlight of the Texas Centennial, it was not the only Catholic element. A replica of another mission, the Alamo, was also built on the grounds and the role of the Church was prominent in the Cavalcade of Texas, an historic panorama acted out on a giant outdoor stage. The show included missionary activities and a life size ship sailing on stage depicting the arrival of La Salle and the establishment of Fort St. Louis.

On October 11, 1936, a special Catholic Day was observed, during which a Military Field Mass was celebrated in the Amphitheater by Dallas Bishop Joseph P. Lynch. Detachments of soldiers, sailors and marines participated. More than 20,000 persons attended the field Mass at which one archbishop, ten bishops and one abbot were present.

When the Texas Centennial Exhibition closed, the Socorro Mission building was carefully disassembled and rebuilt as St. Anthony Church in South Dallas. While the same materials were used, St. Anthony Church does not resemble the Centennial building.

CLICK-LEARNING

> **Texas Centennial**
> **Socorro Mission + Texas**
> **Refugio Mission**

Among the Catholic exhibits was a collection of dolls dressed in the religious habits of the many orders of women religious who have served in Texas.

5 Changing Church

> Second Vatican Council

Ask your grandparents what Mass was like on Sunday when they were your age. You will probably be surprised at their answer. The Mass was celebrated in another language. The homily was in English, but the rest of the Mass was celebrated in Latin. There were other differences, too. The priest had his back to the congregation most of the time. The choir sang almost all the songs. Holy Communion was distributed in only one form, and the priest alone received the wine. There were no lay Eucharistic ministers or readers and no deacons. Only boys could be altar servers.

How did all these changes come about? In 1958 Cardinal Angelo Roncalli, Patriarch of Venice, Italy, was elected Pope and took the name of Pope John XXIII. At age 76, he was expected to be a pope who would look after the affairs of the Church, but not undertake any great changes during his administration. As it turned out, he was anything but a caretaker pope. Less than 100 days after he was elected, he called a new Ecumenical Council, a meeting of all the Catholic bishops of the world. It had been almost a hundred years since a council had been called. Councils usually were called only to address a major problem the Church was facing. Not so for this one. Pope John XXIII called it because he felt the Church needed to be updated.

About 2400 bishops from all over the world met in St. Peter's Basilica at the Vatican for four sessions of several months each in 1962, 1963, 1964 and 1965. They addressed many different aspects of the Catholic Church including Liturgy, the nature of the Church, divine revelation, ecumenism, the priesthood and others. There were also observers from most other Christian religious groups who were invited to express their ideas.

"homily"
The homily is the sermon the priest or deacon preaches at Mass.

"Ecumenical Council"
A council of bishops from the entire world.

CLICK-LEARNING

> "Second Vatican Council" + history

Timeline:

- Diocese of Austin established — 1948
- Korean War — 1950 / 1954
- Diocese of Dallas becomes Diocese of Dallas-Fort Worth — 1954
- Diocese of Galveston becomes Diocese of Galveston-Houston — 1959
- International Congress of Confraternity of Christian Doctrine in Dallas — 1961
- Diocese of San Angelo established — 1961
- **Second Vatican Council** — **1962 / 1965**
- Texas Catholic Conference established — 1964
- Vietnamese War — 1964 / 1975
- Diocese of Beaumont established — 1966
- Permanent Diaconate Restored — 1967
- Diocese of Fort Worth established — 1969
- Diocese of Victoria established — 1982
- Diocese of Lubbock established — 1983
- Diocese of Tyler established — 1986
- Visit of Pope John Paul II to San Antonio — 1987
- Diocese of Laredo established — 2000

When the first session of the Second Vatican Council opened on October 11, 1962, more than 2,400 bishops from throughout the world gathered in St. Peter's Basilica at the Vatican. The Council has been called the most important religious event of the Twentieth Century.

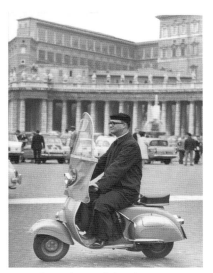

Pope John XXIII died in 1963 before the Council ended, but his successor, Pope Paul VI, carried the Council to its conclusion. He went on to implement many of the reforms it mandated. The changes in Liturgy, that is the Mass, affected the people most. The Mass was to be celebrated in English, and the priest would face the congregation. Holy Communion would be distributed to the congregation in both bread and wine. The congregation would participate more fully in the celebration through common prayers and singing.

There were other changes that were results of the Council. We as Catholics began to work much more closely with other Christians in a new ecumenical dialogue. Similarly, the Church established dialogue with non-Christian religions. Lay men and women became much more involved in Church affairs. Parish Councils and Diocesan Pastoral Councils were established. Lay people were permitted to distribute Holy Communion in church and in visits to the sick. Scriptures, other than the Gospel, began to be read at Mass by lay men and women.

As a result of the Council, married men were recruited and trained to become deacons and were ordained to serve in parishes, hospitals and diocesan offices. Girls were permitted to become altar servers. Catholics were encouraged to read and study scripture. Many lay men and women went on to study theology and become ministers in parishes and dioceses at home and in the foreign missions.

Of course, some people were uncomfortable with the changes. It is difficult to adjust when you have been taught to do things a certain way, and then it is changed. The Second Vatican Council changed the church in many ways. Some Catholics think the Council changed too much. Others believe that it didn't change enough in its renewal efforts.

Ask your grandparents to tell you about how they think the Catholic Church has changed since the Second Vatican Council.

Bishops from all the dioceses in Texas participated in the Second Vatican Council. English language coverage of the first two sessions was coordinated by Texas priest Monsignor James I. Tucek, who served as head of the Rome Bureau of the *Catholic News Service*. He found his Vespa the easiest way to move around busy Rome and the Vatican.

"mandated"
Something that is required is mandated.

"liturgy"
Any formal ceremony of the Church, but the term is most often applied to the Mass or Eucharistic Liturgy.

"ecumenical"
Including all Christian groups.

"parish council"
A group of parishioners who consult with the pastor.

"Scriptures"
The Sacred Writings included in the Old and New Testaments.

"theology"
The study of God and his relation to the world.

Pope John XXIII, on the left, called the Second Vatican Council and presided over the first session in 1962. He died prior to the second session in the fall of 1963. On the right is Cardinal Giovanni Montini, Archbishop of Milan, Italy. He became Pope Paul VI. He presided over the last three sessions of the Council and was responsible for initiating the many reforms in the Catholic Church called for by Vatican II.

> Catholic Acceptance

During the 1930's, non-Anglo immigration was severely restricted by new national-origin immigration quotas. The Church began to shed its immigrant status and defensive attitudes and to move towards acceptance within the American culture. This acceptance was not everywhere, but where there were large numbers of Catholics there was a greater appreciation of their contribution to society.

Catholics became less timid about asserting and even celebrating their faith in public events. The Bicentennial of the founding of San Antonio was celebrated with a military field Mass in the plaza between the cathedral and the city hall on March 5, 1931. Cardinal Patrick Hayes of New York came to preside at the Mass.

> **"bicentennial"**
> Two-hundredth anniversary.

Texas celebrated its century of independence from Mexico not only with civil events but with church ceremonies. The Centennial of the fall of the Alamo was commemorated on March 6, 1936, with a Pontifical High Mass by Archbishop Arthur J. Drossaerts of San Antonio, in front of this shrine of Texas Liberty. Some 20,000 people attended the event.

Lay organizations such as the Knights of Columbus and the Holy Name Societies organized great processions and demonstrations of the faith in the city centers especially for the feasts of Corpus Christi and Christ the King. St. Vincent de Paul societies were organized in many parishes to help the poor.

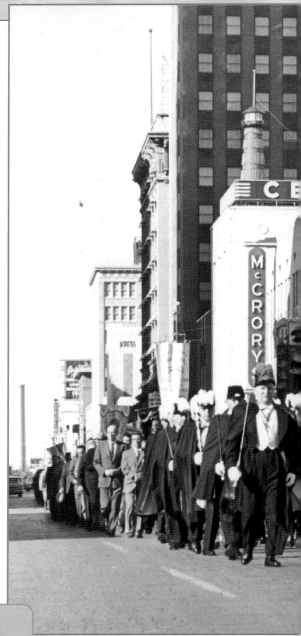

> **"cathedral"**
> The principal church of a diocese; the bishop's church.

> **"centennial"**
> One-hundredth anniversary.

> **"commemorated"**
> The observance of an important anniversary.

> **"culture"**
> The patterns of belief, values, understanding and behavior of a particular group or society.

CLICK-LEARNING

> **Knights of Columbus + Texas**

> **Carlos Eduardo Castañeda + historian**

Timeline:

- Diocese of Austin established — 1948
- Korean War — 1950 / 1954
- Diocese of Dallas becomes Diocese of Dallas-Fort Worth — 1954
- Diocese of Galveston becomes Diocese of Galveston-Houston — 1959
- **International Congress of Confraternity of Christian Doctrine in Dallas** — **1961**
- Diocese of San Angelo established — 1961
- Second Vatican Council — 1962 / 1965
- Texas Catholic Conference established — 1964
- Vietnamese War — 1964 / 1975
- Diocese of Beaumont established — 1966
- Permanent Diaconate Restored — 1967
- Diocese of Fort Worth established — 1969
- Diocese of Victoria established — 1982
- Diocese of Lubbock established — 1983
- Diocese of Tyler established — 1986
- Visit of Pope John Paul II to San Antonio — 1987
- Diocese of Laredo established — 2000

This Christ the King procession through downtown Fort Worth was typical of the increased public demonstrations of their faith by Catholics in the 1950s and 1960s.

> **Carlos Castañeda**

1896 › †1958

Dr. Carlos Castañeda, eminent Catholic historian and author.

Our past is the prologue to our future. That is the motivating principle of this book and any historical writing. It was also the inspiration for the work of Carlos Eduardo Castañeda, Catholic historian and author of the seven-volume, "Our Catholic Heritage in Texas", the first history of our "Texas" Catholic roots.

A native of Mexico, Castañeda moved to Brownsville when he was ten. He attended the University of Texas in Austin and received his doctorate in 1932. The Texas Knights of Columbus commissioned him to write, "Our Catholic Heritage in Texas" "to demonstrate the important role of Catholicism in the history of Texas. It was written over a number of years with the first volume published in 1936. Castañeda, who received many honors for his work, died in 1958.

Catholic publishing in Texas began with the short-lived *Texas Catholic* published in Dallas in the early 1890s. It resumed in the early twentieth century when the Jesuit Fathers published the nationally known *Revista Catolica* newspaper for Spanish-speaking Catholics in El Paso. During this time the lay-edited *Southern Messenger* published in San Antonio, was the official Catholic newspaper for most Texas dioceses. It was directly supported by the Knights of Columbus. Some dioceses developed their own newspapers such as the *Texas Panhandle Register* and the *Alamo Register*. Most Texas dioceses now publish their own newspaper or journal.

"prologue"
Something that goes before, introduces a work or an event and sets the tone for it.

"commissioned"
To give someone an assignment.

"heritage"
Traditions, customs and values passed on from previous generations.

> Texas Catholic Conference

In January of 2003, 300 Catholics who were involved in the work of Catholic Charities traveled to Austin to lobby their state legislators. Their purpose was to meet their representatives and senators and encourage them to "have a heart" and to avoid decreasing funding on state programs for needy people and children. The Texas Catholic Conference coordinated the effort.

"lobbyist"
A lobbyist is a person who attempts to win the support of legislators for a particular cause. The term comes from the fact that they originally waited in the lobby for legislators arriving or leaving and talked to them in the lobby.

"Texas Conference of Churches"
The Texas Conference of Churches is an organization whose membership represents principally Christian religious denominations in Texas. The Conference addresses concerns shared by all member churches.

Callan Graham, center, attorney and founding Executive Director of the Texas Catholic Conference, is shown with Archbishop Francis Furey of San Antonio and Father (later Bishop) John McCarthy who succeeded Graham when he retired in 1973 after nine years in his position.

The primary purpose of the Texas Catholic Conference is to carry out the directives of the Bishops of Texas as they relate to all inter-diocesan offices, ministries and programs within the state. An important, but secondary function, is to provide a voice for the Catholic Church in matters of public policy and legislative concerns. Items of concern to the conference are life issues, parental choice in education, health and human services, environment, criminal justice reform and many others. It also promotes cooperation and communications among the state's 15 Catholic dioceses. The T.C.C. was an outgrowth of the Second Vatican Council in 1963 when the Texas bishops recognized the need for greater communication and coordination among their dioceses. Its first meeting was held in the diocesan offices in Austin on February 15, 1964.

The beginnings of the Conference were modest. Callan Graham, a Catholic attorney and experienced lobbyist, was appointed executive director. At first, meetings included only the bishops. Later departments were established with representatives from the various dioceses. The first groups to be organized were the Catholic school superintendents and directors of Catholic Charities, but others soon followed. Graham credits the conference with "bringing together the vast talents of the people in all the dioceses of the state."

In 1970 the first General Assembly was held in Austin, where representatives of all major ministries in each diocese met for two days to discuss common problems. The board of directors was expanded to include lay people. Work of the conference extends beyond the legislature; it works with other state agencies and other religious bodies like the Texas Conference of Churches.

CLICK-LEARNING

> **Texas Catholic Conference**
> **Texas Conference of Churches**

Diocese of Austin established
Korean War
Diocese of Dallas becomes Diocese of Dallas-Fort Worth
Diocese of Galveston becomes Diocese of Galveston-Houston
International Congress of Confraternity of Christian Doctrine in Dallas
Diocese of San Angelo established
Second Vatican Council
Texas Catholic Conference established
Vietnamese War
Diocese of Beaumont established
Permanent Diaconate Restored
Diocese of Fort Worth established
Diocese of Victoria established
Diocese of Lubbock established
Diocese of Tyler established
Visit of Pope John Paul II to San Antonio
Diocese of Laredo established

1948 | 1950 1954 | 1954 | 1959 | 1961 | 1961 | **1962 1965** | 1964 | 1964 1975 | 1966 | 1967 | 1969 | 1982 | 1983 | 1986 | 1987 | 2000

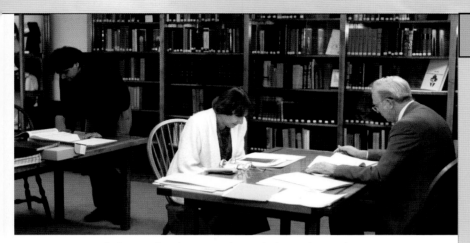

Many scholars and authors visit the Catholic Archives of Texas in Austin where many important documents and other records of the Catholic Church in Texas are kept. The Texas Archivist was a consultant in the preparation of this textbook.

One of its first successes was working with the Texas Education Agency to bring about the accreditation of Catholic schools throughout the state.

Cooperation among Catholic elementary and secondary schools is still one of the main functions of the Texas Catholic Conference. Its Education Department works closely with the Texas Education Agency and the Texas Private School Accreditation Commission. The conference also conducts programs and workshops on pastoral issues including an annual Scripture Seminar for priests and deacons.

Dialogue with the Texas Council of Churches, which did not include Catholic representation, resulted in the establishment of a new body, the Texas Conference of Churches, including all Catholic dioceses.

Graham retired in 1973 and was succeeded by Father (now Bishop) John McCarthy. He was followed in 1979 by Holy Cross Brother Richard Daly, who is the present executive director.

Today the original two groups of school superintendents and Catholic charities directors have expanded to twenty departments ranging from Administration to Youth Ministry. In addition the conference relates to a variety of other Catholic organizations and groups in the state. The work of the Texas Catholic Conference results in a common effort among Catholic dioceses in Texas to achieve the Gospel values all share. Texas had eight dioceses when the Texas Catholic Conference was established; today there are fifteen. In 1964 there were two million Texas Catholics. By 2003 there were 5 1/2 million.

Archives **refer to the beginning of things. They are a place where historical records are kept and preserved. The word archive comes from the Greek word for "the beginning." The Catholic Archives of Texas are concerned with the beginnings of the Catholic Church in Texas. Much of the information and many of the photographs in "Catholic Texans" have come from the Catholic Archives.**

In the Archives can be found documents from four centuries of Catholic history. In 1924 the Knights of Columbus began compiling and publishing a history of the Catholic Church in Texas. Dr. Carlos E. Castañeda, professor of history at the University of Texas, was the historian chosen for the task. He spent years of research for "Our Catholic Heritage in Texas," a seven-volume work that was published beginning in 1936. Casteñeda's papers became the core of the Archives' collection. Originally housed in Amarillo, the collection was moved to Austin where it is housed in the *Chancery Office.*

The Catholic Archives of Texas is now part of the Texas Catholic Conference and is supported by all the dioceses of Texas. Its collection of manuscripts, sacramental records, personal papers, photographs, rare books and maps is recognized as one of the most valuable resources for the history of the Catholic Church in the southwest.

"archives"

Archives are important records, documents, photographs or other items that have a lasting historical significance. The word is also used to denote the place where these items are kept.

"Chancery Office"

The Chancery Office is the center where pastoral activities of a diocese are coordinated. It takes its name from the Chancellor, a person who has the responsibility for keeping official records. It is also the location of the Bishop's Office.

Priests and sisters were prominently involved in support of the farm workers' strike for better pay and working conditions in the Rio Grande Valley. Marches regularly included images of Our Lady of Guadalupe.

> Archbishop Lucey and social action

A champion of social justice, Robert E. Lucey, a priest from Los Angeles, was appointed Bishop of Amarillo in 1934 and Archbishop of San Antonio in 1941. This leader in Catholic education brought several organizations to Texas that he had helped to establish in the Diocese of Los Angeles. He quickly organized the Catholic Welfare Bureau that later became the Catholic Family and Childrens Services, now called Catholic Charities. He also founded the Catholic Action Office, the Council of Catholic Women, and the Council of Catholic Men.

"social justice"
The Church's concern for equal treatment and opportunity for all persons, particularly for the poor and powerless.

Diocese of Austin established

Korean War

Diocese of Dallas becomes Diocese of Dallas-Fort Worth

Diocese of Galveston becomes Diocese of Galveston-Houston

International Congress of Confraternity of Christian Doctrine in Dallas

Diocese of San Angelo established

Second Vatican Council

Texas Catholic Conference established

Vietnamese War

Diocese of Beaumont established

Permanent Diaconate Restored

Diocese of Fort Worth established

Diocese of Victoria established

Diocese of Lubbock established

Diocese of Tyler established

Visit of Pope John Paul II to San Antonio

Diocese of Laredo established

1948 1950 1954 1954 1959 1961 1961 1962 1965 **1964** 1964 1975 1966 1967 1969 1982 1983 1986 1987 2000

The Confraternity of Christian Doctrine, founded by Archbishop Lucey in Los Angeles in 1923 to provide religious instruction to all Catholic youth, spread to the dioceses in Texas. The Missionary Catechists of Divine Providence were founded to teach Hispanic children. In the 1940s Archbishop Lucey was instrumental in developing the national Bishops' Committee for the Spanish-speaking. It was originally planned that this committee's office would rotate among the dioceses with large Hispanic populations. However, it remained in San Antonio until after Archbishop Lucey left office. The Guadalupanas organization was begun with the help of Fr. Carmelo Tranchese, S.J. to serve Hispanic women.

Archbishop Lucey was a friend of President Harry Truman who appointed him to the Commission on Migratory Labor. He was also one of the great defenders of the working man and labor unions. He received awards from both the AFL and the CIO. He encouraged the priests of the Archdiocese of San Antonio to be involved in marches and activities to help the farm workers.

During the 1950s and 1960s the growing Catholic population in Texas increased the need for more parishes and more schools. Fortunately at this time there were a great number of religious and priestly vocations, and schools and churches were established in large numbers.

After the Roe vs. Wade decision by the Supreme Court legalizing abortions in 1983, the movement that began in the previous decade as Right-to-Life, grew into the massive Pro-Life effort to protect the unborn through legal moves, lobbying and demonstrations, and to promote adoption as an alternative to abortion. Progress has been made but Texas Catholics and others continue the fight.

"Pro-Life"
A movement by Catholics and others to protect the lives of unborn babies by working to make abortion illegal and supporting adoption as an alternative.

"labor unions"
Organizations of working people that represent their interests to employers.

CLICK-LEARNING

> **Archbishop Robert E. Lucey**

> **Catholic Charities**

> **Catholic Women**

Father Virgil Elizondo, theologian, author and founder of the Mexican American Cultural Center.

MEXICAN AMERICAN CULTURAL CENTER

> **Mexican American Cultural Center**

The Mexican American Cultural Center in San Antonio is a model of how social action can create an awareness of a need and bring about the means of addressing it. Opened in 1972, the center was the dream of Father Virgil Elizondo, a priest of the Archdiocese of San Antonio. In cooperation with the Texas Catholic Conference, PADRES and Las Hermanas, and groups of Hispanic priests and sisters, he established a national center to study and address the social and religious needs of Hispanics. Its programs, centered on developing awareness of Hispanic culture and the Gospel and social teaching of the Catholic Church, have prepared thousands of priests, sisters and lay persons for ministry to Hispanic communities.

> Lay Ministry

If you lived a half-century ago and wanted to serve God and others in a ministerial role, you would probably have become a priest, religious sister or brother. Today, in Texas there are many opportunities for laypersons to serve others in ministry.

As the world changes, the Church adapts itself to best serve the needs of society at a particular time in history. Today, in Texas, laymen and women are essential to the ministry of the Church. In the very early Church, laymen and women held many ministerial roles, but their work gradually was taken over by priests and religious sisters and brothers. Few lay people were involved in the ministry and administration of the Church.

Lay people's roles in the Church have changed dramatically since the Second Vatican Council. Laymen and women are both ministers and administrators in Texas dioceses and parishes. Some are professional ministers; ministry is their principal work. Many others are volunteers.

Today Catholic laymen and women serve in a variety of ministerial and administrative positions in the Church. Some are presidents of Catholic colleges and universities. Others are Catholic school principals and educators. Many serve in parishes as directors of parish education

"ministry"
Ministry is service to others in the name of Jesus and his Church.

"Eucharistic ministers"
Catholic lay persons who are commissioned to assist priests and deacons in the distribution of the Body and Blood of Christ in the Eucharist (Holy Communion).

The office of Eucharistic Minister is one of the many ministries opened to lay people as a result of the Second Vatican Council's expanded recognition of the role of the laity in the Church.

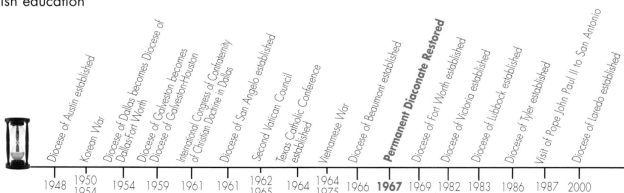

Diocese of Austin established — 1948
Korean War — 1950 1954
Diocese of Dallas becomes Diocese of Dallas-Fort Worth — 1954
Diocese of Galveston becomes Diocese of Galveston-Houston — 1959
International Congress of Confraternity of Christian Doctrine in Dallas — 1961
Diocese of San Angelo established — 1961
Second Vatican Council — 1962 1965
Texas Catholic Conference established — 1964
Vietnamese War — 1964 1975
Diocese of Beaumont established — 1966
Permanent Diaconate Restored — **1967**
Diocese of Fort Worth established — 1969
Diocese of Victoria established — 1982
Diocese of Lubbock established — 1983
Diocese of Tyler established — 1986
Visit of Pope John Paul II to San Antonio — 1987
Diocese of Laredo established — 2000

and youth programs. Large numbers of men and women help others as Catholic social workers. Some are canon lawyers and serve in dioceses as chancellors and other administrative positions. Most Catholic universities in Texas offer graduate degree programs in ministerial areas to prepare students to work as professional ministers.

In your parish, you probably see laymen and women volunteers serving as Eucharistic Ministers and Readers on Sunday. Others assist in the liturgical or music ministry. Some volunteer ministers visit parishioners in the hospital and those who are sick at home. They bring Christ to them, not only in the Eucharist, but also in their presence as ministers.

Service to others is an essential part of being a Catholic Christian. Today, there are many ways of serving others open to us, and the rewards are great. Some people serve through fraternal and service organizations like the Knights of Columbus, The Catholic Daughters, the Catholic Family Fraternal of Texas (KJZT) and others.

Some lay people choose a structured spiritual and apostolic life in groups like the Focolare Movement or the Neo-Catechumenate. Opportunities for spiritual guidance and reflection are provided by a number of Texas retreat houses and movements like the Cursillo and Christian Life.

CLICK-LEARNING

> **Cursillo**
> **Focolare**
> **Knights of Columbus**
> **Neo-Catechumenate**

> Permanent Deacons

Candidates for ordination to the diaconate prostrate themselves as the Litany of the Saints is sung at an ordination Mass. The ancient office of deacon was restored as a full ministry by the Second Vatican Council. One out of every ten deacons in the United States serves in Texas.

Something old is something new in our Catholic tradition. There is a good chance that you have a deacon assigned to your parish working with the priest and lay ministers. The ministry of deacon is one of the oldest in the Church, dating from the days of the Apostles. Yet it is also one of the newest ministries because after centuries of existing only in a ceremonial way for men on the way to the priesthood, the order of deacon was restored as a separate ministry in 1967.

In 1972 the first deacons were ordained for the Archdiocese of San Antonio and the Diocese of Galveston-Houston. The Diocese of Dallas ordained its first deacons in 1973. In 2002 Texas had the largest number of deacons of any state with ten percent of the deacons in the country.

Deacons share the Sacrament of Holy Orders with priests and bishops but are primarily ministers of service not leadership. Many deacons work full time in business or professions and are married and have children. Most men study for their part-time ministry for three to five years before they are ordained. Deacons work in hospitals, jails and in parish ministries. They preach, baptize and witness marriages, but may not hear confessions or celebrate Mass. Deacons remind us of Jesus, who came to serve not be served.

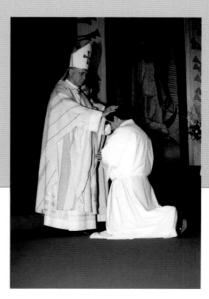

Deacons are ordained by their bishop and participate in the Sacrament of Holy Orders as ministers of service. Many serve as hospital chaplains, teachers, and other service ministries. Most deacons are married and hold positions as business or professional men.

> The new Catholic Mosaic in Texas

Elders of the Sacred Heart of Jesus Christ Vietnamese Catholic Church in Carrollton, Texas, act as the Apostles in the traditional Holy Thursday washing of the feet. Many Asian Catholics have emigrated to Texas adding to the church's rich cultural mix.

Today, the Catholic face of Texas is changing once again. Before Texas' independence from Mexico, the Catholic population was almost entirely Hispanic and Native American. This included Spanish and Mexican as well as mestizo. After independence there was an influx of Catholic immigrants from the United States and Europe. They were principally of European origin.

"mestizo"
A person of mixed European and Indian ancestry.

"influx"
A coming in from the outside.

Diocese of Austin established — 1948

Korean War — 1950 1954

Diocese of Dallas becomes Diocese of Dallas-Fort Worth — 1954

Diocese of Galveston becomes Diocese of Galveston-Houston — 1959

International Congress of Confraternity of Christian Doctrine in Dallas — 1961

Diocese of San Angelo established — 1961

Second Vatican Council — 1962 1965

Texas Catholic Conference established — 1964

Vietnamese War — 1964 1975

Diocese of Beaumont established — 1966

Permanent Diaconate Restored — 1967

Diocese of Fort Worth established — 1969

Diocese of Victoria established — **1982**

Diocese of Lubbock established — 1983

Diocese of Tyler established — 1986

Visit of Pope John Paul II to San Antonio — 1987

Diocese of Laredo established — 2000

CLICK-LEARNING

> **Archbishop Patrick Flores**

> **Cesar Chaves**

"mosaic"
A design composed of many variously colored pieces assembled in such a way as to form a picture or a pattern.

Beginning with the persecution of the Catholic Church in Mexico during the Mexican Revolution in the early twentieth century, increasing numbers of Catholic refugees began to cross the Rio Grande River into Texas. Later in the century, the reason for emigrating from Mexico was mainly for the better paying jobs that were available north of the Rio Grande.

In 2000 about one of every three Texans was Hispanic, an increase from one in five in 1970. The number continues to rise. Not all Hispanics are Catholic, but it is estimated that about three-fourths consider themselves Catholic. Hispanic Catholics have brought with them the celebrations, fiestas and customs of Latin America to enrich the Texas Catholic experience. Their presence is reflected in the increased number of parishes where Spanish is the first language. It is also reflected in the Catholic hierarchy of Texas, with six of the fifteen bishops who head dioceses being of Hispanic origin. This number includes Archbishop Patrick Flores of San Antonio, the first Hispanic raised to the American church hierarchy.

Our Catholic mosaic has also been enhanced by a large number of Catholics who have come from Asian countries. The earliest arrivals from Asia came from the Philippine Islands following World War II. The Korean War resulted in many Korean Catholics coming to Texas. The largest number of new Texas Catholics from Asia came from Vietnam following the end of the Vietnamese War in 1975. Others have migrated from India and China as well as countries of the Middle East and Africa. Each group contributes to the beauty of the Texas Catholic mosaic and reminds us of how truly "catholic" or universal our church really is.

"fiestas"
Celebrations, usually marking a saint's day, holy day or holiday.

"hierarchy"
Ordained leaders of the church, usually bishops, archbishops and the Pope.

"Viva la Raza"
The meaning of "Viva la Raza" is "long live the race", it usually refers to Mexican-American culture and tradition.

Newly consecrated Bishop Patrick Flores blesses the crowd that filled the old San Antonio City Auditorium in 1970 for his elevation as the first Mexican-American in the North American hierarchy.

> Archbishop Patrick Flores

1929 >

Amid shouts of "Viva la Raza", one-time migrant worker Patrick Fernandez Flores, a priest of the Galveston-Houston Diocese, became the first Mexican-American bishop in the United States. He was consecrated auxiliary bishop of San Antonio in that city's old Arena on "Cinco de Mayo", May 5, 1970, Mexico's national holiday.

In 1978, after eight years as auxiliary bishop, Flores was installed as the Bishop of El Paso. Less than two years later, he was named Archbishop of San Antonio.

The archbishop has been heavily involved in social justice issues both nationally and internationally. Farm labor leader Cesar Chaves, a personal friend, acted as lector at his consecration. He loves music and has given away many guitars to poor youth. He also has a wonderful gift of paying attention to everyone in a crowd around him.

> The Pope Comes to Texas

On September 13, 1987, a chartered airliner touched down at Kelly Air Force Base in San Antonio. The event marked the beginning of the first visit by a Pope to Texas. Two years of preparations had been made for Pope John Paul II's second pastoral visit to the United States. On his first U.S. visit, eight years earlier, the Pontiff had visited the major cities of the Northeast and Midwest. His 1987 visit was primarily to the South, southwest and the west coast. The Pope's pilgrimage to Texas was unique in that all fourteen dioceses in the state were hosting the visit, not just one archdiocese or diocese.

More than 300,000 Catholics from throughout Texas greeted Pope John Paul II upon his arrival at the outdoor Mass site. Many had been waiting for hours in 100+ Texas heat for the Pontiff's arrival.

The Holy Father was driven directly to the site for the outdoor Mass where more than 300,000 Catholics from throughout the state were gathered. Many had come by bus, train and car. Some left their homes in the middle of the night and had been waiting for hours in the hot Texas sun.

A large cathedral-like structure had been constructed on the Mass site in the Westover Hills area of San Antonio. Two days before the visit a severe wind and rain storm demolished the structure and its twin towers. Crews labored around the clock to build a temporary structure to replace the destroyed portion. When the crowds arrived for the Mass, everything had been cleaned up.

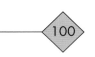

Diocese of Austin established
Korean War
Diocese of Dallas becomes Diocese of Dallas-Fort Worth
Diocese of Galveston becomes Diocese of Galveston-Houston
International Congress of Confraternity of Christian Doctrine in Dallas
Diocese of San Angelo established
Second Vatican Council
Texas Catholic Conference established
Vietnamese War
Diocese of Beaumont established
Permanent Diaconate Restored
Diocese of Fort Worth established
Diocese of Victoria established
Diocese of Lubbock established
Diocese of Tyler established
Visit of Pope John Paul II to San Antonio
Diocese of Laredo established

| 1948 | 1950 1954 | 1954 | 1959 | 1961 | 1961 | 1962 1965 | 1964 | 1964 1975 | 1966 | 1967 | 1969 | 1982 | 1983 | 1986 | **1987** | 2000 |

Pope John Paul II passes the Alamo in his Popemobile during his historic visit to San Antonio in 1987.
(Courtesy of Goldbeck Panoramic Photography, San Antonio)

The towers were gone, but most people were completely unaware of the frantic work of the final two days.

Upon arrival at the Mass site, the Pope and Archbishop Flores of San Antonio drove around the Mass site in the glass-covered Popemobile to the delight of the crowds who caught an up-close look at the Pope. Pilgrims who had spent hours in the scorching Texas sun forgot about the heat as they cheered the Pontiff.

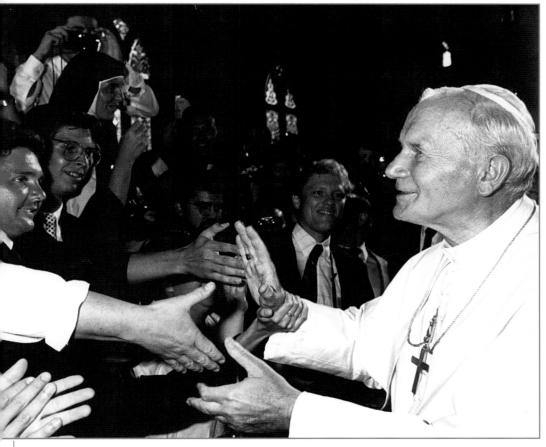

Seminarians and sisters in formation reach out to greet the Pope upon his arrival at San Fernando Cathedral where he addressed the young people preparing for service to the Church.

After Mass the Papal party departed for downtown San Antonio for a parade, to drive by the Alamo, and to address representatives of Catholic organizations from throughout the nation. Later at San Fernando Cathedral, the oldest parish in Texas, Pope John Paul II spoke to men and women preparing for the priesthood and religious life from seminaries and houses of formation throughout the state.

The Pontiff's final activity of this momentous day was a visit to Our Lady of Guadalupe Church where he spoke in Spanish to a plaza packed with Hispanic Catholics. He was entertained by mariachi band, Mexican dancers and a song by the guitar-playing Archbishop Flores.

Later that evening Pope John Paul II held a private audience with parishioners from St. Mary's Church in Panna Maria, Texas, the oldest Polish settlement in the United States. He presented an elegant, gold and jewel-encrusted chalice to the church.

Exhausted but exhilarated, hundreds of thousands of Catholics returned home in their buses, cars and trains with memories of a papal visit that they would never forget.

CLICK-LEARNING

> Pope John Paul II

This was the logo for the Pope's visit.

The Church in Texas today

> How the Church is organized:

For most of us Church means our parish, maybe our school. Our pastor represents the leadership of the Church for us. When a pastor is reassigned it is always a sad thing; it is like losing a member of the family, particularly if he has been in the parish a long time. When the bishop comes to administer Confirmation, it is a big occasion, particularly if you are an altar server and get to hold the bishop's crozier or his miter.

Bishop Bernard Ganter, a former Bishop of Beaumont, told of standing outside the church in all his vestments with his crozier and miter, when a seven-year-old girl came up to him. She looked him over and said "Hi king!" He told her that he wasn't a king. He was a pastor of many parishes instead of one, and that together the many parishes and their people are called a diocese. He further explained that one of the marks of his pastoral office was a crozier, or pastoral staff. It is similar to a shepherd's staff, because, like a shepherd, he looks after his flock.

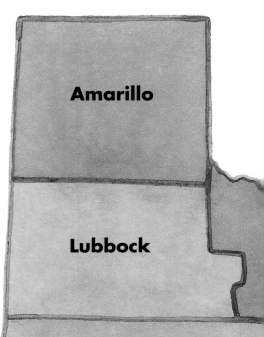

In Texas there are 15 dioceses, each with a chief pastor who is a bishop. There are more than 15 bishops in Texas because some are auxiliary bishops, and some are retired. The chief pastor of Texas and the whole Church is the Pope. He is chief pastor because he is the successor of St. Peter, who was appointed by Jesus to be the leader of the Church. Later he became the first Bishop of Rome. The Pope is Pope because he is the Bishop of Rome and, as such is the successor of Peter as the leader of the church. Does it surprise you that the Pope is only a bishop like your bishop? Actually, there are only three pastoral offices in the church. They are deacon, priest and bishop. All share in the sacrament of Holy Orders, which is the sacrament of leadership. Titles like monsignor, archbishop, cardinal, even Pope, are titles of honor or office given to bishops and priests.

If your pastor is a monsignor then he is a priest whose pastoral service to the church has been recognized. Bishops of certain important dioceses are called archbishops and their dioceses are called archdioceses, like the Archbishop of the Archdiocese of San Antonio. Cardinals are bishops who have been chosen as papal electors. There are no cardinals in Texas, but some have been born here. All Texas bishops work directly with the Pope and do not report to an archbishop or a cardinal. Once every five years, Texas bishops meet with the Pope to discuss pastoral affairs in Texas dioceses.

Priests and deacons work with the bishop and represent him in parishes for which the bishop has pastoral responsibility. All leadership offices in the church are offices of service. The Pope is called the Servant of the Servants of God. All members of the Christian church are Servants of God, and our bishops, priests and deacons are servant leaders.

Ft. North

Dallas

Tyler

Austin

Beaumont

Galveston-Houston

Victoria

Corpus Christi

Brownsville

> The Church in Texas

By 2003 there were 15 dioceses in Texas. When the first Spanish explorers arrived about 500 years ago, there were none. Texas was part of the dioceses of Guadalajara, Durango and Linares-Monterrey. Mexican jurisdiction ended in 1840 with the establishment of the Vicariate Apostolic of Texas. When Texas entered the Union, the Vicariate Apostalic became the Diocese of Galveston in 1847. There are now 15 dioceses in Texas, the newest of which is the Diocese of Laredo, established in July, 2000.

How much do you know about your diocese? How much do you know about the other dioceses of Texas? In this chapter of the book you will find the stories of how your diocese and other Texas dioceses came to be and how each has been an important part of Texas history. As you study this section, try to imagine what the area of your diocese looked like 100 or 200 years ago when the only light came from fire, and horses were the most important means of transportation.

> Diocese of Galveston-Houston

Before the coming of the railroads, water was the fastest and most dependable means of transport. Rivers and seas were the highways of commerce and of faith. During the days of the Republic and early statehood, most people came to Texas by ship, and the most important cities were the seaports.

Right Reverend
Jean Marie Odin, C.M.
First Bishop of Galveston

Galveston Island had been the home of Indians, pirates and revolutionaries long before French-Canadian Catholic Michael B. Menard began plans for the City of Galveston in 1833. The American Navy forced pirate Jean Lafitte off the island in 1821. Mexico designated the Island a port of entry in 1824. During Texas' War of Independence the island served as the base for the Texas Navy, and the refuge for many fleeing the invading Mexican Army. Following the Battle of San Jacinto, Mexican prisoners of war and General Santa Anna were housed on the Island.

In 1839 the Texas Congress incorporated the City of Galveston with Menard as principal founder. It was December 27, 1838, when Father John Timon arrived from New Orleans to inspect the church situation in Texas and happened upon Menard, whom he had known as a missionary in Missouri. It was on New Year's Eve in 1838 that the first plans for St. Mary's Church were made, before the official incorporation of the city.

In July 1841, the new Vicariate Apostolic of Texas was established under Bishop Jean Marie Odin. After his consecration in New Orleans in the spring of 1842, he made Galveston the seat or headquarters of the new Vicariate. In September the newly completed St. Mary's was destroyed by a storm. Reconstruction began immediately and was completed by March, 1843. Ground was broken for a new brick church in 1847 and was underway when the Diocese of Galveston was established in May 1847 with Bishop Odin as the first Ordinary. The present cathedral was dedicated in November, 1848. In 1979 Pope John Paul II designated the cathedral a Minor Basilica, an honor reserved for historically significant churches.

As Texas grew and the number of Catholics increased, other dioceses were established. In 1874 territory for the Diocese of San Antonio and Vicariate Apostolic of Brownsville was taken from the Galveston Diocese. The northern section of the diocese (about one-third of the state) became the Diocese of Dallas in 1890. In 1966 the eastern portion of the diocese became the Diocese of Beaumont. More territory was transfered in 1982 to the Diocese of Victoria and in 1986 to

Sacred Heart Co-Cathedral, Houston

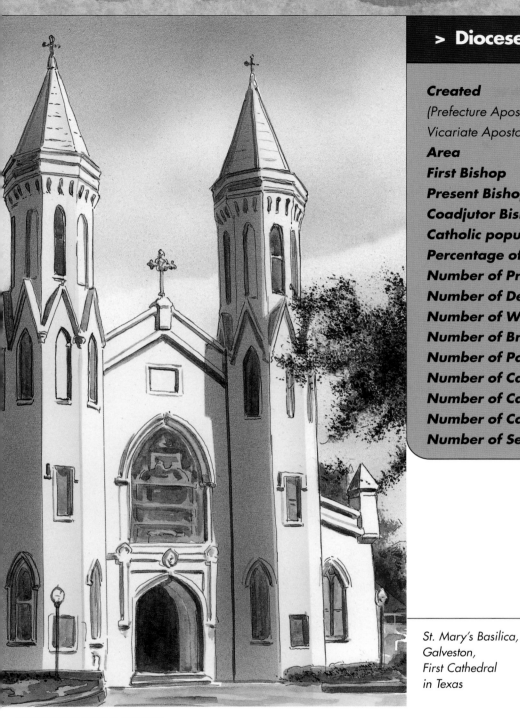

Created	**May 4, 1847**
(Prefecture Apostolic of Texas, 1839, Vicariate Apostolic of Texas, 1841)	
Area	**8,880 Square Miles**
First Bishop	**Most Rev. Jean Marie Odin, C.M.**
Present Bishop	**Most Rev. Joseph Anthony Fiorenza**
Coadjutor Bishop	**Most Rev. Daniel N. DiNardo**
Catholic population	**1,041,123**
Percentage of total population	**21**
Number of Priests	**452**
Number of Deacons	**362**
Number of Women Religious	**499**
Number of Brothers	**12**
Number of Parishes and Missions	**158**
Number of Catholic Elementary Schools	**52**
Number of Catholic High Schools	**8**
Number of Catholic Colleges or Universities	**2**
Number of Seminaries	**1**

CLICK-LEARNING

> **Diocese of Galveston-Houston**
> **Jean Lafitte**
> **Texas Navy**

*St. Mary's Basilica,
Galveston,
First Cathedral
in Texas*

the Diocese of Tyler. In 1959 the name of the diocese was changed to Galveston-Houston. The chancery and bishop's residence were later moved to Houston, and Sacred Heart Church, Houston, was named the Co-Cathedral.

Today fifteen dioceses have been created from of the original Diocese of Galveston, still the largest diocese in Texas with 1,041,123 Catholics. The mother diocese that once embraced the entire state of Texas now includes 10 counties and a territory of 8.880 square miles. It is the 10th largest diocese in the United States. Most Rev. Joseph Fiorenza is the present Bishop of Galveston-Houston.

*Silver monstrance that belonged to Bishop Odin,
now in the Ursuline Archives, Dallas*

> Archdiocese of San Antonio

When Texas won its independence from Mexico, the center of political activity shifted from Spanish Texas around San Antonio further to the east, where most Anglo-American colonies existed. The first diocese in Texas was established at Galveston, the busy Gulf port in 1847. San Antonio, however, continued to thrive as a center of Catholic activity with Ursuline Academy established in 1851, St. Mary's Institute, now St. Mary's University in 1852 and Santa Rosa Hospital in 1869.

In 1874 San Antonio became the second diocese to be established in Texas. San Fernando, the first parish church in the state, was designated the cathedral of the new diocese. When Bishop Anthony Pellicer was installed as first Bishop of San Antonio in December, 1874, the only portion of the old cathedral that remained was the sanctuary. The rest of the building had been rebuilt and expanded.

His new diocese had few of the amenities that Bishop Pellicer had enjoyed in the Diocese of Mobile, Alabama. Although San Antonio had a population of 13,000, it was still very much a frontier town. It would be three more years before the railroad reached the city from Houston. Most of his 90,000 square mile diocese was accessible only by stagecoach, wagon or horseback.

"secular"

Secular priests are assigned to a diocese as opposed to religious priests who are members of an order or community.

St. Mary's College was the cultural center of San Antonio and of the diocese, but Bishop Pellicer felt that his new diocese needed a seminary for the formation of secular priests. It would have the principal responsibility for ministry in the diocese. An attempt in the later 1870s by exiled Jesuits from Mexico ceased when they were allowed to return to that country. But with remarkable energy and dedication Father Lawrence Wyer in Victoria succeeded in running a basically one-teacher seminary during the 1880s and 1890s for candidates from several Texas dioceses. In 1881 a charter was granted for Incarnate Word Academy, which is now the University of the Incarnate Word. The cornerstone of Our Lady of the Lake University was laid in 1895. The Oblates of Mary Immaculate opened the San Antonio Theological Seminary (now Oblate School of Theology) in 1903, St. John's Diocesan Seminary (now Assumption Seminary) was opened in 1915.

The responsibility of a large frontier diocese and poor health took their toll on the Bishop. It was not unusual for him to be away from San Antonio for months on journeys of one or two thousand miles that took him to the far reaches of his diocese. As his health failed he leaned heavily on his vicar general, Father Jean Neraz, one of the pioneer missionary priests from France. In spite of his illness Bishop Pellicer kept up his duties until his death in April, 1880. His vicar general, Father Neraz, was named to succeed him.

"pallium"

A wool collar-like vestment worn only by the Pope and archbishops.

An archdiocese in Texas had long been discussed. Indeed Dallas' first two bishops openly campaigned to have the North Texas diocese made the Metropolitan See, but it was not to be. In 1926 the Diocese of San Antonio became an archdiocese and the Archbishop's pallium fell upon Bishop Arthur Drossaerts, who became first Metropolitan of the Province of San Antonio.

San Fernando Cathedral, San Antonio
First Parish Church in Texas

CLICK-LEARNING

> Mexican-American Cultural Center

> Archdiocese of San Antonio

> Bishop Anthony Pellicer

Today San Antonio is the center of Catholic education and culture in Texas with three Catholic universities, a Catholic school of theology, the Mexican American Cultural Center and a Catholic history that goes back three centuries. Tourists from throughout the world visit the San Antonio missions, four of which function as active churches, and the Alamo, the first mission which became a fort and the cradle of Texas liberty.

Because of its long Catholic history, San Antonio was chosen as one of the cities to be visited by Pope John Paul II during his trip to the United States in 1987. The Holy Father spoke to a group of student priests and sisters at San Fernando Cathedral and celebrated an outdoor Sunday Mass attended by 300,000 at Westover Hills on September 13, 1987.

Few cities can claim such a rich Catholic heritage as San Antonio. Today the archdiocese has an area of 23,180 square miles and embraces all or part of 19 counties with a Catholic population of 667,667. Most Reverend Patrick F. Flores is the present archbishop.

> Archdiocese of San Antonio

Created (Archdiocese August 3, 1926)	**August 28, 1874**
Area	**23,180 Square Miles**
First Bishop	**Most Rev. Anthony Dominic Ambrose Pellicer**
Present Bishop	**Most Rev. Patrick F. Flores**
Catholic population	**667,667**
Percentage of total population	**33%**
Number of Priests	**350**
Number of Deacons	**313**
Number of Women Religious	**822**
Number of Brothers	**78**
Number of Parishes	**139**
Number of Missions	**34**
Number of Catholic Elementary Schools	**40**
Number of Catholic High Schools	**10**
Number of Catholic Colleges or Universities	**4**
Number of Seminaries	**11**

Most Rev. Anthony Dominic Ambrose Pellicer First Bishop of San Antonio

> Diocese of Dallas

Most Rev.
Thomas Francis Brennan
First Bishop of Dallas

*Cathedral Santuario
Guadalupe, Dallas
Originally Sacred Heart
Cathedral*

Bishop Claude Dubuis established Dallas' first parish, Sacred Heart, in 1872. No longer was the population of Texas concentrated on the coast and the borderlands. With the arrival of the railroads, Dallas had become the commercial center of North Texas.

In 1881 an ill Bishop Dubuis returned to France and Nicholas A. Gallagher was consecrated bishop and named administrator of the Diocese of Galveston.In concert with the other bishops of the New Orleans province, Bishop Gallagher appealed to Pope Leo XIII in 1890 that "The Diocese of Galveston is too large to be conveniently and properly attended from Galveston, which is at the southern extremity of the diocese." He recommended to the Holy Father that Dallas, which he described as the largest and most important city in the area, should become the See city of a new diocese.

"See"

See refers to the city of the diocese where the bishop resides.

On July 15, 1890, Pope Leo XIII established the Diocese of Dallas. The new diocese would include all of North Texas from Louisiana to New Mexico. It would cover 108,000 square miles and contain an estimated 15,000 Catholics. In 1892, at the urging of the Jesuit priests in El Paso County who were having serious disagreements with the Bishop of the Vicariate of Arizona. The El Paso district remained part of the Dallas diocese until the creation of the new Diocese of El Paso in 1914.

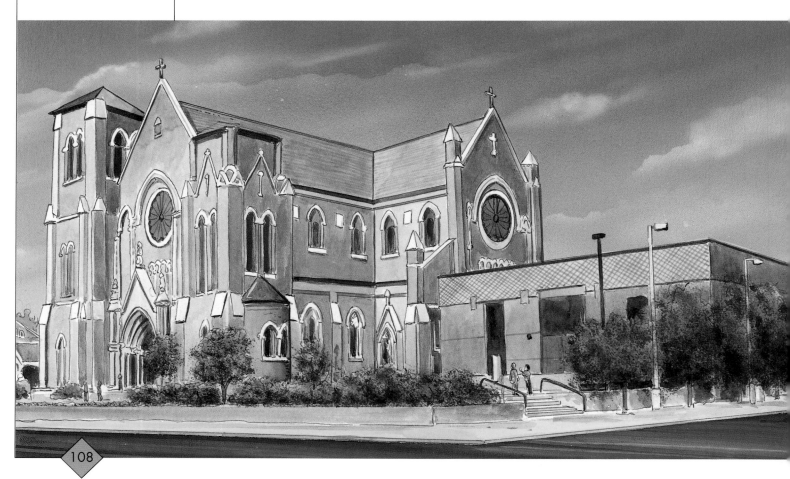

Chosen to head the new diocese was 37-year-old Thomas Francis Brennan, a sophisticated, highly educated cleric from Pennsylvania. Born in County Tipperary, Ireland, in 1855, his parents brought him to America when he was 8. After priestly studies in France and Austria he was ordained at 24.

During his first year the number of priests increased by 11, four new religious communities were brought to the diocese and 12 new churches were built. This was accomplished despite an economic depression and heavy indebtedness inherited by the new diocese.

Sacred Heart School, staffed by Ursuline Nuns, was Dallas first parochial school

But all was not well. The Ursuline nuns accused him of claiming ownership of property belonging to their community. Priests of the diocese charged that he was a tyrant using "spies" to intimidate them. They also claimed that he was prideful and not always virtuous. In his brashness, Bishop Brennan began a campaign for Dallas to be made an archdiocese with him appointed as archbishop. This action antagonized the other bishops of the province.

"ad limina"

The term used to describe the visit each bishop must make to the Pope every five years.

Unaware of the complaints sent forward by the Ursulines and priests of the diocese, the bishop went to Rome for his *ad limina* visit in 1892. Instead of becoming an archbishop, he was confronted by Rome with the complaints and resigned. He was replaced by Bishop Edward Joseph Dunne.

Dallas is the mother diocese of all or portions of the dioceses of El Paso, Amarillo, San Angelo, Austin, Fort Worth, Lubbock and Tyler. From its original 108,000 square miles, the present diocese embraces only 7,523 square miles and nine counties in North Central Texas. Most Rev. Charles V. Grahmann is the present Bishop of Dallas and Most Rev. Joseph Galante, J.C.D. is coadjutor.

> Diocese of Dallas

Created	**July 15, 1890**
Area	**7,523 Square Miles**
First Bishop	**Most Rev. Thomas Francis Brennan**
Present Bishop	**Most Rev. Charles Victor Grahmann**
Catholic population	**930,352**
Percentage of total population	**26%**
Number of Priests	**180**
Number of Deacons	**162**
Number of Women Religious	**142**
Number of Brothers	**7**
Number of Parishes	**67**
Number of Missions	**8**
Number of Catholic Elementary Schools	**33**
Number of Catholic High Schools	**9**
Number of Catholic Colleges or Universities	**1**
Number of Seminaries	**1**

CLICK-LEARNING

> **Diocese of Dallas**

> **Pope Leo XIII**

> Diocese of Corpus Christi

Alonso de Pineda and his crew were the first Europeans and the first Catholics to view what is now Corpus Christi Bay as they explored the Texas coast in 1519. Less than a decade later, Alvar Núñez Cabeza de Vaca and his companions trekked across the area on their incredible journey across Texas to New Spain.

Both France and Spain sought to colonize the area. LaSalle established his ill-fated Fort St. Louis near Matagorda Bay in 1685. The Spanish later established the La Bahia Presidio and Mission at the same location in 1722. Nuestra Señora del Refugio, the last of the missions, was established in 1793 at the juncture of the San Antonio and Guadalupe rivers, and moved to the present site of Refugio in 1795.

Many Irish Catholic colonists settled in the Refugio and San Patricio area prior to the War of Independence against Mexico. They had been encouraged by the Mexican Government to emigrate in order to provide a buffer against the influx of largely Protestant Anglo-American colonists.

Most Rev. Dominic Manucy
Vicar Apostolic
of Brownsville
Predecessor to Diocese
of Corpus Christi

It was not until 1839 that the first permanent settlement was made on Corpus Christi Bay. Bishop Jean Marie Odin, the first Bishop of Galveston, visited Corpus Christi in 1850. In 1874 the Pope established the Vicariate Apostolic of Brownsville and Bishop Dominic Manucy was named vicar apostolic. He soon moved to Corpus Christi.

In 1912 the vicariate was raised to a diocese and designated the Diocese of Corpus Christi. Bishop Paul Joseph Nussbaum became its first Bishop. The South Texas diocese has endured a unique set of challenges because of its location on the Gulf and its proximity to Mexico. A number of hurricanes have struck the Corpus Christi area over the years bringing extensive damage and loss of life and property. Rebuilding church structures damaged by storms was an ongoing process. Assistance was given by other dioceses and the Catholic Church Extension Society.

Corpus Christi Cathedral

In the period from 1910 to the mid 1930s, the diocese received thousands of refugees from the persecution of the Catholic Church by the government of Mexico. The original territory of the diocese has been reduced three times by the creation of other dioceses. In 1965 the southernmost four counties became part of the newly established Diocese of Brownsville. When the Diocese of Victoria was established in 1982 the eastern portion of the diocese was taken. In 2000, three and one-half counties on the Rio Grande were attached to the new Diocese of Laredo.

Today the Diocese of Corpus Christi covers an area of 10,951 square miles and includes all or part of twelve counties with a Catholic population of 384,308. The present Bishop of Corpus Christi is Most Rev. Edmond Carmody.

CLICK-LEARNING

> Diocese of Corpus Christi

> Corpus Christi Bay

> Catholic Church Extension Society

> Diocese of Corpus Christi

Created	**March 23,1912**
(Vicariate Apostolic of Brownsville, August 28, 1874)	
Area	**10,951 Square Miles**
First Bishop	**Most Rev. Peter Verdaguer**
	(Most Rev. Dominic Manucy, V.A. Brownsville)
Present Bishop	**Most Rev. Edmond Carmody**
Catholic population	**384,308**
Percentage of total population	**70%**
Number of Priests	**160**
Number of Deacons	**62**
Number of Women Religious	**182**
Number of Brothers	**13**
Number of Parishes	**67**
Number of Missions	**33**
Number of Catholic Elementary Schools	**16**
Number of Catholic High Schools	**1**
Number of Catholic Colleges or Universities	**1**
Number of Seminaries	**0**

> Diocese of El Paso

There is no better monument to the Catholic history of El Paso than the 42 foot statue of Christ the King that was erected nearly 70 years ago atop Mount Cristo Rey. It seems appropriate that Mount Cristo Rey is located on the border of Texas, New Mexico because Catholicism has played such an important role in their histories.

El Paso takes its name from the gap in the mountains that provided access to New Mexico to the early Spanish explorers. They named it "El Paso del Norte" or "The Pass to the North." The area later provided refuge for those fleeing the Pueblo Revolt in New Mexico in 1680. Two villages established by the refugees became the first missions in Texas.

Franciscan friars from Chihuahua ministered to the old settlements of Socorro, Ysleta and San Elizario until 1852 when secular priests from the Diocese of Durango took over. Twenty years later, El Paso County became part of the Vicariate Apostolic of Arizona. By that time the new town of Franklin, next to the American military post of El Paso established in 1849, had itself been renamed El Paso.

Father Carlos Persone arrived with the first group of Jesuit priests in 1881 to assume pastoral responsibility for the parishes and missions in the area. In 1892 El Paso became part of the new Diocese of Dallas. The change was prompted by the Jesuits whose relationship with Tucson Bishop Peter Bourgade had been stormy. Bishop Brennan visited El Paso briefly in April 1892, before resigning his post in Dallas. The area was briefly administered by Bishop Edward Fitzgerald of Little Rock until the appointment of Bishop Edward J. Dunne as second Bishop of Dallas.

Bishop Dunne bestowed the faculties of Vicar General of the El Paso area on Jesuit superior Father Carlos Pinto. Bishop Dunne visited the area once, in November 1895. Upon his death in 1910, Bishop Joseph P. Lynch was named his successor. Bishop Lynch realized that his diocese was too large to be properly administered from Dallas.

Most Rev. Anthony Joseph Schuler, SJ Bishop of El Paso 1915-1944

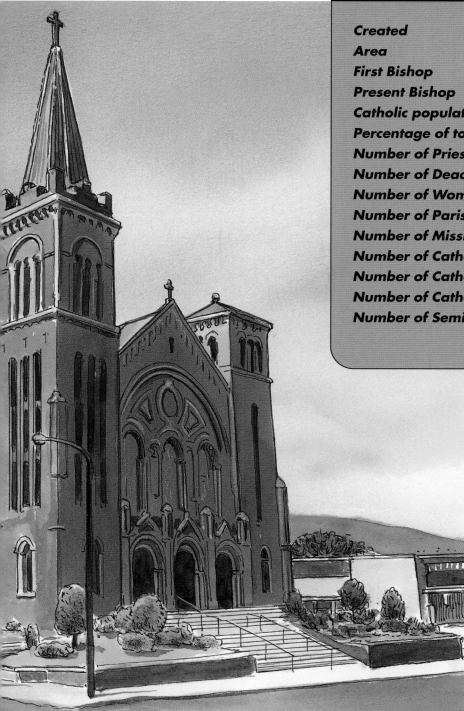

> Diocese of El Paso

Created	March 3,1914
Area	26,686 Square Miles
First Bishop	Most Rev. Anthony Joseph Schuler, SJ
Present Bishop	Most Rev. Armando Xavier Ochoa
Catholic population	656,035
Percentage of total population	81%
Number of Priests	119
Number of Deacons	10
Number of Women Religious	254
Number of Parishes	58
Number of Missions	22
Number of Catholic Elementary Schools	12
Number of Catholic High Schools	3
Number of Catholic Colleges or Universities	0
Number of Seminaries	3

He had to cross part of the Diocese of San Antonio to reach El Paso which was not contiguous with the rest of the Dallas diocese. He petitioned Rome to separate the far west Texas area from Dallas.

In March 1914 the Pope established the Diocese of El Paso and the region so rich in Catholic history became a separate jurisdiction embracing a larger part of West Texas and also southern New Mexico. The first bishop named to El Paso, Jesuit Father John J. Brown, declined the office because of ill health. The episcopal appointment went then to another Jesuit, Father Anthony Joseph Schuler, who served in that post until 1942.

CLICK-LEARNING

> Diocese of El Paso
> Mount Cristo Rey
> El Paso del Norte

Portions of the Diocese of San Angelo and the Diocese of Las Cruces, New Mexico, have been taken from the original Diocese of El Paso. Today the diocese includes 26,686 square miles and ten counties situated along the Rio Grande and in far West Texas. The present Bishop of El Paso is Most Rev. Armando Xavier Ochoa.

> Diocese of Amarillo

Most Rev. Rudolph
Aloysius Gerken
First Bishop of Amarillo

Catholicism first came to the Texas panhandle in 1541 when Coronado's expedition crossed into Texas seeking the elusive riches of Quivira. He was accompanied by Friar Juan de Padilla, who was to become North America's first martyr.

Few settlers came to the area until the establishment of the Indian Territory (the future Oklahoma) in 1875. Tom O'Loughlin, an Irish Catholic, operated a hotel in Fort Elliott and had extensive ranch lands. First mention of a Panhandle city by the Official Catholic Directory was in 1880 when Fort Elliott was listed as a mission of Windthorst, north of Fort Worth. Benedictines from Kansas also made the long trip to minister to the Catholics at Fort Elliott.

Mass was held in Old Tascosa at first by priests from New Mexico, where a former schoolhouse was converted into a chapel. In 1892 Dallas Bishop Thomas F. Brennan administered Confirmation there but by 1916 the town had been abandoned.

More Catholics arrived with the railroads. In 1881, the Texas and Pacific Railroad crossed the South Plains running from Fort Worth to Sweetwater and Colorado City. Six years later the Fort Worth and Denver and the Southern Kansas railroads crossed at Amarillo assuring that city's dominance of the Panhandle. Priests from Gainesville served the area.

In 1890 the Texas Panhandle became part of the new Diocese of Dallas. In 1891 Bishop Thomas Brennan made the whole Panhandle a mission of Henrietta much further to the east. In 1892, St. Mary's Church was built at Clarendon at a cost of $1,700, becoming the first Catholic church in the Panhandle. St. Mary's Academy was opened in the same town in 1899 by the Sisters of Charity of the Incarnate Word, even though there was still not a resident priest in the Panhandle. The area grew rapidly after the breakup of the large ranches. Many German Catholic immigrants began to farm the land.

> Diocese of Amarillo

Created	**August 25, 1926**
Area	**25,800 square miles**
First Bishop	**Most Rev. Rudolph Aloysius Gerken**
Present Bishop	**Most Rev. John W. Yanta**
Catholic population	**43,651**
Percentage of total population	**10**
Number of Priests	**55**
Number of Deacons	**51**
Number of Women Religious	**106**
Number of Brothers	**1**
Number of Parishes	**35**
Number of Missions	**13**
Number of Catholic Elementary Schools	**6**
Number of Catholic High Schools	**1**
Number of Seminaries	**0**

CLICK-LEARNING

> **Diocese of Amarillo**

> **Texas Panhandle**

The Diocese of Amarillo was established by the Pope in August, 1926 and Father Rudolph A. Gerken was named the first Bishop of Amarillo. In 1933 he was named Archbishop of Santa Fe and was replaced the following year by Bishop Robert E. Lucey, who would later become Archbishop of San Antonio.

In 1961 the southernmost portion of the diocese was split off to help establish the Diocese of San Angelo, twenty additional counties were removed to create most of the Diocese of Lubbock in 1983.

Today the Diocese of Amarillo covers an area of 25,800 square miles and includes 26 counties in the Panhandle with more than 43,651 Catholics. The present bishop is Most Rev. John W. Yanta.

St. Laurance Cathedral

> Diocese of Austin

Catholic roots of the Diocese of Austin are found in the establishment of three East Texas Missions, and the El Camino Real, or Kings Highway, which connected the missions to San Antonio and to Mexico. Early missionaries and conquistadors travelled the Camino which was south of the site of present-Austin. The East Texas missions were abandoned in 1730 and were temporarily combined and relocated on the south side of the Colorado River near present-day Town Lake, before being moved to San Antonio.

In a sense, Austin was the birthplace of modern Catholic history in Texas. The city was a year old when Vincentian Fathers John Timon and Jean Marie Odin arrived in the new capital to negotiate for the return of all church lands which had been confiscated by the new Republic after the War of Independence. Had they not been successful, the reintroduction of Catholicism would have been much more difficult.

St. Mary's Cathedral

The capital would become the see city of the new Diocese of Austin 107 years later. When Bishop Louis J. Reicher was named first Bishop of Austin, all the city's parishes were staffed by religious order priests. The city itself had been divided between two dioceses, the Diocese of Galveston and the Archdiocese of San Antonio.

Most Rev. Louis Joseph Reicher
First Bishop of Austin

St. Edwards University, operated by the Holy Cross Brothers, was one of the earliest educational institutions in the state with its founding in 1874. Also unique to the new diocese was the presence of the oldest parish for African-American Catholics in Texas, Blessed Virgin Mary Church located at "Old Washington," or Washington-on-the-Brazos. The parish was established by the Spann family for the slaves on their plantation in the 1840s and was called Our Lady of the Most Holy Rosary. It has continuously served a small African-American congregation.

Strategically important because of its location at the state capital, Austin also serves as the headquarters of the Texas Catholic Conference and the location of the Catholic Archives of Texas. The diocese is also responsible for the important Catholic campus ministries at the University of Texas and Texas A&M University.

In 1961 four counties were removed from the Austin diocese to form the Diocese of San Angelo, leaving it with its present 23 and one-half counties of 19,511 square miles. The current Catholic population is 401,541. The present Bishop of Austin is the Most Rev. Gregory M. Aymond.

> Diocese of Austin

Created	November 15, 1947
Area	19,511 Square Miles
First Bishop	Most Rev. Louis Joseph Reicher
Present Bishop	Most Rev. Gregory Michael Aymond
Catholic population	401,541
Percentage of total population	19
Number of Priests	194
Number of Deacons	191
Number of Women Religious	97
Number of Brothers	46
Number of Parishes	104
Number of Missions 2	22
Number of Catholic Elementary Schools	16
Number of Catholic High Schools	5
Number of Catholic Colleges or Universities	1
Number of Seminaries	0

CLICK-LEARNING

> Diocese of Austin

> El Camino Real

> Washington-on-the-Brazos

> Diocese of San Angelo

As is the case with so many of Texas' fifteen dioceses, the Catholic roots run deep in the Diocese of San Angelo. Two of the earliest lengthy missionary visits among Indians took place within the boundaries of the present diocese in the 17th century.

The first was by Friar Diego León among Jumanos near present day San Angelo, in response to a visit to New Mexico by a group of Jumanos. They explained that the "Woman in Blue had instructed them" to seek priests for instruction.

Some 50 years later the Spanish explorer Juan Dominguez de Mendoza and Friar Nicolas Lopez returned to the area. They remained a month and a half among the Jumanos south of Ballinger on the Colorado River.

The first formally founded mission in the area was the ill-fated Santa Cruz de San Saba which was established in 1757 among the Apaches. It was destroyed a year later following an Indian attack by tribes hostile to the Apaches. Seventeen Indians and eight Spaniards, including two Franciscan Friars were killed.

> Diocese of San Angelo

Created	**October 16, 1961**
Area	**37,433 Square Miles**
First Bishop	**Most Rev. Thomas Joseph Drury**
Present Bishop	**Most Rev. Michael David Pfeifer, OMI**
Catholic population	**82,734**
Percentage of total population	**12%**
Number of Priests	**51**
Number of Deacons	**35**
Number of Women Religious	**23**
Number of Brothers	**0**
Number of Parishes	**49**
Number of Missions	**24**
Number of Catholic Elementary Schools	**3**
Number of Catholic High Schools	**0**
Number of Catholic Colleges or Universities	**0**
Number of Seminaries	**0**

An interesting footnote to history is that Friar Junipero Serra, who is credited with founding the California missions, was posted to San Saba. He was sent to California instead after the Indian attack.

In 1961 Pope John XXIII established the Diocese of San Angelo with territory taken from the Dioceses of Amarillo, Austin, El Paso and Dallas-Fort Worth. The area around San Angelo was sparsely populated until the coming of the Texas and Pacific and the Santa Fe railroads in the 1870s and 1880s. Many of the earliest Catholic settlers in the diocese came with the construction of the railroads. Others were soldiers assigned to Fort Concho which was established in 1867. Sacred Heart Church in San Angelo was built in 1906, replacing a much older red sandstone structure built in 1884. When the diocese was established, the present Sacred Heart Church was designated as the Cathedral of the Sacred Heart.

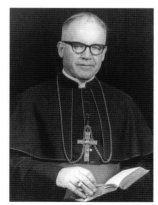

Most Rev.
Thomas Joseph Drury
First Bishop of San Angelo

Today, the Diocese of San Angelo embraces 37,433 square miles and 29 counties with a Catholic population of more than 82,000. The present Bishop of San Angelo is Most Rev. Michael D. Pfeiffer, O.M.I.

Sacred Heart Cathedral, San Angelo

> Diocese of Brownsville

The Diocese of Brownsville is a land filled with tales of martyrs, pirates and treasure. It is located in the southernmost part of Texas and the U.S. mainland where the Rio Grande River meets the Gulf of Mexico. First seen by Alonso de Pineda in 1519 the area later became one of the lairs of Pirate Jean Lafitte. The lighthouse at Point Isabel (Port Isabel) was a welcome sight to many a mariner.

When Texas won its independence from Mexico, the area remained under Mexican control until 1846. When Texas became a state, United States troops established Fort Texas, which later became Fort Brown. After the Mexican War the City of Brownsville was founded and the area, which had been part of the Mexican Diocese of Monterrey, became part of the Diocese of Galveston. A group of priests and brothers of the Oblates of Mary Immaculate arrived in 1849 to take care of this area known as the Lower Rio Grande valley.

Most of the Catholics in the area lived on ranchos and the priests rode on horseback to reach their people, thus gaining the title of the Cavalry of Christ. Today, state historical markers, indicate the Oblate Fathers Trail which begins in Port Isabel and follows the Rio Grande River to Brownsville, Hidalgo, La Lomita, Rio Grande City and Roma to San Ignacio below Laredo.

In 1874, Brownsville became its own Vicariate Apostolic which covered an area extending beyond the Lower Rio Grande country that would later become the Dioceses of Corpus Christi, Brownsville and Laredo. The first bishop of the area was Dominic Manucy, a priest of the Diocese of Mobile. He moved his residence from Brownsville to Corpus Christi and subsequently was made Bishop of Mobile. He retained administrative control of the vicariate until his death.

Two religious communities, the Oblates and the Sisters of the Incarnate Word and Blessed Sacrament served the Church in the Lower Rio Grande Valley in the early days. In 1912, the Vicariate became the Diocese of Corpus Christi.It was not until 1965 that the present Diocese of Brownsville, consisting of the Lower Rio Grande Valley, was carved out of the Diocese of Corpus Christi. In 1948 an Oblate priest, Fr. Jose Azpiazu,

Immaculate Conception Cathedral

CLICK-LEARNING

> **Diocese of Brownsville**

> **Cavalery of Christ**

> **Oblate Fathers Trail**

and the local Mexican people founded the Shrine of Our Lady of San Juan of the Valley, which draws tens of thousands of pilgrims every week and is now a basilica. The first bishop of the new diocese was Bishop Adolph Marx, who died the year he was appointed while attending the Second Vatican Council in Europe.

Of the residents of the diocese, 85 percent are Catholic and the majority of them speak Spanish as their first language. Although covering only a little over 4,000 square miles, the diocese has a Catholic population of more than 831,000. The present bishop is Most Reverend Raymundo Peña.

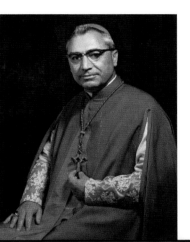

Most Rev. Adolph Marx
First Bishop of Brownsville

> Diocese of Brownsville

Created	*July 10, 1965*
Area	*Area 4,226 Square Miles*
First Bishop	*Most Rev. Adolph Marx*
Present Bishop	*Most Rev. Raymundo Joseph Peña*
Catholic population	831,613
Percentage of total population	85%
Number of Priests	98
Number of Deacons	64
Number of Women Religious	120
Number of Brothers	17
Number of Parishes	65
Number of Missions	44
Number of Catholic Elementary Schools	9
Number of Catholic High Schools	2
Number of Catholic Colleges or Universities	0
Number of Seminaries	1

> Diocese of Beaumont

Some of the earliest Catholic missionary activity by the Spanish occurred in what one day would be the northern counties of the Diocese of Beaumont, counties which later became part of the Diocese of Tyler. The first East Texas missions were very different from the adobe-type buildings with domes and bell towers that people usually associate with Texas missions. They were located in the deep forests of East Texas and were simple log structures and sometimes, little more than lean-tos.

In the days of the Republic and early statehood the area became the center of missionary activity for priests from France under the guidance of Bishop Jean Marie Odin, the Vicar Apostolic of Texas and later Bishop of Galveston. Areas of Texas that were among the first centers of population were among the last to be removed from the diocesan jurisdictions established in the mid- and later nineteenth century.

Such was the case with the Diocese of Beaumont. It was separated from the Diocese of Galveston-Houston in 1966 with Most Rev. Vincent Harris as its first bishop.

> Diocese of Beaumont

Created	*September 29, 1966*
Area	*7,878 Square Miles*
First Bishop	*Most Rev. Vincent Madeley Harris*
Present Bishop	*Most Rev. Curtis John Guillory, SVD*
Catholic population	*89,403*
Percentage of total population	*15%*
Number of Priests	*71*
Number of Deacons	*32*
Number of Women Religious	*42*
Number of Brothers	*1*
Number of Parishes	*45*
Number of Missions	*8*
Number of Catholic Elementary Schools	*6*
Number of Catholic High Schools	*1*
Number of Catholic Colleges or Universities	*0*
Number of Seminaries	*0*

Most Rev.
Vincent Madeley Harris
First Bishop of Beaumont

There were some 83,000 Catholics in the 13 county diocese which covered most of southeast Texas. It found its greatest concentration of Catholics in the Beaumont-Port Arthur-Orange area currently known as the Golden Triangle. When the Vatican established the Diocese of Tyler in northeast Texas in 1986, it acquired six counties from the Beaumont diocese.

Following the war in Viet Nam, large numbers of Vietnamese refugees relocated in the area. The diocesan resettlement program of the late 1970s was very successful. The Vietnamese Catholics added a new dimension to the rich ethnic mix of Hispanic, Italian, German, African-American and Cajun Catholics.

Today the Catholic Faith still thrives in the area where it was first planted in Texas over three hundred years ago. The Diocese of Beaumont has a Catholic population of nearly 100,000 in an area of 7,878 square miles embracing nine counties. The Most Rev. Curtis J. Guillory, S.V.D., is present Bishop of Beaumont.

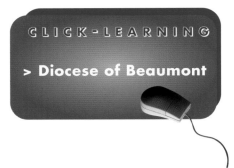

CLICK-LEARNING

> **Diocese of Beaumont**

> Diocese of Fort Worth

As more settlers moved into North Central Texas and the Indian wars subsided, the City of Fort Worth developed at the site of a frontier fort named for General William Worth, a hero of the Mexican War. One of the first Catholics in the area was Maxime Guillot, a French immigrant who was a wagon maker for the army. Guillot moved to Dallas and used his skills to make stylish carriages.

Early Catholics in the area were served by missionary priests from Nacogdoches, which served as the mother church for Catholicism in North Central Texas. Among the early circuit riders was Father Mathurin Perrier, who was French, as were most of the priests in the early days of statehood and the Republic. Father Perrier visited Fort Worth twice a year. Mass was celebrated in the Carrico home until a small frame church, St. Stanislaus, was built in 1876. In 1892 a new and larger church was built nearby, and the name of the parish was changed to St. Patrick.

In 1890 Fort Worth became part of the Diocese of Dallas, the state's third diocese which extended across the northern third of the state from Texarkana to New Mexico. As the number of Catholics increased in west Texas, new dioceses were carved out of the territory of the Dallas diocese. The increasing importance of Fort Worth was recognized by the Vatican in 1953 when the Diocese of Dallas was redesig-nated the Diocese of Dallas-Fort Worth. St. Patrick Church was raised then to the status of co-Cathedral.

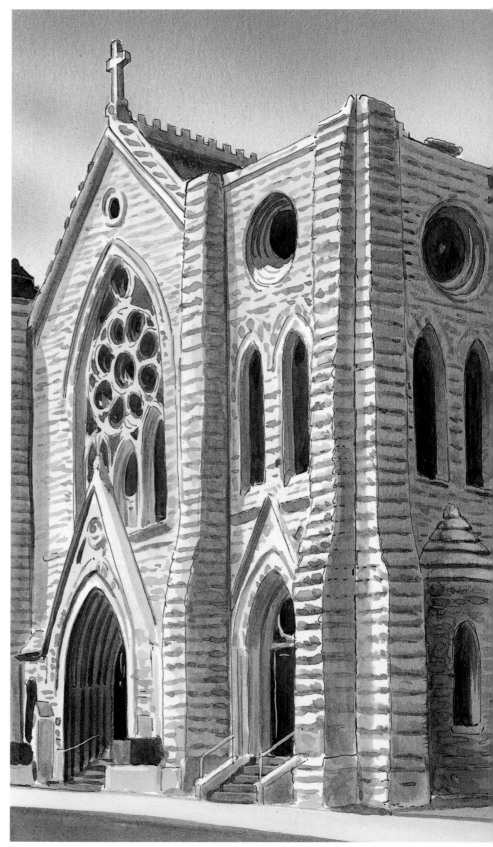

Pope Paul VI created the Diocese of Fort Worth in 1969, essentially splitting the Diocese of Dallas in half. The new diocese had a Catholic population of 67,000 residing in 28 counties. Most Rev. John Cassata, a priest of the Galveston-Houston diocese, was named first Bishop of Fort Worth.

Since its establishment the number of Catholics in the Diocese of Fort Worth has more than quintupled to about 400,000. The present bishop is Most Rev. Joseph Delaney.

Most Rev. John J. Cassata
First Bishop of Fort Worth

> Diocese of Fort Worth

Created	*August 9, 1969*
Area	*23,950 Square Miles*
First Bishop	*Most Rev. John J. Cassata*
Present Bishop	*Most Rev. Joseph Patrick Delaney*
Catholic population	*400,000*
Percentage of total population	*7%*
Number of Priests	*112*
Number of Deacons	*80*
Number of Women Religious	*90*
Number of Brothers	*13*
Number of Parishes	*87*
Number of Missions	*3*
Number of Catholic Elementary Schools	*17*
Number of Catholic High Schools	*4*
Number of Catholic Colleges or Universities	*0*
Number of Seminaries	*0*

St. Patrick Cathedral, Fort Worth

> Diocese of Victoria

A strong Catholic heritage is part of the history of the Diocese of Victoria. Located in this diocese was Fort St. Louis, the ill-fated colony of Sieur De La Salle where the first European baby born in Texas was baptized. There is also Goliad, with its fort and two mission sites dating back to the mid-1700s. Along the Gulf Coast is the site of Linnville, named for John Linn, a Catholic who was prevented from signing the Texas Declaration of Independence by the Mexican Army. It was at Linnville where Father Jean Marie Odin would first arrive on Texas soil as vice prefect apostolic of Texas. He would go on to become the first Texas bishop.

Bishop Charles V. Grahmann,
first Bishop of Victoria

Victoria was part of the Catholic colony of Martin De Leon which was established under the Republic of Mexico when the Mexican government was anxious to find Catholic immigrants. The city's original name, Guadalupe Victoria, became Victoria after Texas' War of Independence. It was one of the first three cities chartered under the Republic. Its first mayor was John Linn.

The area became part of the Diocese of San Antonio in 1874 when Bishop Claude Dubuis asked that the Diocese of Galveston be divided. Victoria remained part of the Archdiocese of San Antonio for more than a century. In 1982 the new Diocese of Victoria was formed from the Archdiocese of San Antonio and the Dioceses of Galveston-Houston and Corpus Christi. Most Rev. Charles V. Grahmann, a native son of the new diocese, was named first Bishop of Victoria. There are more than 100,000 Catholics in the Victoria diocese representing 40 percent of the population. The present bishop is Most Rev. David Fellhauer.

> Diocese of Victoria

Created	May 29, 1982
Area	9,609 Square Miles
First Bishop	Most Rev. Charles Victor Grahmann
Present Bishop	Most Rev. David Eugene Fellhauer, JCD
Catholic population (approximate)	100,000
Percentage of total population	40%
Number of Priests	72
Number of Deacons	26
Number of Women Religious	90
Number of Brothers	1
Number of Parishes	50
Number of Missions	18
Number of Catholic Elementary Schools	12
Number of Catholic High Schools	3
Number of Catholic Colleges or Universities	0
Number of Seminaries	0

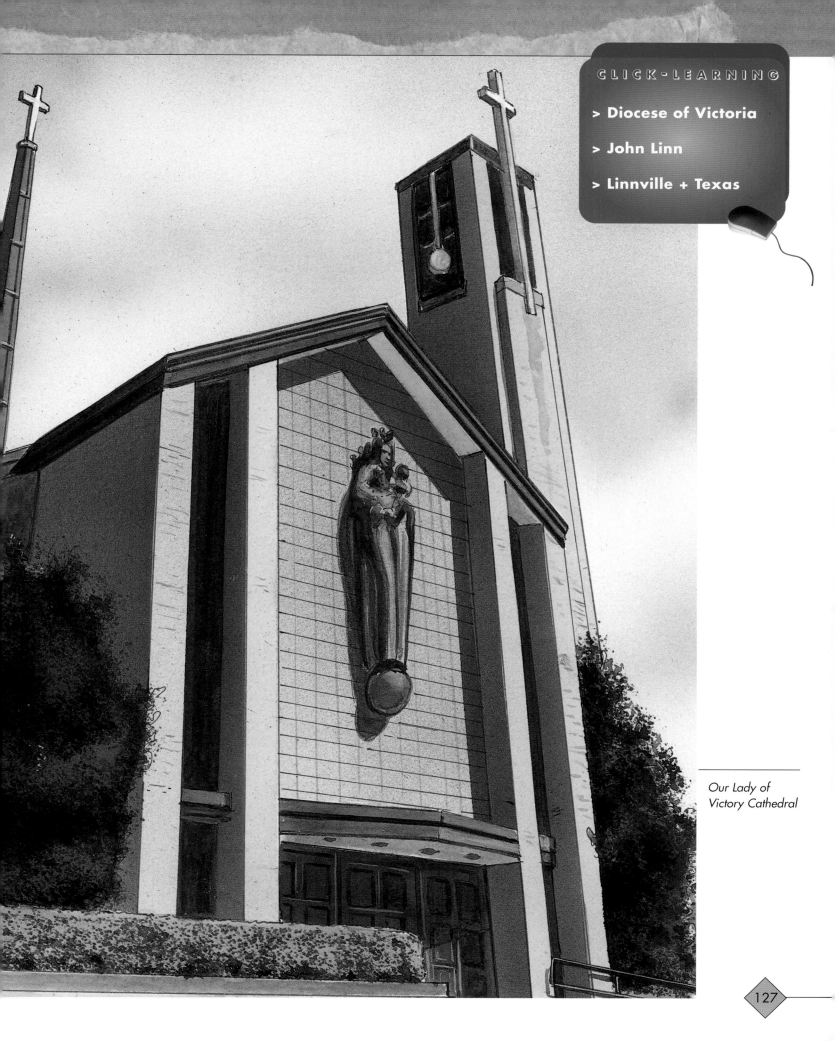

CLICK-LEARNING

> Diocese of Victoria

> John Linn

> Linnville + Texas

Our Lady of
Victory Cathedral

> Diocese of Lubbock

Catholicism first came to the area of Texas destined to become the Diocese of Lubbock in 1541. Priests celebrated the sacraments with the Spanish explorers as the Coronado expedition made its way across the Llano Estacado. In 1629 two Franciscan Friars from the Mission of San Agustin de Isleta near Santa Fe crossed through the area in response to a delegation of 50 Jumano Indians seeking a priest. They told the missionaries in New Mexico that they had been told by a mysterious Lady in Blue to find a priest.

The High Plains were largely ignored until the middle of the 19th Century, when the danger of Indian attack lessened and ranchers and farmers began to settle in the area. Lubbock County was organized in 1876, but the City of Lubbock was not incorporated until 1909. The earliest churches built in the diocese were St. John's in Hermleigh (1907), which only had a permanent pastor for three years, St. Alice's in Plainview (1911) and St. Joseph's in Slaton (1912), the first to have a permanent resident priest.

Missionary priests, known locally as sky-pilots, crisscrossed the area on horseback and later by train. A chapel car, a converted railroad car, donated by the Catholic Church Extension Society, was used extensively in the area. Anti-Catholic and anti-Mexican sentiment was occasionally a problem in acquiring land for churches. Pastors would sometimes have others make land purchases for them to circumvent the prejudice of the seller.

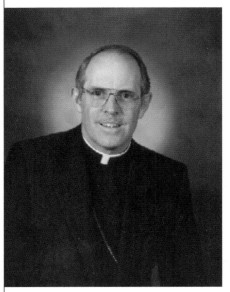

In 1926 the area, which had been a part of the Diocese of Dallas, was separated from the Dallas diocese with the establishment of the Diocese of Amarillo. In 1983 Lubbock itself became a See city with the establishment of the Diocese of Lubbock by Pope John Paul II. The Catholic population of the 20 counties taken from the dioceses of Amarillo and San Angelo was 51,846. The first bishop was Most Rev. Michael J. Sheehan, who served in that post until named Archbishop of Santa Fe in 1994. Today the Catholic population is nearly 81,000. The present bishop is Most Rev. Placido Rodriguez, CMF.

Most Rev. Michael Jarboe Sheehan, JCD
First Bishop of Lubbock

> Diocese of Lubbock

Created	**June 17, 1983**
Area	**23,382 Square Miles**
First Bishop	**Most Rev. Michael Jarboe Sheehan, JCD**
Present Bishop	**Most Rev. Placido Rodriguez, CMF**
Catholic population	**80,742**
Percentage of total population	**16%**
Number of Priests	**46**
Number of Deacons	**49**
Number of Women Religious	**23**
Number of Brothers	**0**
Number of Parishes	**34**
Number of Missions	**28**
Number of Catholic Elementary Schools	**2**
Number of Catholic High Schools	**0**
Number of Catholic Colleges or Universities	**0**
Number of Seminaries	**0**

Christ the King Cathedral

CLICK-LEARNING

> Diocese of Lubbock

> Llano Estacado

> Diocese of Tyler

> Diocese of Tyler

Created	**December 12, 1986**
Area	**22,971 Square Miles**
First Bishop	**Most Rev. Charles E. Herzig**
Present Bishop	**Most Rev. Alvaro Corrada del Rio, S.J.**
Catholic population	**56,127**
Percentage of total population	**4%**
Number of Priests	**97**
Number of Deacons	**62**
Number of Women Religious	**62**
Number of Brothers	**4**
Number of Parishes	**40**
Number of Missions	**23**
Number of Stations	**3**
Number of Catholic Elementary Schools	**4**
Number of Catholic High Schools	**1**
Number of Catholic Colleges an Universities	**0**
Number of Seminaries	**0**

In a real sense, the young Diocese of Tyler can rightly claim to be the birthplace of Catholicism in the eastern half of Texas. Probably the first Catholics and the first priests entered East Texas in 1542 as part of the De Soto expedition led by Luis de Moscoso Alvarado.

Worried by a French presence in Louisiana, New Spain marked its northeastern frontier with the San Francisco de las Tejas mission in 1690. It was abandoned by the Franciscans in three years, but reestablished along with additional missions in 1716. San Antonio, the Presidio de Bexar and Mission San Antonio de Valero (Alamo),were established as supply bases for the East Texas missions.

After the War of Independence from Mexico, Vincentian Father John Timon, prefect apostolic for Texas, and his vice prefect Jean Marie Odin, visited Crockett and Nacogdoches. Missionary priests from Nacogdoches founded most Catholic communities in north and north central Texas, including Dallas and Fort Worth. Jefferson was the site of St. Mary's School, the first Catholic school, and the first Catholic hospital in north Texas, both established in the 1860s by the Daughters of Charity of St. Vincent de Paul.

Originally part of the Diocese of Galveston, in 1890 the area became part of the newly established Diocese of Dallas, which stretched from the Louisiana border to New Mexico. In 1986 Pope John Paul II established the Diocese of Tyler with counties taken from the dioceses of Dallas, Galveston-Houston and Beaumont.

Most Rev. Charles E. Herzig
First Bishop of Tyler

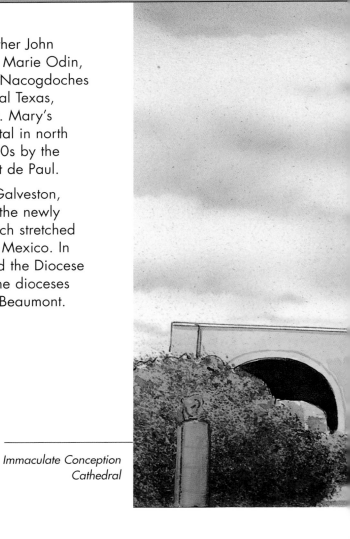

Immaculate Conception
Cathedral

The new diocese includes 32 counties with an area of 23,000 square miles in northeast Texas with a Catholic population of 29,153. Most Rev. Charles E. Herzig was named the first bishop.

Today the Diocese of Tyler has a Catholic population of about 54,000. The present bishop is the Most Rev. Alvaro Corrada del Rio, S.J.

CLICK-LEARNING
> **Diocese of Tyler**
> **San Francisco de las Tejas**

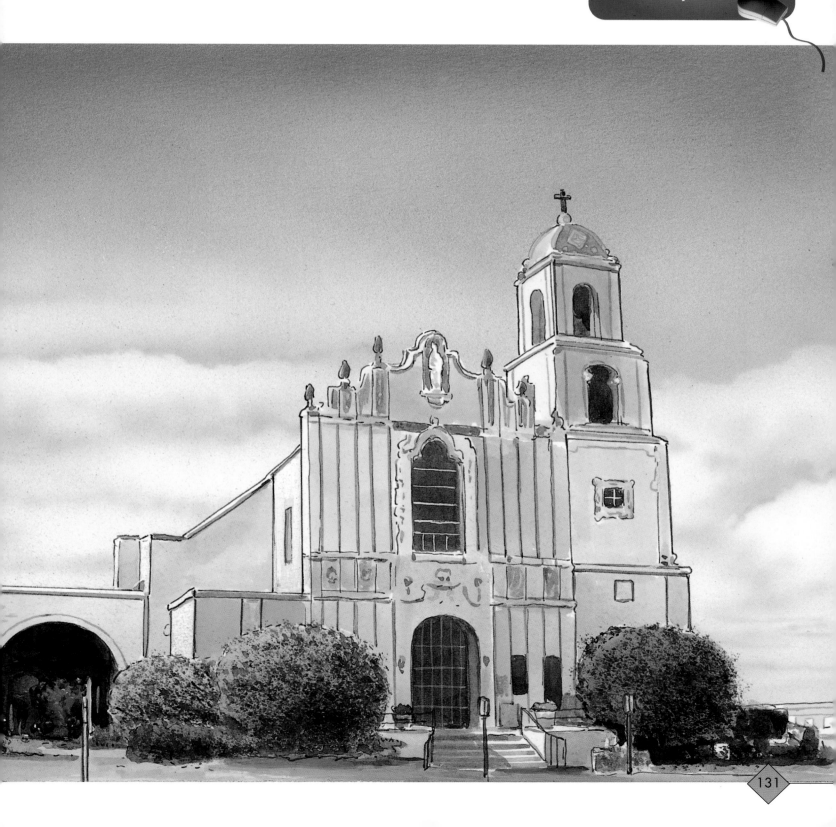

> Diocese of Laredo

Laredo, the youngest diocese in Texas, was established in 2000. It is rich in Catholic history. El Camino Real, the King's Highway, crossed the Rio Grande about 30 miles below the city of Eagle Pass. Spanish missionaries used this route in establishing the missions in San Antonio and East Texas. San Juan Bautista on the Mexican side served as a departure point for a number of Spanish entradas.

The area was not part of the Mexican state of Texas, but rather of Texas' companion states of Coahuila and Tamaulipas and continued under Mexican control until the Mexican War. After the war it became a part of Texas. In 1850 it came under the jurisdiction of the Galveston Diocese. But the old parish of San Agustin in Laredo continued to be served by secular priests from the Mexican Diocese of Linares-Monterrey until 1853, when diocesan clergy from Texas arrived. The Eagle Pass district continued to be served by Mexican clergy until 1863 if not later.

Most Rev. James Anthony Tamayo
First Bishop of Laredo

When the Vicariate Apostolic of Brownsville was formed in 1874, the area became part of the new vicariate. But in an exchange of counties three years later, the Eagle Pass district was transferred to the new Diocese of San Antonio. Bishop Pedro Verdaguer, the second Vicar Apostolic of Brownsville, moved his residence to Laredo and San Agustin Church became the de facto cathedral until his death in 1911. The following year the vicariate was renamed the Diocese of Corpus Christi and the Laredo area became part of the new diocese.

In 1990 the area around Laredo was established as the Western Vicariate of the Diocese of Corpus Christi with Monsignor James A. Tamayo as its first Episcopal Vicar. After a term as auxiliary bishop of Galveston-Houston, he was named as the first Bishop of Laredo when Pope John Paul II established the new diocese in 2000. The new diocese also took some counties, including the Eagle Pass district from the San Antonio archdiocese.

Today the Diocese of Laredo covers 10,614 square miles with a Catholic population of about 220,000. San Agustin Church, established in 1760, is once again a cathedral with Most Rev. James A. Tamayo as bishop.

CLICK-LEARNING

> Diocese of Laredo

> Diocese of Laredo

Created	July 3, 2000
Area	10,614 Square Miles
First Bishop	Most Rev. James Anthony Tamayo
Present Bishop	Most Rev. James Anthony Tamayo
Catholic population	222,000
Percentage of total population	75%
Number of Priests	54
Number of Deacons	27
Number of Women Religious	76
Number of Brothers	8
Number of Parishes	32
Number of Missions	19
Number of Catholic Elementary Schools	6
Number of Catholic High Schools	1
Number of Catholic Middle Schools	1
Number of Catholic Colleges or Universities	0
Number of Seminaries	0

San Agustin Cathedral

> Photo and illustration credits

Cover	Texas Catholic Archives; Texas State Library and Archives, Archdiocese of San Antonio Archives
Preface	Patrice Thébault
Introduction (p. 4-5)	Institute of Texan Cultures
Introduction (p. 6-7)	University of Texas
Pages 10-11	Hendricks-Long; Dominique Bach
Pages 12-13	Institute of Texan Cultures
Pages 14-15	Dominique Bach
Pages 16-17	Institute of Texan Cultures; Dominique Bach
Pages 18-19	Institute of Texan Cultures; Dominique Bach; Steve Landregan
Pages 22-23	Diocese of Beaumont; Institute of Texan Cultures; Dominique Bach
Pages 24-25	Institute of Texan Cultures; Archdiocese of Santa Fe
Pages 28-29	Lufkin, Texan Chamber of Commerce
Pages 34-35	Institute of Texan Cultures
Pages 36-37	Institute of Texan Cultures
Pages 38-39	Dominique Bach; Order of Friars Minor
Pages 40-41	Institute of Texan Cultures; Zvardon; Dominique Bach
Pages 42-43	University of Texan Center for American History; Institute of Texan Cultures
Pages 44-45	Texas State Library and Archives
Pages 46-47	Star of Texas Museum; Texas State Library and Archives
Pages 48-49	Judy Courtwright; Texas State Library and Archives; Rosenberg Library
Pages 50-51	Institute of Texan Cultures
Pages 52-53	Louisiana State Museum; Texas Catholic Archives
Pages 54-55	Texas State Library and Archives; University of Texas Barker Texas Library; Rosenberg Library
Pages 56-57	St. Mary Cathedral, Galveston
Pages 58-59	U.S. Coast and Geodetic Survey; Texas State Library and Archives
Pages 60-61	Congregation of the Mission; Institute of Texan Cultures
Pages 62-63	Texas Catholic Archives; Diocese of Dallas Archives
Pages 64-65	Marist Archives; Diocese of Dallas Archives
Pages 66-67	Texas Catholic Archives
Pages 68-69	Diocese of Dallas Archives
Pages 70-71	Ursulines Archives, Dallas; Diocese of Dallas Archives
Pages 72-73	Texas Catholic Archives; Sherry Thorup
Pages 74-75	Institute of Texas Cultures; Texas Catholic Archives
Pages 76-77	Rosenberg Library
Pages 78-79	Diocese of Dallas Archives
Pages 80-81	Diocese of Beaumont; Diocese of Dallas Archives
Pages 82-83	Extension Soc; Oregon Catholic Historical Society; Diocese of Dallas Archives
Pages 84-85	University of Texas Center for American History; Diocese of Dallas Archives
Pages 86-87	Diocese of Dallas Archives
Pages 88-89	Catholic News Service; Diocese of Dallas Archives
Pages 90-91	Diocese of Dallas Archives; Texas Catholic Archives
Pages 92-93	Texas Catholic Archives
Pages 94-95	Institute of Texan Cultures; Mexican-American Cultural Center
Pages 96-97	Diocese of Dallas Archives
Pages 98-99	Diocese of Dallas Archives; Steve Landregan
Pages 100-101	Goldbeck Panoramic Photography, San Antonio; Today's Catholic
Pages 104-105	Texas Catholic Archives; Ursulines Archives, Dallas
Pages 106-107	Diocese of Dallas Archives
Pages 108-109	Diocese of Dallas Archives; Ursulines Archives, Dallas
Pages 110-111	Texas Catholic Archives
Pages 112-113	Diocese of Dallas Archives
Pages 114-115	Texas Catholic Archives
Pages 116-117	Texas Catholic Archives
Pages 118-119	Texas Catholic Archives
Pages 120-121	Texas Catholic Archives
Pages 122-123	Diocese of Dallas Archives
Pages 124-125	Diocese of Dallas Archives
Pages 126-127	Diocese of Dallas Archives
Pages 128-129	Texas Catholic Archives
Pages 130-131	Texas Catholic Archives
Pages 132-133	Texas Catholic Archives
Back cover	Main altar at San Fernando Cathedral, San Antonio

> Bibliography | Compiled by Patrick J. Foley, Ph.D. editor, Catholic Southwest

Almaraz, Felix D. Jr., *Knight Without Armor: Carlos Eduardo Castaneda, 1896-1958* College Station: Texas A&M University Press, 1999)

_____. *The San Antonio Missions and Their System of Land Tenure* (Austin: University of Texas Press, 1989)

_____. *Tragic Cavalier: Governor Manuel Salcedo of Texas, 1808-1813* (College Station: Texas A&M University Press, 1971, 1991)

Baker, T. Lindsay, *The First Polish Americans: Silesian Settlements in Texas* (College Station and London: Texas A&M University Press, 1979)

Bayard, Ralph, C.M., *Lone-Star Vanguard: The Catholic Re-Occupation of Texas (1838-1848)* (Saint Louis: The Vincentian Press, 1945)

Butler, Anne M., "Building Justice: Mother Margaret Murphy, Race, and Texas," *Catholic Southwest: A Journal of History and Culture* vol. 13 (2002)

Castaneda, Carlos Eduardo, *Our Catholic Heritage in Texas, 1519-1936*, 7 vols. (Austin: Von Boeckmann-Jones Company, 1936-58)

Cruz, Gilbert R.; foreword by Donald C. Cutter, *Let There Be Towns: Spanish Municipal Origins in the American Southwest, 1610-1810* (College Station: Texas A&M University Press, 1988)

Doyon, Bernard, O.M.I., *The Cavalry of Christ on the Rio Grande* (Milwaukee: Catholic Life Publications, Bruce Press, 1956)

Dworaczyk, Rev. Edward J., *The First Polish Colonies of America in Texas* (San Antonio: The Naylor Company, 1936)

Flannery, John Brendan, *The Irish Texans* (San Antonio: The University of Texas Institute of Texan Cultures, 1980)

Foley, Patrick, Jean-Marie Odin, C.M., Missionary Bishop Extraordinaire of Texas, *Journal of Texas Catholic History and Culture* vol. 1, no. 1 (March 1990)

_____. "From Linares to Galveston: Texas in the Diocesan Scheme of the Catholic Church to the Mid-Nineteenth Century," *Catholic Southwest: A Journal of History and Culture* vol. 8 (1997)

Giles, Robert C.; researched by Mary Ann Acosta, and Kenny J. Cluse, *Changing Times: The Story of the Diocese of Galveston-Houston in Commemoration of its Founding* (Houston: John L. Morkovsky, S.T.D., 1972)

Habig, Marion A., O.F.M., *San Antonio's Mission San Jose: State and National Historic Site, 1720-1968* San Antonio: The Naylor Company, 1968)

_____. *The Alamo Mission: San Antonio de Valero, 1718-1793* (Chicago: Franciscan Herald Press, 1977)

Hackett, Sheila, O.P., *Dominican Women in Texas: From Ohio to Galveston and Beyond* (Houston: D. Armstrong Company, Inc., 1986)

Hanks, Nancy, "American Diocesan Boundaries in the Southwest, 1840 to 1912," *Catholic Southwest: A Journal of History and Culture* vol. 11 (2000) Hebert, Rachel Bluntzer, *The Forgotten Colony, San Patricio de Hibernia: The History, The People and the Legends of the Irish Colony of McMullen-McGloin* (Burnet, Texas: Eakin Press, 1981)

Hegarty, Sister Mary Loyola, C.C.V.I., *Serving With Gladness: The Origin and History of the Congregation of the Sisters of Charity of the Incarnate Word, Houston, Texas* (Houston: The Bruce Publishing Company, 1967)

Hoover, William R.; eds. Malinda R. Crumley and Kay Fialho, *St. Patrick's: The First 100 Years* (Fort Worth: St. Patrick's Cathedral, 1988)

LaFleur, M. Monica, C.C.V.I., "They Ventured to Texas: The European Heritage of Women Religious in the Nineteenth Century," *Catholic Southwest: A Journal of History and Culture* vol. 8 (1997)

Landregan, Steve; eds. and compilers, Staff of the Diocese of Dallas Archives, *Circuit Rider to Cathedral: How the Diocese of Dallas Came to Be* (Strasbourg, France: Éditions du Signe, 2001)

Linn, John J., *Reminiscences of Fifty Years in Texas – A Facsimile Reproduction of the Original* (Austin, Texas: State House Press, 1986, originally published in 1888)

Matovina, Timothy M., *Tejano Religion and Ethnicity: San Antonio, 1821-1860* (Austin: University of Texas Press, 1995)

_____. "Religion and Ethnicity in San Antonio: Germans and Tejanos in the Wake of United States Annexation," *Catholic Southwest: A Journal of History and Culture* vol. 10 (1999)

Miller, Randall M., and Wakelyn, Jon L., eds., *Catholics in the Old South* (Macon, Georgia: Mercer University Press, 1983)

Moore, James Talmadge, *Through Fire and Flood: The Catholic Church in Frontier Texas, 1836-1900* (College Station: Texas A&M University Press, 1992)

_____. *Acts of Faith: The Catholic Church in Texas, 1900-1950* (College Station: Texas A&M University Press, 2001)

Marquardt, Dona B. Reeves- and Lewis R., "Catholic Germans From Russia to Texas," *Journal of Texas Catholic History and Culture* vol. 4 (1993)

Oberste, William H., *The Restless Friar: Venerable Fray Antonio Margil de Jesus: Missionary to the Americas–Apostle of Texas* (Austin: Von Boeckmann-Jones Company, 1970)

Teja, Jesus F. de la, "The Catholic Legacy at Paso del Norte, Gateway to Nuevo Mexico: Photographs from the Catholic Archives of Texas," *Catholic Southwest: A Journal of History and Culture* vol. 9 (1998)

Wangler, Rev. Msgr. Alexander, ed., *Archdiocese of San Antonio, 1874-1974* (San Antonio: Francis J. Furey, Archbishop of San Antonio, 1974)

Williams, Donald Mace, *Italian POWS and a Texas Church: The Murals of St. Mary's* (Lubbock: Texas Tech University Press, 1992)

Wright, Robert E., O.M.I., "Pioneer Religious Congregations of Men in Texas Before 1900," *Journal of Texas Catholic History and Culture* vol. 5 (1994)

Vanderholt, James F.; Martinez, Carolyn B.; and Gilman, Karen A., *The Diocese of Beaumont: The Catholic Story of Southeast Texas* (Beaumont, Texas: Catholic Diocese of Beaumont, 1991)

A

Acoma Pueblo 25
Ad limina 109
Adobe 16, 18, 30, 122
African-American Catholics 80, 81, 117
African-Americans 67, 78, 79, 81
Agreda, Mother Maria de Jesús de 22, 23
Aguayo, Marques de 35, 36, 37
Alabama 16, 106
Alamo Register 91
Alarcón, Martin de 34
Alsace 73
Altar servers 88, 89
Amarillo 41, 78, 80, 93, 94, 109, 114, 115, 119, 128
American pioneers 42

Amerindians 11, 15, 16, 18, 19, 21, 22, 23, 29, 30
Angelina 29, 63
Angelina County 29
Anglicization 43
Anglo-American 43, 44, 45, 79, 106, 110
Annexation 56, 59, 75, 135
Anti-Catholicism 78
Apache 38, 118
Apostle to El Paso 65
Apostle to Texas 135
Archbishop 72, 84, 89, 90, 92, 94, 95, 99, 101, 107, 115,
Archbishop of Mexico 23
Archbishop of New Orleans 57
Archbishop of Santa Fe 115, 128
Archdiocese of San Antonio 41, 79, 97, 99, 106, 107, 126, 132, 134, 135

Arizona 41, 56, 59, 108, 112
Arkansas 16, 43, 51, 82
Arroyo De León 28
Asian Catholics 98
Augusta, Texas 28
Austin 54, 55, 65, 67, 69, 75, 79, 84, 91, 92, 93, 109, 116, 117, 119
Austin, Moses 43
Austin, Stephen G. 43, 45, 47, 49
Austin's Colony 44, 48
Auxiliary Bishop 81, 83, 99, 132
Aymond, Gregory M., Bishop 117
Aztec 19, 25

B

Bakanowski, Father Adolph 74
Baltimore 53, 56, 58

Baltimore Council 59
Baptism 7, 15, 38
Basilica 89, 104, 105, 121
Bastrop, Baron de 43
Beaumont 22, 80, 81, 104, 122, 123, 130, 134, 135
Beaumont - Port Arthur - Orange 123
Belgium 9
Benavides, Colonel Santos 73
Benavides, Friar Alonso de 23
Benedictines 114
Bexar 48, 49, 130
Bicentennial of the founding of San Antonio 90
Bigotry 82, 83, 85
Bishop 13, 53, 56, 57, 58, 59, 60, 61, 63, 64, 65, 66, 67, 70, 72, 73, 74, 75, 80, 81, 83, 86, 87, 92, 93, 104, 105, 106, 107, 108, 109, 110, 111, 112, 113, 114, 115, 117, 119, 120, 121, 122, 123, 125, 126, 128, 129, 130, 131, 132, 133, 135
Bishop-elect 15, 72
Bishops Committee for Spanish-speaking 95
Bishops of Texas 59, 92
Black Catholics 80, 81
Blanc, Bishop Antoine 50, 51, 52, 53, 60, 72
Blandine, Mother Mary 74
Blessed Virgin 19, 61, 80, 117
Blessed Virgin Mission, Old Washington 80
Bogel, Philip Henri Nering 43
Bourgade, Peter, Bishop 112
Bower, John White 47
Bowie, Jim 48, 49, 87
Brannan, Father Patrick 82, 83
Brazoria County Museum 48
Brazos River 7, 47, 117
Brennan, Thomas F., Bishop 108, 109, 112, 114
Brockbank, Father S. R. 83
Brothers 13, 39,
Brown, Father John J., SJ 113
Brownsville 64, 66, 72, 73, 74, 75, 104, 110, 111, 120, 121, 132
Bruté, Bishop Simon 52
Bryan, Texas 71
Buffalo, New York 60
Burnet, David 45, 47, 135

C

Cabeza de Vaca, Alvar Nuñez 12, 13, 14, 15, 16, 17, 19, 80, 110
Caddo 29
Cadillac, Governor de 32
California 41, 56, 79, 119
Canada 27, 51, 64
Canary Islands 40, 47
Canonization 35
Capital 24, 25, 33, 37, 55, 116, 117
Capital of the Republic 55
Cardinal 54, 88, 89, 90
Carlos I, King 13
Carmelite Fathers 65, 85
Carmody, Edmond, Bishop 111
Cassata, John J., Bishop 125
Castañeda, Carlos 16
Castañeda, Dr. Carlos Eduardo 90, 91, 93
Castroville 59, 67, 73
Cathedral 19, 24, 34, 40, 57, 60, 61, 81, 85, 90, 101, 104, 105, 106, 107, 108, 110, 112, 115, 116, 119, 120, 123, 124, 125, 127, 129, 130, 132, 133, 134, 135
Cathedral Santuario de Guadalupe, Dallas 85
Catholic Action 94
Catholic Archives of Texas 93, 117, 135
Catholic Charities 92, 93, 94, 95
Catholic Church Extension Society 83, 110, 128
Catholic Colonies 44, 72, 74
Catholic Daughters 97
Catholic Day 87
Catholic Diocese 13, 92, 93, 135
Catholic Education 65, 68, 71, 94, 107
Catholic Exhibit 86, 87
Catholic Family and Childrens Services 94
Catholic Family Fraternal of Texas (KJZT) 97
Catholic Heroes 43, 48
Catholic Hierarchy of Texas 99
Catholic Immigrants 50, 72, 74, 98, 114, 126
Catholic Legislators 8, 54
Catholic Majesties 11
Catholic News Service 89, 134
Catholic Publishing 91
Catholic Religious Orders 69

Catholic Schools 68, 69, 71, 93
Catholic Settlers 9, 119
Catholic Truth Society 79, 82
Catholic Welfare Bureau 94
Catholicity 44
Cavalcade of Texas 86, 87
Chambodut, Father Louis 73, 74, 75
Chancery Office 93
Chapel Cars 82, 83
Chargé d'affaires 55
Chaves, Cesar 99
China 9, 10, 99
Chipman, Dr. Donald 12, 37
Cholera 21, 38, 49, 60
Christ the King Cathedral, Lubbock 129
Christ the King Procession 91
Christian 5, 14, 15, 17, 19, 24, 25, 29, 38, 68, 70, 88, 89, 92, 95, 97
Christian Life Communities 97
Christianize 24, 38, 40
Church in Texas 3, 37, 40, 50, 57, 73, 80, 84, 93, 102, 103, 104, 107, 135
Cibola 21
Ciudad Juarez 65
Civil war 3, 7, 8, 9, 42, 58, 71, 72, 73, 78, 84, 85
Clayton, Nicholas 61
Coadjutor Bishop 53, 54, 109
Coahuila y Texas 30, 34, 36, 43, 45, 47, 132
Colonists 13, 42, 43, 44, 45, 50, 51, 60, 61, 110
Colonization 42, 44
Colorado 22, 58, 114, 116, 118
Colorado City, Texas 114
Colorado River 22, 116, 118
Columbus, Christopher 6, 10, 11, 39, 93
Communities 9, 40, 61, 62, 64, 65, 66, 67, 69, 71, 95
Concepción 33, 86
Confederate 71, 72, 73, 74, 75, 82
Confraternity of Christian Doctrine 95
Congregation of the Holy Cross 65
Congregation of the Incarnate Word and Blessed Sacrament 66
Congregation of the Mission 50, 64, 134
Congress of Mexico 47
Conquistador 7, 11, 19, 25, 38, 116
Conrad, Edwin 47
Consecration 56, 60, 70, 99, 104
Constitution 46, 47, 49, 51, 85
Constitution of 1824 46, 47, 49

Convent 23, 60, 66, 67, 70, 73, 74, 75, 79, 81, 82, 109
Convention 44, 51
Conventual Franciscans 65
Converts 29, 30, 53, 83
Coronado, Francisco Vázquez de 6, 18, 19, 20, 21, 24, 114, 128
Corpus Christi 7, 8, 9, 26, 66, 67, 74, 110, 111, 120, 121, 126, 132
Corpus Christi Cathedral 110
Cortés, Hernán 11, 12, 13, 17, 25
Cos, Gen. Martin Perfecto de 45, 49
Council of Catholic Men 94
Council of Catholic Women 94
County Tipperary, Ireland 109
Courtwright, Judy 48, 134
Crockett, Davy 49, 130
Crozier 41
Culture 5, 7, 15, 20, 29, 38, 40, 55, 70, 71, 90, 95, 99, 107, 134, 135
Cursillo Movement 97
Czechoslovakia 9, 79

D

Daingerfield, William Henry 52, 53
Dallas 9, 19, 59, 63, 65, 66, 67, 69, 71, 78, 79, 81, 85, 86, 87, 91, 97, 104, 105, 106, 108, 109, 112, 113, 114, 119, 124, 125, 128, 130, 134, 135
Dallas Ursulines 71
Daly, Brother Richard, CSC 93
Daughters of Charity of St. Vincent de Paul 67, 130
Daughters of the Republic of Texas 75
De la Cruz, Friar Juan 20, 21
De León 28, 29, 30
De Niza, Friar Marcos 16, 17, 18, 20
De Saligny, Alphonse Dubois 54, 55
De Soto, Hernando 15, 16, 17, 19, 130
Deacons 88, 89, 93, 96, 97, 105, 107, 109, 111, 113, 114, 117, 119, 121, 122, 125, 126, 129, 130, 133
Declaration of Independence, Texas 46, 47, 51, 86, 126
Del Rio, Alvaro Corrada, SJ, Bishop 130, 131
Del Rio, José Mora, Archbishop 84
Delaney, Joseph, Bishop 125
Delille, Henriette 80, 81
Denison 67
Detroit 54
Dimmit, Philip 47

DiNardo, Daniel N., Bishop 105
Diocesan Pastoral Councils 89
Diocese 13, 15, 102
Diocese of Amarillo 41, 76, 78, 80, 82, 84, 86, 114, 115, 128
Diocese of Austin 90, 92, 94, 96, 98, 100, 116, 117
Diocese of Beaumont 90, 92, 94, 96, 98, 100, 104, 122, 123, 130, 134, 135
Diocese of Brownsville 111, 120, 121
Diocese of Corpus Christi 78, 80, 82, 84, 86, 110, 111, 120, 132
Diocese of Dallas 19, 59, 65, 76, 78, 80, 82, 84, 86, 90, 92, 94, 96, 97, 98, 100, 104, 108, 109, 112, 114, 124, 125, 128, 130, 134, 135
Diocese of Durango 41, 112, 103
Diocese of El Paso 76, 78, 80, 82, 84, 86, 108, 112, 113
Diocese of Fort Worth 90, 92, 94, 96, 98, 100, 125
Diocese of Galveston 7, 8, 41, 44, 46, 48, 50, 52, 54, 56, 57, 58, 59, 60, 61, 62, 64, 66, 68, 70, 72, 73, 74, 90, 92, 94, 96, 97, 98, 100, 103, 104, 105, 108, 117, 120, 122, 126, 130, 135
Diocese of Galveston-Houston 65, 81, 97, 99, 104, 105, 122, 130, 132, 135
Diocese of Guadalajara 41, 103
Diocese of Laredo 90, 92, 94, 96, 98, 100, 103, 111, 132, 133
Diocese of Linares-Monterrey 41, 44, 45, 50, 103, 132
Diocese of Los Angeles 94
Diocese of Lubbock 90, 92, 94, 96, 98, 100, 115, 128, 129
Diocese of Lyon, France 57
Diocese of Mexico City 41
Diocese of Mobile 106, 120
Diocese of San Angelo 109, 113, 115, 117, 118, 119
Diocese of San Antonio 75, 76, 78, 80, 82, 84, 86, 95, 104, 106, 108, 113, 126, 132
Diocese of Tyler 90, 92, 94, 96, 98, 100, 105, 122, 123, 130, 131
Diocese of Victoria 90, 92, 94, 96, 98, 100, 104, 111, 126, 127
Discalced Carmelite Fathers 85
Diseases 16, 21, 30
Dominican Sisters 67, 80
Dowling, Lieutenant Dick 73, 74
Drexel, St. Katharine 81
Drossaerts, Arthur J., Archbishop 90, 106

Drury, Thomas Joseph, Bishop 119
Dubuis, Claude Marie, Bishop 59, 63, 67, 72, 73, 74, 75, 108, 126
Dunne, Edward j., Bishop 81, 112
Dutchman 43

E

Eades, Father B. G. 19
East Texas 6, 16, 27, 28, 29, 30, 31, 32, 33, 34, 35, 37, 38, 39, 40, 41, 63, 67, 116, 122, 130, 132
Ecumenical 88, 89
Ecumenical Council 88
Education Department, Texas Catholic Conference 93
El Camino Real 116, 117, 132
El Dorado 18, 19
El Paso 9, 25, 28, 38, 40, 41, 50, 59, 65, 67, 78, 86, 87, 91, 99, 108, 109, 112, 113, 119
El Paso County 108, 112
El Paso del Norte 112, 113
Elizando, Father Virgil 95
Empresarios 44
Escalona, Friar Luis de 20, 21
Esteban the Moor 14, 15, 17
Estevanico (see Esteban) 17, 18
Eucharist 63, 96, 97
Eucharistic ministers 88, 96, 97
Europe 5, 10, 36, 52, 56, 57, 60, 61, 69, 73, 74, 98, 121
Europeans 5, 10, 12, 110
Evangelization 64
Evangelize 20, 38
Expedition 5, 10, 11, 12, 13, 14, 15, 16, 17, 18, 19, 20, 21, 22, 24, 26, 27, 28, 32, 33, 34, 36, 37, 47, 114, 128, 130
Explorers 7, 10, 11, 21, 64, 103, 112, 128

F

Fagan, Nicholas 47
Famine 56
Farm workers 94, 95
Father of Texas 43
Federalists 46
Fellhauer, David, Bishop 126
Ferdinand, King 10, 11, 81

Fiorenza, Joseph, Bishop 105
First Texans 10
Fitzgerald, Edward, Bishop 112
Flag 75
Flores, Patrick Fernandez, Archbishop 99, 101, 107
Florida 11, 13, 14, 15, 16, 17, 42, 76
Focolare Movement 97
Fontcuberta, Friar Miguel de 29, 30
Fort Brown 120
Fort Concho 119
Fort Elliott, Texas 114
Fort St. Louis 7, 26, 27, 37, 87, 110, 126
Fort Texas 120
Fort Worth 67, 91, 109, 114, 119, 124, 125, 130, 135
Franciscan 13, 15, 17, 20, 21, 22, 23, 28, 29, 32, 35, 36, 37, 38, 39, 40, 41, 48, 64, 65, 112, 118, 128, 130
Francisco, Father Manuel de, CM 85
Fransoni, James, Cardinal 54
Fredericksburg 59
French 5, 7, 8, 17, 26, 27, 28, 29, 31, 32, 33, 34, 37, 50, 51, 54, 55, 59, 63, 64, 65, 67, 69, 73, 74, 104, 124, 130
French Legation 55

G

Gabriel, Mother 76
Gallagher, Nicholas, Bishop 73, 80, 108
Galveston 7, 8, 9, 14, 45, 47, 50, 51, 52, 53, 56, 57, 58, 60, 61, 63, 64, 65, 66, 67, 70, 71, 72, 73, 74, 75, 76, 77, 78, 79, 80, 81, 103, 104, 105, 106, 108, 110, 122, 125, 126, 130, 132, 134, 135
Galveston Hurricane 77
Galveston Island 13, 15, 63, 77, 104
Galveston Ursulines 60, 71
Garay, Francisco de 11, 12
Genoa 10
Georgia 16, 82, 135
Gerken, Rudolph A., Archbishop 114, 115
German Catholics 60
Germany 9, 69, 79
Godfather of Texas 43
God's Cavalry 62
Gold 11, 14, 17, 18, 19, 24
Golden Triangle 123
Goliad 41, 47, 50, 56, 126

Goliad Declaration 47
Goliad Presidio 49
Gonzalez 47
Gospel 5, 6, 7, 11, 20, 22, 23, 28, 31, 38, 39, 66, 70, 93, 95
Graham, Callan 92, 93
Grahmann, Charles V., Bishop 109, 126
Grandfather of Texas 43
Great Storm of 1900 61
Guadalupanas 95
Guadalupe Victoria 126
Guatemala 35
Guillory, Curtis John, SVD, Bishop 80, 81, 122, 123
Guillot, Maxime 124
Gulf coast 9, 11, 12, 13, 15, 38, 52, 76, 126
Gulf of Mexico 11, 26, 58, 70, 76, 77, 120

H

Haas, Father Charles OMI 83
Halletsville, Texas 66
Handbook of Texas 38
Harris, Vincent, Bishop 122, 123
Hayes, Patrick, Cardinal 90
Healy-Murphy, Margaret Mary (Mother Margaret Mary) 67, 81
Hennessy, Father Thomas 62, 63, 80
Henrietta, Texas 114
Herzig, Charles E., Bishop 130, 131
Hewitson, James 44
Hidalgo, Friar Francisco 30, 31, 32, 33
Hierarchy 99
Hispanic Catholics 40, 41, 61, 72, 99, 101
Hispanic settlements 7, 40
Hispanicize 40
Hispaniola 11, 12, 13
Holly 71
Holy Communion 88, 89, 96
Holy Cross Brothers 65, 117
Holy Name Societies 90
Honduras 35
Hostile 7, 8, 15, 20, 21, 26, 38, 60, 118
Hostyn, Texas 45
Houston, President Sam 47, 49, 51, 54, 72
Houston, Texas 44, 46, 53, 74, 80, 104, 105, 106, 135
Huastec Indians 11, 12
Hurricane Carla 71

I

Illinois 50, 51
Illinois River 27
Immaculate Conception Cathedral, Brownsville 120
Immaculate Conception Cathedral, Tyler 130
Immigrants 8, 9, 43, 44, 47, 54
Incarnate Word College 87
Independence 7, 8, 38, 41, 42, 44, 45, 47, 48, 50, 55, 90, 98, 106, 120, 130
Independence, Texas Declaration of 7, 8, 44, 46, 47, 51, 126
Independence, Texas War of 45, 50, 104, 110, 116, 126
India 9, 11, 99
Indian Territory 114
Indiana 52, 82
Indians 7, 8, 11, 15, 16, 17, 22, 24, 25, 28, 29, 30, 33, 38, 39, 40, 51, 60, 64, 118, 128
Ireland 9, 42, 44, 45, 67, 69
Irish Catholics 47
Isabella, Queen 10, 11
Italian Catholics 65
Italy 9, 10, 54, 65, 88, 89

J

Jamaica 11, 12, 13
Jefferson, Texas 62, 63, 67, 130
Jesuit 27, 65, 85, 108, 112, 113
Jesuits 65, 106, 112
Jewish 5, 78
Jordan, Mary 79, 81
Josephite Fathers 80, 81
Juan Diego 19
Jumano 6, 22, 23, 118, 128
Juneteenth 73

K

Kansas 18, 19, 20, 58, 114
Karankawas 27, 38
Kelly Air Force Base 100
Kentucky 48, 54
Kerr, Dr. James 47, 51

King of France 26
King of Spain 13, 36
King's Highway 132
Kirwin, Father James M. 77
Knights of Columbus 79, 82, 90, 91, 93, 97
Know-Nothings 79
Knox, Jim 29
Korea 9
Korean Catholics 99
Ku Klux Klan 8, 78, 79

L

La Bahia 6, 37, 39, 40, 110
La Grange, Texas 45
La Junta 6, 28, 38, 40
Labor unions 95
Lamar, President Mirabeau B. 51, 54
Lamy, John B., Bishop 59
La Salle, René Robert Cavelier, Sieur de 6, 26, 27, 37, 86, 87, 126
Laredo 7, 50, 66, 73, 120, 132
Las Hermanas 95
Lavaca Bay 53
Lay brother 20, 39
Lay Ministry 96
Leven, Stephen, Bishop 83
Linn, John J. 44, 47, 51, 53, 126, 127, 135
Linnville 52, 53, 126, 127
Llebaria, Fr. Juan 50, 51
López, Friar Diego 22
Los Adaes 37
Los Angeles 94, 95
Louis of France, King 27
Louis Philippe, King 55
Louisiana 16, 31, 32, 33, 43, 48, 53, 63, 80, 108, 130, 134
Lower Rio Grande 6, 50, 61, 74, 120
Lubbock 9, 102, 109, 115, 128, 129
Lucey, Robere E., Archbishop 94, 95, 115
Lufkin 29, 134
Lynch, Joseph P., Bishop 87, 112
Lyon, France 57, 66, 73

M

Manucy, Dominic, Bishop 110, 111, 120
Margil de Jesús, Friar Antonio 32, 35

Marianists 65, 69
Martyr 7, 21, 114, 120
Marx, Adoph, Bishop 121
Mass, first 7, 50, 51, 63, 83, 85, 87, 88, 89, 90, 97, 100, 101, 107, 114, 124
Massanet, Friar Damián 28, 29, 30
Matagorda Bay 26, 27, 37, 110
Matamoros 45, 67, 72
McCarthy, John, Bishop 92, 93
McGloin, James 44, 135
McMullen, John 44, 135
Medicine men 25
Menard, Michael (Michel) B. 47, 50, 51, 104
Mestizo 98
Mexican American Cultural Center 95, 107
Mexican border 9
Mexican Catholics 80, 84
Mexican dioceses 41
Mexican Independence 38, 42
Mexico 8, 9, 11, 12, 13, 16, 17, 18, 19, 20, 21, 25, 27, 28, 29, 30, 31, 35, 37, 40, 41, 42, 44, 45, 46, 49, 50, 51, 55, 56, 58, 59, 63, 67, 68, 72, 84, 85, 86, 90, 91, 98, 99, 104, 106, 110, 111, 112, 116, 120, 126, 130
Mexico City 14, 15, 19, 25, 32, 33, 41, 45, 84, 85
Middle East 9, 99
Milam, Benjamin Rush (Ben) 44, 45, 48, 49
Ministry 38, 39, 56, 61, 63, 64, 65, 79, 85, 93, 95, 96, 97, 106
Minor Basilica 61, 104
Mission Concepción 33
Mission Dolores 33, 37
Mission Espiritu Santo de Zúñiga 37
Mission Guadalupe 33
Mission Nuestra Señora de la Concepción de Pueblo de Socorro 86, 87
Mission Nuestro Padre San Francisco de los Tejas 29, 33
Mission San Francisco Solano 34
Mission San José de Aguayo 33, 35, 36
Mission San Miguel de los Adaes 33, 36
Mission Santa Cruz de San Saba 118, 119
Mission Santissimo Nombre de Maria 29, 30
Missionary 8, 13, 16, 17, 20, 23, 35, 50, 51, 57, 59, 63, 79, 82, 83, 87,

95 104, 106, 118, 122, 124, 128, 130, 135
Missionary Catechists of Divine Providence 95
Missionary priests 8, 16, 63, 106, 124, 128, 130
Missions, Queen of Texas missions 35, 36
Mississippi 16, 26, 27, 53
Mississippi River 26, 27
Missouri 48, 51, 52, 53, 57, 82, 104
Miter 41
Moctezuma 25
Monarchy 42
Monsignor 59, 86, 89, 132
Montreal 51, 61
Moor 15, 17, 80
Moore, James Talmadge 74, 80, 85
Mosaic 98, 99
Moscoso, Luis de 16, 17, 130
Mount Cristo Rey 112, 113
Muldoon Catholics 44, 50
Muldoon, Father Michael 44, 45, 48
Murphy, Father Max 79, 81
Muslim 5, 15, 78

N

Nacogdoches 33, 40, 41, 51, 59, 63, 124, 130
Namur 67, 69, 75
Narváez, Pánfilo de 12, 13, 14, 15, 16, 17
Natchez, Mississippi 53
Natchitoches 33, 37, 40
Native American 38, 98
Navarro, José Antonio 47, 51
Neo-Catechumenate 97
Neri, Philip Enrique 43
New Braunfels 60
New Mexico 16, 18, 19, 21, 22, 23, 24, 25, 28, 41, 56, 58, 59, 108, 112, 113, 114, 118, 124, 128, 130, 135
New Orleans, Louisiana 50, 51, 52, 55, 56, 57, 60, 66, 70, 72, 73, 76, 80, 104, 108
New Spain 12, 13, 15, 16, 17, 19, 21, 26, 35, 41, 110, 130
New World 11, 13, 15, 17, 21, 26, 27, 39
New York 49, 52, 53, 56, 60, 85, 90
Nicaragua 35
Normann, Charles and Fanny 46
North America 10, 13, 26, 41, 99, 114

North Central Texas 109, 124, 130
Northeastern frontier 26, 27, 33, 36, 130
Nueces River 50
Nuestra Señora del Refugio 87, 110
Nueva Vizcaya 28
Nussbaum, Paul Joseph, Bishop 110

O

Oblate Fathers Trail 120, 121
Oblates of Mary Immaculate 61, 64, 106, 120
Ochoa, Armando Xavier, Bishop 113
Odin, Jean Marie, C. M., Bishop 53, 54, 55, 56, 57, 58, 59, 60, 61, 64, 65, 66, 67, 70, 72, 73, 80, 104, 105, 110, 116, 122, 126, 130, 135
O'Donohoe, Monsignor Joseph G. 86
Oklahoma 20, 58, 114
Old Washington 80, 117
Olivares, Friar Antonio 34
Olivetan Benedictine Sisters 67
O'Loughlin, Tom 114
Oñate, Juan de 24, 25
Orange County 63, 81
Order of Deacon 97
Order of Friars Minor 39, 134
Ordinary 57, 104
Orient 7, 10, 11, 17, 26
O'Rourke, Father John 62
Ortega, Friar Juan de 22
Our Catholic Heritage in Texas 91, 93, 135
Our Lady of Good Counsel Academy, Dallas 69
Our Lady of Guadalupe 19, 85, 94, 101
Our Lady of Guadalupe Church, Dallas 85
Our Lady of Guadalupe Church, San Antonio 101
Our Lady of San Juan of the Valley Shrine 121
Our Lady of the Lake College (University) 67
Our Lady of Victory Cathedral, Victoria 127
Our Lady Star of the Sea Church, Port Isabel 120

P

Padilla, Friar Juan de 20, 21, 114
Padilla, Juan Antonio 47
Padres 63, 95
Panhandle Register 91
Panna Maria, Texas 61, 74, 101
Papal Bull 58
Parish Councils 89
Parisot, Father Pierre, OMI 59, 63, 82
Parochial schools 69, 109
Pastor 34, 41, 45, 61, 62, 63, 72, 80, 86, 89, 128
Pectoral Cross 41
Peña, Raymundo, Bishop 121
Pennsylvania 53, 109
Permanent Diaconate 89, 97
Perrier, Father Mathurin 63, 124
Persecution 44, 50, 82, 84, 85, 99, 111
Persone, Father Carlos, S.J. 112
Pfeiffer, Michael D. OMI, Bishop 119
Pilgrimage 100
Pineda, Alonso Alvarez de 11, 12, 110, 120
Pinto, Father Carlos S. J. 65, 112
Pirates 26, 104, 120
Plenary Council (Baltimore) 56
Point (Port) Isabel 120
Poland 9, 61
Polish 65, 72, 74, 78, 79, 101, 135
Polk County 63
Pontifical Mass 87, 90
Poor Clare 23
Popé 25
Pope Clement VII 13
Pope John Paul II 19, 61, 100, 101, 104, 107, 128, 130, 132
Pope John XXIII 88, 89, 119
Pope Leo XIII 108, 109
Pope Paul VI 89, 125
Pope Pius XII 19
Popemobile 101
Pope's pilgrimage to Texas 100
Port Arthur 81
Portugal 10, 15, 17
Portuguese 10
Power, James 44, 47
Powers, John Joseph 47
Prefect Apostolic 50, 53, 64, 126, 130
Prefecture Apostolic of Texas 41, 105
Prejudice 78, 79, 82, 83
Presidio 14, 28, 32, 33, 34, 37, 40, 41, 110, 130
Presidio de los Adaes 33, 37

Presidio de los Tejas 37
Presidio San Antonio de Bexar 130
Pro, Father Miguel 85
Pro-Life, 95
Prologue 91
Protestant 42, 51, 79, 82, 83, 110
Public schools 5, 69
Pueblo 24, 25, 28, 38, 112
Pueblo de Socorro 86
Pueblo Nations 24
Pueblo Revolt 22, 24, 25, 28, 38, 112

Q

Quauhtlatoatzin 19
Queen of Texas missions 36
Quivira 18, 19, 20, 21, 114

R

Railroads 9, 78, 83, 104, 108, 114, 119
Reconstruction 74, 75, 104
Refugees 24, 38, 45, 77, 79, 84, 85, 99, 111, 112, 123
Refugio 38, 40, 41, 44, 45, 47, 50, 87, 110
Reicher, Louis J., Bishop 117
Religious Communities of Men 61, 64, 65, 69
Religious Communities of Women 61, 66, 67, 69
Religious persecution 84, 85
Religious priests 64, 69, 106
Reminiscences of a Texas Missionary 63
Republic 8, 42, 44, 45, 46, 47, 49, 50, 51, 52, 53, 54, 55, 56, 58, 59, 64, 70, 75, 104, 116, 122, 124, 126
Republic, Texas 44, 45, 49, 50, 51, 52, 53, 54, 55, 58, 59, 64, 75
Restoration of Church Lands 55
Resurrectionist Fathers 65
Revista Catolica 91
Río de las Palmas 12, 13, 15
Rio Grande 12, 27, 28, 32, 33, 34, 40, 50, 54, 56, 58, 59, 61, 94, 99, 111, 113, 120, 132, 135
Río Pánuco 11, 12, 16
Rio Soto la Marina 12
Rodriguez, Placido CMF, Bishop 128, 129

Roman Union 71
Roncalli, Angelo, Pope John XXIII 88, 89
Rosati, Joseph, Bishop 53
Rosenberg Library 55, 134
Royal Charter 13, 19, 26
Ruiz, Francisco 47
Ryan, W. M. 43

S

Sabine Pass, Battle of 73, 74
Sacrament of Holy Orders 97
Sacred Heart Academy, Galveston 77
Sacred Heart Cathedral, Dallas 85, 108
Sacred Heart Cathedral, San Angelo 119
Sacred Heart Co-Cathedral, Houston 104
Salas, Friar Juan de 22
Sam Houston Normal (University) 75
San Agustin Cathedral, Laredo 132, 133
San Angelo 22, 83, 109, 113, 115, 117, 118, 119, 128
San Antonio 8, 9, 30, 31, 34, 35, 36, 37, 38, 39, 40, 41, 43, 45, 47, 48, 49, 50, 51, 52, 56, 59, 65, 66, 67, 69, 71, 72, 73, 75, 79, 81, 82, 83, 84, 85, 86, 87, 90, 91, 92, 94, 95, 97, 99, 100, 101, 104, 106, 107, 108, 110, 113, 115, 116, 117, 126, 130, 132, 134, 135
San Antonio de Bexar, Presidio 40, 41, 130
San Antonio de Padua 30
San Antonio de Valero 8, 34, 40, 87, 130, 135
San Antonio River 28, 31, 34, 79
San Augustine County 63
San Clemente 22
San Elizario 50, 112
San Fernando Cathedral 37, 40, 101, 107, 134
San Francisco de los Tejas 28, 29, 33
San Gabriel 24
San Isidro 22
San Jacinto, Battle of 47, 48, 49, 75, 104
San Juan Bautista 32, 33, 34, 132
San Miguel de los Adaes 33
San Patricio 41, 44, 50, 110, 135
San Salvador 11
Santa Anna, General 45, 46, 47, 49, 104
Santa Cruz de San Saba 118

Santa Fe 24, 25, 40, 47, 59, 115, 119, 128, 134
Santa Rosa Infirmary, San Antonio 67
Santo Domingo 13
Schuler, Anthony Joseph, SJ, Bishop 112, 113
Scriptures 89
Second Vatican Council 88, 89, 92, 96, 97, 121
Secular priests 34, 64, 106, 112, 132
Secularization 38
Secularized 38
See 72, 106, 108, 128
Seguin, Juan 48, 49, 51, 79
Seminarians, 60, 73
Seminary 45, 53, 72, 79, 106
Serra, Friar Junipero 119
Seven Cities of Gold 17, 18, 19
Shaman 21, 25
Shamrock and Cactus 43
Sheehan, Michael Jarboe, Archbishop 128, 129
Sherman, Texas 67, 86
Shiner, Texas 66
Siege 46, 47, 49
Sister Mary Evangelist 71
Sister Servants of the Holy Ghost and Mary Immaculate 67
Sisters of Charity of the Incarnate Word 66, 67, 74, 75, 76, 114, 135
Sisters of Divine Providence 67
Sisters of St. Mary Namur 67, 69, 75
Sisters of the Holy Family 80
Six Flags Over Texas 75
Slavery 72, 73, 80
Slaves 41, 58, 72, 80, 117
Small Pox 21, 38
Smith County 63
Smith, Erastus (Deaf) 48, 49
Social action 94, 95
Social justice 94, 99
Society of Jesus 27, 64, 65
Society of Mary 65
Socorro 28, 38, 40, 41, 86, 87, 112
South Plains 114
South Texas 41, 62, 64, 73, 110
Southern Messenger 91
Spaniards 15, 16, 17, 19, 20, 24, 25, 28, 30, 31, 38, 50, 86, 118
Spanish Missouri 48
Spanish Texas 37, 43, 106
St. Anthony Church, Dallas 87
St. Denis, Louis Juchereau de 32, 33, 37
St. Edward's College (University) 65, 117

St. Francis of Assisi 13, 39, 53
St. Joseph Church, Panna Maria 60
St. Laurance Cathedral, Amarillo 115
St. Louis Cathedral, New Orleans 56, 57
St. Mary Church, Cathedral 56, 60, 104, 86
St. Mary Church, Clarendon 114
St. Mary of the Barrens Seminary 53
St. Mary's Church, Panna Maria 101
St. Mary's College (University) 64, 65, 106
St. Mary's Infirmary, Galveston 66, 67, 76
St. Mary's Orphanage 76, 77
St. Patrick 44, 77, 79, 85, 112, 124, 125, 135
St. Patrick Cathedral, El Paso 85, 112
St. Patrick Cathedral, Fort Worth 124, 125
St. Paul Sanitarium, Dallas 67
St. Peter's Basilica 88, 89
St. Peter's Church, Dallas 81
St. Stanislaus, Fort Worth 124
St. Vincent de Paul 50, 53, 90
St. Vincent de Paul Societies 90
Star of the Republic Museum 46
Statehood 7, 42, 87, 104, 122, 124
Statistics, Diocesan 105, 107, 109, 111, 113, 114, 117, 119, 121, 122, 125, 126, 129, 130, 133
Steamboat Meteor 53
Steamer Palmétto 70
Steamship Henry 53
Storming of Bexar 48, 49
Strait of Anian 11
Suárez, Friar Juan 12, 13, 15

T

Tamayo, James Anthony, Bishop 132, 133
Taylor, Charles S. 47
Tejanos 49, 135
Tennessee 16, 49
Terán de los Ríos, Domingo 30, 31
Tewa nation 25
Texans, first 10
Texas Catholic 6, 7, 8, 72, 80, 91, 92, 93, 95, 99, 117, 134, 135
Texas Catholic Conference 92, 93, 95, 117
Texas Centennial 86, 87
Texas Centennial, Catholic Day 87
Texas City 77

Texas Coast 11, 12, 15, 27, 110
Texas Conference of Churches 92, 93
Texas Congress 7, 54, 104
Texas Constitutional Convention 51
Texas Council of Churches 93
Texas Education Agency 93
Texas Independence 42, 43, 49
Texas Navy 104, 105
Texas Panhandle 20, 114
Texas War of Independence 45, 50, 126
Tiguas 21
Timon, John, C.M., Bishop 50, 51, 52, 53, 54, 55, 56, 60, 64, 67, 104, 116, 130
Tranchese, Father Carmelo, SJ 95
Travis, William 49
Trinity 7, 16, 34, 36
Tucek, Monsignor James I. 89
Turk 18

U

Union 8, 55, 71, 73
United States 8, 21, 41, 42, 43, 47, 53, 56, 57, 58, 59, 65, 66, 67, 75, 77, 79, 85, 97, 98, 99, 100, 101, 105, 107, 120, 135
Ursuline 60, 61, 66, 68, 69, 70, 71, 73, 75, 77, 79, 81, 82, 105, 106, 109, 134
Ursuline Academy 60, 71, 75, 77, 81, 106
Ursuline Archives 105
Ursuline Nuns 61, 66, 68, 70, 71, 81, 82, 109
U.S. citizens 42

V

Vatican 50, 53, 54, 57, 88, 89, 92, 96, 97, 121, 123, 124
Vehlin, Joseph 45
Vera Cruz 47
Veramendi, Ursula 49
Vicar 8, 9, 44, 56, 65, 73, 106, 110, 112, 122, 132
Vicar Apostolic 56, 64, 70, 110, 122, 132
Vicar General 73, 106, 112
Vicariate Apostolic of Arizona 59, 112
Vicariate Apostolic of Brownsville 75, 104, 110, 111, 132
Vicariate Apostolic of Texas 58, 103, 104, 105
Vice-prefect 53
Viceroy 17, 18, 28, 29, 30, 31, 32, 34, 36, 45
Victoria 41, 44, 47, 56, 66, 106, 126
Vietnamese Catholics 123
Vietnamese Refugees 123
Villa San Fernando 34
Vincentian 50, 51, 53, 54, 57, 64, 85, 116, 130, 135
Viva Cristo Rey 85
Viva la Raza 99

W

Waco 67, 75
Washington 55, 79
Washington-on-the-Brazos 47, 80, 117
West Virginia 67
Wichita 18
Wichita Falls 67
Wichitas 20
Windthorst, Texas 114
Woman in Blue 22, 23, 28, 29, 118
Wright, Father Robert E. OMI 38, 40, 135
Wyoming 58

Y-Z

Yanta, John W., Bishop 114, 115
Yellow Fever 60, 62, 66, 67, 70, 71, 74
Ysleta 28, 38, 40, 41, 50, 112
Zapata, Captain Octaviano 73
Zavala, Adina Emilia de 75
Zavala, Lorenzo de 44, 45, 47
Zuni 17, 18, 19